lonely planet

BEST ROAD TRIPS JAPAN

ESCAPES ON THE OPEN ROAD

SELENA TAKIGAWA HOY, LOUISE GEORGE KITTAKA, KIMBERLY HUGHES, JESSICA KORTEMAN, CRAIG MCLACHLAN

Contents

RUSSIA
CHINA
NORTH KOREA
SOUTH KOREA
JAPAN
Sakhalin
Sea of Okhotsk
HOKKAIDŌ p153
Wakkanai
Kuril Islands
Asahikawa
Kitami
Hokkaidō
Sapporo
Tomakomai
Kushiro
Hakodate
CENTRAL HONSHŪ p59
Aomori
Hirosaki
Hachinohe
SEA OF JAPAN (EAST SEA)
Akita
Morioka
Sakata
TŌHOKU p125
Sendai
WESTERN HONSHŪ p109
Niigata
Fukushima
Noto Peninsula
Nagaoka
Iwaki
Toyama
Nagano
Utsunomiya
Kanazawa
Mito
Fukui
Matsue
Maizuru
Gifu
Honshū
TOKYO
AROUND TOKYO p35
Okayama
Kyoto
Nagoya
Hiroshima
Osaka
Hamamatsu
Kitakyūshū
Matsuyama
Nara
Fukuoka
Tokushima
Oita
Kochi
Izu-Shoto
Nagasaki
Kyūshū
Shikoku
KANSAI p81
Kagoshima
Miyazaki
NORTH PACIFIC OCEAN
East China Sea
Ōsumi
SHIKOKU p177
Nampo-Shoto
KYŪSHŪ & OKINAWA p201
Naha
0 200 km
0 100 miles

Welcome to Japan

Known for its buzzing cities, superlative food and cutting-edge technology, Japan is a place that inspires wonder. And those lively cities are wonderful – as well as being complicated and crowded.

Away from the crowds, much of Japan is delightfully unbusy, yet just as deserving of attention. From the drift-ice-dotted seas of the frozen north to the subtropical hopscotch of islands in the south, with the great ridge of mountain ranges that makes up the country's spine in between, Japan stretches for 2800km from north to south, much of it not covered by the admittedly excellent rail network.

Enter the road trip. With the 36 drives in this guide, you'll see another side of Japan: surprising scenery, exquisite crafts, fascinating folklore and kind people who are glad you've made the extra effort to see something more.

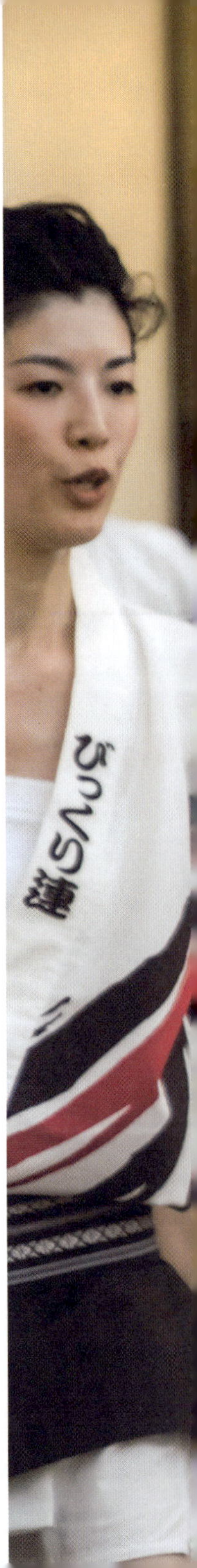

Dancers at the Koenji Awa-odori festival (p37), Tokyo

CANYALCIN/SHUTTERSTOCK

びっくり連
びっくり連

My Perfect Drive

Craig McLachlan

SHIRETOKO NATIONAL PARK TO KUSHIRO

P.170

I love the wide-open expanses of Hokkaidō, where you can drive great distances without seeing a traffic light. This drive is my favourite, taking in three national parks – with chances of seeing a *higuma* (brown bear), wild Ezo-shika (Hokkaidō deer), salmon hurtling themselves at a waterfall, trying to get upriver to spawn, and elegant red-crowned cranes swooping across the sky. There's amazing volcanic scenery plus lakeside onsen in which to relax.

Jessica Korteman

KIRISHIMA KINKŌWAN NATIONAL PARK & KAGOSHIMA CITY

P.216

One of the most fascinating aspects of this trip is how locals find ways to live side by side with Sakura-jima, and even more so that a few thousand people choose to reside on this (very) active volcano. From school children making their commute in mandatory helmets and residents sweeping up the constant sprinkling of volcanic ash into dedicated municipal garbage bags, I'm always struck by just how different life is here.

FLORIAN AUGUSTIN/SHUTTERSTOCK

Shimanami Kaidō (p22)

Top 5 Scenic Drives

1. **Shimanami Kaidō** Hopscotch across half a dozen small islands in the Inland Sea.
2. **Kanazawa to Hakuba** Sea views, emerald rice terraces and the Kurobe Gorge.
3. **Shiretoko NP to Kushiro** Two national parks, wildlife, volcanoes and caldera lakes.
4. **Kyoto to Kōya-san** Wind through hamlets to a sacred mountaintop.
5. **Kumamoto, Aso, Takachiho** An active volcano, waterfalls and a dramatic gorge.

Louise George Kittaka

AROUND THE SHIMOKITA PENINSULA

P.142

Hotokegaura (Buddha's Cove) on the remote Shimokita Peninsula is a majestic stretch of rock formations sculpted by weather and waves over millions of years. Enjoy breathtaking views from the cliffside parking area, or follow a 1.4km trail down to the beach for a different perspective. In this ruggedly beautiful spot, which you may well have all to yourself, it almost feels like you've attained nirvana.

KANUMAN/SHUTTERSTOCK

Mt Fuji view, Lake Kawaguchi (p52)

Top 5 Family Drives

Fuji Five Lakes
Cycling, pleasure boats, museums and beautiful views delight at a resort getaway.

Matsumoto to Nozawa Onsen
Choose from adventure sports, wildlife and hot springs.

San'in-Shimane & Tottori
Find mythology, a splendid art museum and a pretty castle.

Okinawa Main Island
Theme parks, beach time and plenty of tasty treats – perfect.

Hakone
Tokyo's favourite hot-spring weekender town offers more than sulphuric thermal waters.

Selena Takigawa Hoy

SAPPORO TO ASAHIKAWA

P.162

Did someone say ice cream? The drive between Hokkaidō's first and second largest cities is dreamlike, with long roads unfurling like a ribbon into the unblemished countryside. The flower fields of Biei and Furano are painted in pleasing colourful stripes, and a delicious lavender-scented cloud hangs over the whole thing in summer. Stop for a lavender soft serve and an ear of freshly grilled corn with a generous pat of Hokkaidō butter.

Kimberly Hughes

CHIBA'S BŌSŌ PENINSULA

P.42

Between the warm weather, tropical foliage, stunning coastal views and calm vibe along the Bōsō Peninsula, particularly near its southern tip, I can literally feel the stress of the city melting away. The historical shrines, along with numerous local organic farms – some with cafes serving fresh, nourishing meals – infuse the region with a truly unique and special energy.

History

BEST HISTORICAL DRIVES

In the land of samurai and shogun, merchants and monks, pilgrims and poets, you're never far from a site of historical significance. On these drives, you can step into the sandals of the people who shaped this land and culture, from the 88 temple pilgrimage in Shikoku to the homes of lords and their retainers to the work camps of Hokkaidō.

COLLECTABLES

Collect *goshuin* from temples and shrines – calligraphy signatures written by shrine and temple staff; available for a few hundred yen.

Western Kagawa

Trace a section of Shikoku's 88 temple pilgrimage on this trip.

P.194

Nagoya to Matsumoto

Bookended with castles, you'll also encounter a famous swordsmithing town and sections of the old Nakasendō road.

P.62

Yamaguchi Prefecture

Highlights include centuries-old temples, limestone caves and a samurai quarter in a castle town.

P.112

CRIS FOTO/SHUTTERSTOCK

ROAD SAFETY

There's no right turn on red lights in Japan.

Road signs, Tokyo

Asahikawa to Shiretoko National Park

Learn about Abashiri's history as a prison colony and traverse the roads that prisoners built.

P.166

Kyoto – Lake Biwa Loop

Visit Hikone Castle with its cute cat mascot and National Treasure designation.

P.88

Right: Traditional Japanese *kominka*

WHERE TO EAT & STAY

Look for cafes and accommodation in farmhouses or *kominka*, traditional Japanese houses, more common in the countryside.

ONSEN ETIQUETTE

It's imperative to wash your body thoroughly before entering the shared bath; soap and shampoo is almost always provided.

Hot-Spring Sojourn

KIMBERLY HUGHES/LONELY PLANET

BEST ONSEN DRIVES

Taking little trips to dip in restorative waters is a national pastime in Japan, and thanks to its position on the Pacific Ring of Fire, there are more than 27,000 hot springs nationwide. You could easily build your entire trip around visiting different springs purporting to soothe various ailments. Make sure to try *rotemburo*, open-air baths often overlooking nature.

TOWELS

Towels are not provided at many onsen, though you can buy or rent one for a small fee.

Izu Peninsula

Waterfalls and temples are paired with hot springs and beaches for a relaxing escape.

P.46

Matsumoto to Kanazawa

Appreciate deep nature, secluded hot spring towns and the lively old-fashioned town of Takayama.

P.70

COST OF ENTRY

Entering hot springs is free if you're staying in an *onsen ryokan*. Otherwise, you'll need to pay a day-use fee of ¥400-3000.

Onsen ryokan

NANO CALVO/ UNIVERSAL IMAGES GROUP/GETTY IMAGES

Hakodate to Sapporo

Stop in two premier onsen towns, learn about Ainu culture, and appreciate Japan's answer to Scottish whisky.

P.156

Kyoto to Kinosaki Onsen

Wend through rural Japan, visit mountain villages and finish at one of the country's best hot springs.

P.84

Kunisaki, Beppu, Usuki

Visit 'seven hells' baths, sandbathe in thermal heat and luxuriate in one of more than 2000 springs.

P.208

Onsen, Izu Peninsula (p46)

Oceanside

BEST COASTAL DRIVES

Unsurprisingly for an archipelago, Japan has a lot of oceanfront. At almost 30,000km, the country has the sixth-longest coastline in the world. The ocean is an indivisible part of the culture, from fishing villages (and the accompanying seafood) to surfing, water sports and beachcombing. These trips will take you there, for the views, the food and the fun.

BEACH SEASON

Beach season is generally only in summer, beginning after rainy season (usually June). The season is longer in Okinawa, and for surfers.

LUCAS SHU/SHUTTERSTOCK

Chiba's Bōsō Peninsula

Surfers and hippies have retreated to this peninsula to grow organic vegetables and luxuriate on Onjuku Beach.

P.42

Tobishima Kaidō

A leisurely potter across a string of islands with a ferry ride, beaches and fishing towns.

P.26

Yakushima

Circumnavigate this lush green island populated with sea turtles and primeval cedar forests.

P.212

GE ZHENG/SHUTTERSTOCK

NARROW ROADS

Coastal roads can be narrow and you may need to pull over to let someone pass.

Road, Tokushima (p184)

Tokushima to Kōchi Coast

Whirlpools, surfing and craggy cliffs characterise this remote stretch of Shikoku.

P.184

Iwate Coast & Tōno

The Sanriku Coast is known for its rugged cliffs and charming bays, as well as its Michinoku hiking trail.

P.146

DANGERS

Keep an eye out for ocean-related hazards like typhoons and tsunamis, and head for secure quarters and high land if there's any doubt.

Beach, Okinawa (p220)

Country Living

BEST RURAL DRIVES

Though much of the countryside is becoming depopulated as people move to urban centres, Japan's countryside has plenty to offer. In these rural areas, get a glimpse, and a taste, of a way of life that's rapidly disappearing from cities.

BODY FUEL

Fruits and vegetables in the country are a fraction of the big city price. Dig in!

Iya Valley

This remote valley is so far off the map it has a village populated mostly by scarecrows.

P.188

Aizu Bandai, Fukushima

Travel from candy-coloured lakes to an inhabited settlement of thatch-roofed farmhouses.

P.128

Sapporo to Asahikawa

Wide-open pastoral landscapes are dotted with farms where you can stop and sample local produce.

P.162

Kōya-san to Nachi Grand Shrine

Visit an ancient pilgrimage trail that winds through mountainous villages.

P.98

Matsumoto to Kanazawa

Wind through mountains and valleys and stop at two famous thatch-roofed farm settlements.

P.70

CREEPY CRAWLIES

Insects in the Japanese countryside are no joke. Bring bug spray.

WORLDROADTRIP/SHUTTERSTOCK

Vine bridge, Iya Valley (p191)

Chilling and Thrilling

BEST ADVENTURE DRIVES

Whether it's adventure sports or weird and wonderful folk legends, these drives are for those who savour that spine-tingling sensation.

GHOST STORIES

If you like Japanese ghosts and monsters, pick up a copy of the classic *Kwaidan.*

Kirishima Kinkōwan National Park & Kagoshima City

Hike over lava fields through a series of active volcanoes.

P.216

Iya Valley

Swing on vine bridges crossing deep gorges like the samurai who fled here centuries ago.

P.188

Zaō & Ginzan Onsen

Glimpse snow monsters in this remote former silver mining area.

P.132

PACK SNACKS

Most petrol stations don't stock snacks so be sure to stock up at convenience stores instead.

STREETVJ/SHUTTERSTOCK

Namahage (p137)

Around the Shimokita Peninsula

Osorezan, or Fear Mountain, has both heavenly and hellish attributes.

P.142

Akita & Aomori Coast

Visit the home of Namahage, mythological ogres that keep the locals in line.

P.136

When to Go

Spring through autumn are grand for driving; in winter, snow and ice will make driving in Hokkaidō, Tōhoku and mountainous areas dicey.

I LIVE HERE

I LOVE DRIVING HERE

Selena Takigawa Hoy is a writer in Tokyo, always chasing coffee and hot springs. @selenahoy

There's a road near my city that's lined on both sides with cherry trees. They bloom into a cotton-candy tunnel in late March, and the street is transformed into a doll's world. The best time is about a week after the moment when petals start falling in a fluttering shower – driving through it feels like entering the portal to an enchanted dimension. The whole *sakura* season only lasts a week or two, so you have to savour it while you can.

During the spring, chasing flowers is practically a national pastime, and no one will look askance at you if you go decked out in pink. In summer, locals beat the heat by heading to either the beach or mountains, while searching for fall foliage is the done thing in autumn. Snow takes over in Hokkaidō and Tōhoku from at least November until March, so head south during these times: there's plenty to see in the southern islands.

Accommodation

Hotels fill up fast around holidays and festivals, so be sure to book ahead if your trip will coincide with Golden Week (end of April and early May), school holidays (at the end of March),

ARTEM MISHUKOV/SHUTTERSTOCK

Awa-odori Matsui, Tokushima (p179)

Weather Watch

JANUARY	FEBRUARY	MARCH	APRIL	MAY	JUNE
Avg daytime max: **9°C.**	Avg daytime max: **10°C.**	Avg daytime max: **14°C.**	Avg daytime max: **18°C.**	Avg daytime max: **23°C.**	Avg daytime max: **25°C.**
Days of rainfall: **3**	Days of rainfall: **5**	Days of rainfall: **7**	Days of rainfall: **8**	Days of rainfall: **8**	Days of rainfall: **9**

AREZA TAQWIM/SHUTTERSTOCK

Sanja Matsuri

TOP TIP

The rainy season, *tsuyu*, hits the country in June and July, bypassing Hokkaidō.

or O-Bon (mid-August). Make sure your lodging has parking, especially in cities.

Snowbound

Hokkaidō and northern Honshū are covered in snow through the winter, as are many of the mountainous areas. Some roads may close entirely for the season. If open, these regions are likely to require snow tyres or chains, as well as snow-driving know-how. Be prepared.

ISLAND-HOP

Okinawa has a subtropical climate, meaning that even in the winter, the temperature averages about 15°C. In direct opposition to Hokkaidō, road trips are convenient year-round. Public transportation is relatively sparse down here, and most people get around by car.

MAJOR FESTIVITIES

The already lively neighbourhood of Asakusa positively vibrates during the **Sanja Matsuri**, where 100 portable shrines are hoisted by thousands of scantily clad, sometimes tattooed and inebriated, bearers *(www.japan.travel/spot/1705)*. **May**

Japan's biggest LGBTIQ+ Pride festival, **Tokyo Rainbow Pride**, is held yearly in Yoyogi Park, drawing over 200,000 people to a weekend of musical performances, booths and a huge parade through Shibuya *(tokyorainbowpride.org)*. **June**

Extravagant, gilded floats pay homage to sea god Susano-o in the thousand-year-old Shinto festival **Gion Matsuri**, one of Japan's top three celebrations *(yasaka-jinja.or.jp/en/gion_fes)*. **July**

One of Japan's biggest festivals, **Summer Sonic** happens simultaneously in Chiba and Osaka, drawing major international and domestic acts. Spread over a main stage and several smaller stages, there are a few dozen performers, most playing in both cities *(summersonic.com)*. **August**

JULY	AUGUST	SEPTEMBER	OCTOBER	NOVEMBER	DECEMBER
Avg daytime max: **29°C**.	Avg daytime max: **31°C**.	Avg daytime max: **27°C**.	Avg daytime max: **22°C**.	Avg daytime max: **17°C**.	Avg daytime max: **12°C**.
Days of rainfall: **10**	Days of rainfall: **8**	Days of rainfall: **9**	Days of rainfall: **8**	Days of rainfall: **6**	Days of rainfall: **4**

Get Prepared for Japan

Useful things to load in your bag, your ears and your brain.

WATCH

The Boyfriend
(Netflix; 2024) Reality dating show featuring a group of men living and running a coffee truck together as they try to form relationships.

My Neighbor Totoro
(Hayao Miyazaki; 1988) Children take a cat bus to an enchanted parallel world.

Our Little Sister
(Hirokazu Kore-eda; 2015) An estranged half-sister comes to live with her three older sisters after their father dies.

Solitary Gourmet
(Netflix; 2023) A travelling businessman visits independent restaurants and dines alone; based on a famous manga.

Clothing and Gear

Sun protection: Control road glare with sunglasses, hat, sunblock and UV-protective layers.

Backpack: Theft is not a big problem in Japan, but you'll still want to take essential valuables with you when you leave the vehicle.

Layered clothing: Consider including comfortable, breathable layers and a windbreaker.

Comfortable shoes: Suitable for long stretches in the car and side quests.

Rain protection: A folding umbrella will be invaluable in a sudden squall.

Gloves: Especially for longer drives.

Water bottle: Don't forget to hydrate.

Snacks: Convenience stores have plenty of fun options for driving nibbles.

First-aid kit: A mini kit with basic antiseptic, bandages and gauze will come in handy for minor mishaps.

Mobile phone and spare battery: Not all rental cars have charging ports.

Car phone mount: If you're planning to use your phone's map apps, this little device will come in handy, and is not a regular fixture in car rentals.

CLOCKWISE FROM TOP LEFT: SERGIY KUZMIN/SHUTTERSTOCK, ATLASSTUDIO/SHUTTERSTOCK, ANATOLIY BERISLAVSKIY/SHUTTERSTOCK, TIMQUO/SHUTTERSTOCK, PIXIEME/SHUTTERSTOCK, TARZHANOVA/SHUTTERSTOCK, C12/SHUTTERSTOCK

Words

Chairudō shīto Car seat

Enjin Engine

Gasorin Petrol

Panku Flat tyre

Jidōsha Automobile

Kuruma Car

Rentakā Rental car

Unten menkyō Driver's license

Abunai! Danger!

Ganbatte! Good luck/You can do it!

Ki o tsukete Be careful

Konbanwa Good evening

Konnichiwa! Hello!

Mata ne See you later

Ohayō gozaimasu Good morning

Sayōnara Goodbye

...made wa dono gurai desu ka? How far until ...?

...wa doko desu ka? Where is...?

Chikai Near

Tōi Far

Hidari Left

Massugu Straight

Migi Right

Kado Corner

Kudarizaka Downhill

Noborizaka Uphill

Saka Slope

Chūshajō Parking

Shingō Traffic signal

Dōro/michi Road

Kosoku dōro Highway

Koko wa nan to iu tokoro desu ka? What is this place called?

Kono michi wa ...e ikimasu ka? Does this road go to...?

Kyō no tenki wa ikaga desu ka? How's the weather today?

Ashita no tenki wa ikaga desu ka? How's the weather tomorrow?

Ii otenki desu ne! Nice weather!

Atsui Hot

Hare Sunny

Ame Rain

Samui Cold

Byōin Hospital

Hoteru Hotel

Konbini Convenience store

Kyanpujō Campsite

Mizu Water

Neru Sleep

Nomimono Drink

Resutoran Restaurant

Tabemono Food

Yasumu Rest

...wa ikura desu ka? How much is...?

Yōyaku o onegaishimasu I'd like to make a reservation

Kyūkyūsha o yonde kudasai Please call an ambulance

LISTEN

Sweet Soul Revue
(Pizzicato Five; 1993) Sparkly and bright, this swingy pop is great for a summer road trip.

Yuzu Ikka
(Yuzu; 1998) The folk-pop duo's debut album brought them from street performers to the national stage.

Japan Eats!
(Apple Podcasts) Hosted by Akiko Katayama, every episode explores an aspect of Japanese food culture.

The Guy Perryman Show
(InterFM) Broadcast four mornings a week from Tokyo, the show mixes music, news and commentary. 89.7 FM in Tokyo.

READ

Before the Coffee Gets Cold
(Toshikazu Kawaguchi; 2020) A set of connected short stories taking place in a time-travelling cafe.

The Art of Simple Living
(Shunmyo Masuno; 2019) A Zen monk shares lessons on living a minimalist life.

Saint Young Men
(Hikaru Nakamura; 2019) A manga exploring what it would be like if Jesus and Buddha were 20-something roommates in Tokyo.

ROAD TRIPS

Hakodate (p145), Hokkaidō
SEAN PAVONE/SHUTTERSTOCK

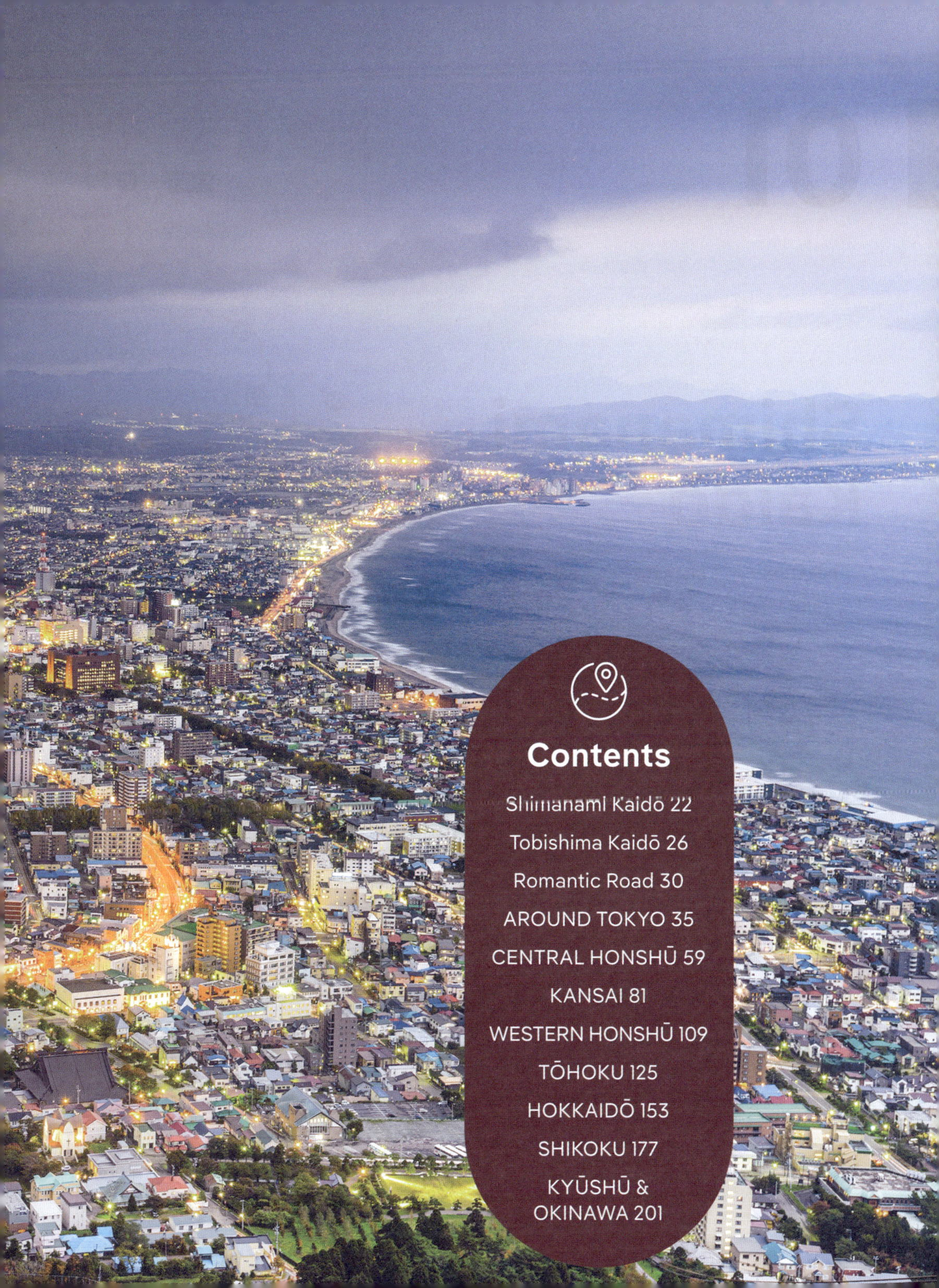

Contents

01

Shimanami Kaidō

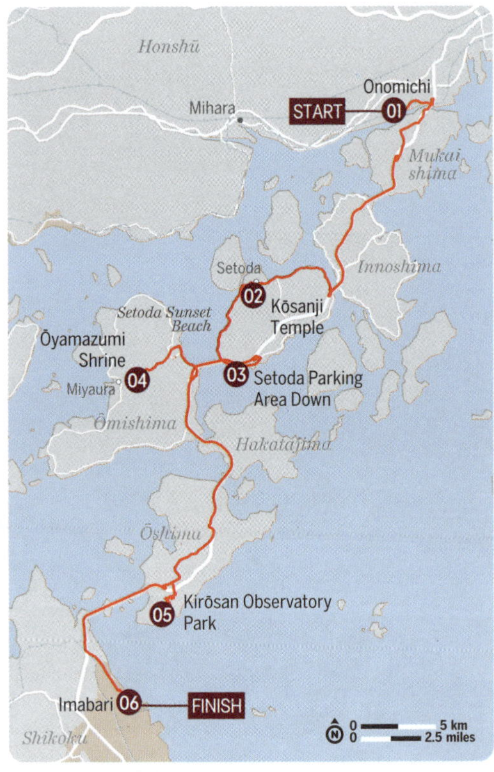

TANYA JONES/SHUTTERSTOCK

DURATION	DISTANCE	GREAT FOR
2 days	96km	Sea views, bridges, island life, art museums & architecture

BEST TIME TO GO	Year-round (but many eateries keep irregular hours in winter)

The Shimanami Kaidō connects Onomichi, Hiroshima Prefecture, with Imabari, Ehime Prefecture, crossing the Inland Sea via six islands and seven bridges. Opened in 1999, the route has become a mecca for cycling enthusiasts worldwide, but also makes for a wonderful drive, full of breathtaking views and island charm. Enjoy an evocative mix of culture and creativity along the way, from shrines and temples to contemporary art. Note that the driving route is a toll road. Although the driving and cycling routes frequently diverge, you'll share the road with cyclists at times, so drive with care to ensure everyone's safety.

Link Your Trip

02 Tobishima Kaidō

For another scenic island route, set off from Imabari to Hiroshima.

31 Western Kagawa

Drive from Imabari along the coast to Kanonji for about 90 minutes to pick up this drive.

01 ONOMICHI (尾道)

Start your trip in the port city of Onomichi before heading out over the islands. Take the ropeway up to the summit of **Mt Senkōji** to reach **Senkōji Temple**, the city's iconic vermilion landmark. The Tadao Ando–designed **Onomichi City Museum** is located nearby. Make your way back down through the narrow streets of **Senkōji**, dotted with tiny shops and quirky cafes. Animal lovers will enjoy spotting the felines that make their

Ropeway, Onomichi

BEST FOR SCENERY

Enjoy stunning panoramic views of the Inland Sea from Kirōsan Observatory Park.

When Life Hands You Lemons

The town of **Setoda** on Ikuchijima is famous for the lemons that grow well on the island's sunlit slopes. Yellow lemon fields dominate the landscape during the autumn and winter, as most farmers here cultivate them. Lemon-themed objects make for fun photo ops, including the huge citrus fruit outside the Setoda Town Tourist Information Centre. **Dolce** gelato shop, a five-minute drive from Kōsanji Temple, is a Shimanami favourite for its range of handmade citrus gelato flavours. Other local food products include Shimagokoro lemon cakes, jams, pickles, salad dressings and even lemon ramen.

home along **Neko no Hosomichi** (Cat Alley).

THE DRIVE Most major points of interest are on the third and fourth of the Seto islands (Ikuchijima and Ōmishima). It's a 21km drive to Ikuchijima from central Onomichi, via Rte 2 and then onto the Shimanami Expressway toward Imabari. Cross Mukaishima and Innoshima Islands on the way, then get off at the Ikuchijima-kita IC. With the sea on your right, follow Rte 81 for another 7km to Kōsanji Temple.

02 KŌSANJI TEMPLE (耕三寺)

The designated car park for Kōsanji Temple (opposite the petrol station) offers convenient access to several attractions. The interesting temple complex was built by a businessman-turned-priest in homage to his mother, along with **Miraishin no Oka** (Hill of Hope), a garden full of glittering marble sculptures behind the temple. Nearby is the **Hirayama Ikuo Museum of Art**, featuring works by this revered artist. Then, take a 15-minute walk past shops and citrus orchards up to peaceful **Kōjōji Temple** to see the three-story pagoda (a designated National Treasure). Don't be tempted to drive – the roads are extremely steep and narrow.

THE DRIVE Continue 4km around the coast on Rte 81 via Sunset Beach, then on Rte 317 for 6km, and take the Ikuchijima-Minami entrance to get back on the Shimanami Expressway. Drive 1.5km to the parking area on the left.

03 SETODA PARKING AREA (DOWN) (瀬戸パーキングエリア (下り))

It isn't usually possible to stop when driving over the bridges, so take the chance to pause here for good views of the **Tatara Bridge**, which links Ikuchijima and Ōmishima.

THE DRIVE Continue 4km, crossing the Tatara Bridge, and exit at the Ōmishima IC on to Ōmishima (and into Ehime Prefecture). Drive 7km along Rtes 317 and 21 to the Ōyamazumi Shrine car park.

04 ŌYAMAZUMI SHRINE (大山祇神社)

Ōyamazumi Shrine is the oldest in Ehime and was once an important place of worship for samurai. Points of interest include a huge **sacred camphor tree**, thought to be over 2600 years old, and one of Japan's best collections of samurai armour and weaponry at the **museum**. Over the road is the **Ōmishima Art Museum**, featuring contemporary Japanese paintings within an atmospheric building with traditional washi paper interiors.

THE DRIVE It's only a short 70km hop back. Drive 19km, back the way you came on Rtes 21 and 317 and then back onto the Shimanami Expressway in the direction of Imabari. Cross briefly over to the fifth island, Hakatajima, before proceeding to Ōshima. Exit at Ōshima-kita IC and then drive 9km via Rte 317 up to the observatory.

Take a Break

ZAKKA CAFÉ is located on Ōmishima, just past the exit off the Tatara Bridge. Sip on barista-brewed coffee paired with superb views of the bridge and surrounding islands. The cafe also has lunch plates and indulgent desserts, perfect for a relaxed break. It's closed on Tuesday and, like many eateries along the island route, keeps irregular hours in the winter months. For those staying longer, a variety of year-round accommodation options are available at Zakka, including cottages, dome tents and budget-friendly dormitories.

MUSASHI2001/SHUTTERSTOCK

Kurushima-Kaikyo Bridge

05 KIRŌSAN OBSERVATORY PARK (亀老山展望公園)

The majestic Kurushima-Kaikyo Bridge, which links Ōshima Island with Imabari, is the world's first triple-suspension bridge. Designed by eminent architect Kengo Kuma, the Kirōsan Observatory on Ōshima offers spectacular views of the bridge and the surrounding Inland Sea. The observatory deck is accessed from the stairs behind the car park.

THE DRIVE
Wend your way back down and take the Shimanami Expressway toward Imabari. Travel 17km, crossing the bridge and exiting at Imbari-kita IC. Head toward Central Imabari.

Artful Discoveries

The 'Island-Wide Art Museum' on **Ikuchijima** has 17 outdoor sculptures created by contemporary artists, each thoughtfully placed to suit its surroundings. The works are scattered across the island, but you don't need to track down every piece to enjoy the experience – just take in the art as you come across it. Several installations are conveniently located on Sunset Beach. For more sculptures, the **Tokoro Museum** on Ōmishima displays contemporary works by Japanese and international artists along descending terraces that lead to a wonderful seascape. The striking building is a work of art in itself, resembling a modern Noah's Ark.

06 IMABARI (今治)

Just over the final bridge lies photogenic **Imabari Castle**, with distinctive moats filled with seawater. Although relatively little remains of the original buildings from the early 17th century, the faithful reconstruction is impressive nonetheless. **Imabari City** is also known for producing top-quality towels, and an eclectic range of exhibits are housed in the expansive **Towel Museum**, including fabric art and a Moomin-themed collection. Drive 13km via Rte 155 from the castle to reach the museum.

02

BEST FOR HISTORY

The well-preserved townscape of Mitarai is a seaside gem.

Tobishima Kaidō

DURATION	DISTANCE	GREAT FOR
2 days	96km	Sea views, island life, maritime history & historic towns

BEST TIME TO GO	Year-round (but many eateries keep irregular hours during the winter)

MUSASHI2001/SHUTTERSTOCK

Imabari Castle

The Tobishima Kaidō offers a great option for island-hopping in the Inland Sea. Connecting seven islands between Kure, Hiroshima Prefecture, and Imabari, Ehime Prefecture, it is much quieter than the popular Shimanami Kaidō (p22). While primarily a cycling route, it's also tailor-made for a leisurely drive; it's mostly toll-free with little traffic, plus there's a scenic ferry ride. While you can start at either end, the suggested route leads to Hiroshima City, ideal for further exploration in Western Honshū (p109). Discover an area still largely untapped by international tourism and relax – you're on island time.

Link Your Trip

01 Shimanami Kaidō

For another Inland Sea adventure, connect to Drive 1 in Imabari.

17 Yamaguchi Prefecture

Drive 130km from Hiroshima City to Yamaguchi to start Drive 17.

01 IMABARI (今治)

The city is home to the striking **Imabari Castle**, renowned for its seawater-filled moats and carefully reconstructed architecture. Imbari is also famous for its premium towel production, showcased at the expansive **Towel Museum**, which features an eclectic range of exhibits.

THE DRIVE

Your trip starts with a refreshing ferry ride to Okamurajima Island. The Sekizen ferry runs four daily

vehicle services from Imabari, starting at 8.25am. Enjoy the views during the hour-long journey to Okamurajima Port. With the sea on your left, follow the road for 3km and then take a sharp right onto Rte 177 (Orange Line). Drive 5km, crossing over two tiny islands, Nakanoshima and Heira, and then turn left onto Rte 355 toward Mitarai on Ōsakishimojima Island. Park in the free municipal lot on the outskirts; cars are not permitted in the historic town centre.

MITARAI (御手洗)

Entering the small harbour town of Mitarai feels like stepping back in time. The narrow streets are lined with well-preserved **traditional wooden houses**, merchant shops and inns, offering countless photo opportunities. Pick up a map at the tourism information centre near the main car park, or simply wander the streets to soak in the nostalgic atmosphere. Among the notable buildings are the **Former Kaneko Residence**, the home of a wealthy merchant family built in 1823, and the **Shinkō Clock Shop**, still in business and unchanged since 1919.

THE DRIVE
Return along the coastal road (Rte 355) for 14km, the sea on your right, and take the Toyohama Bridge to the island of Toyoshima. Cross over to the next island, Kamikamagari, and then drive 4km, turning left to reach the beach.

Ferrying Around

Sekizen car ferries leave Imabari for Okamurajima at 8.25am, noon, 2.45pm and 5.50pm. (From Okamurajima, they depart at 6.50am, 9.35am, 1.30pm and 4.15pm.) The ferry from Imabari is rarely full. Staff will show you where to line up and assist with purchasing tickets at the cash-only machine; prices depend on vehicle size. You'll need to show your car's registration (usually it's in the rental's glove box). Alternatively, drive 45km on the Shimanami Expressway to Munakata Port on Ōmishima Island (on Drive 1, p22), then take the 23-minute Ōmishima Blue Line car ferry to Okamurajima; five sailings a day.

03 CITIZEN'S BEACH/ KENMIN-NO-HAMA (県民の浜)

Take a dip in the sea during Japan's short swimming season (July–August) or stroll along one of the country's most attractive beaches. **Kagayaki-no-Yakata**, a beachside facility, has a cafe and various accommodation options, including Western and Japanese-style rooms and cottages. **Yasuragi-no-Yakata** onsen adjacent is open to day visitors from 3pm to 8pm.

THE DRIVE
Drive 1km back the way you came, turn left onto Rte 287 and continue for 8km along the coast, crossing the Kamagari Bridge to Shimokamagari Island, and entering the Sannose port area. Shōtōen is a just a few minutes from the bridge; there is free parking nearby on the same side of the road.

04 SHŌTŌEN (松濤園)

Shimokamagari Island (下蒲刈島) offers an impressive cluster of historical and cultural facilities along a charming, paved coastal road in the Sannose neighbourhood. If you only visit one, make it Shōtōen. This complex features collections of historical documents, lamps and ceramics, a 17th-century guardhouse and a beautiful Japanese garden. Other sites include the **Rantōkaku Art Museum** and **Hakusetsurō House**, where you can sip a cup of green tea in a traditional tearoom. Inquire about a pass for discounted access if you plan to visit multiple sites.

THE DRIVE
Travel 4km on Rte 74 toward Kure, crossing the Akinada Bridge back to the mainland, and drive via Rte 185 for 14km, following signs for Central Kure.

05 KURE (呉)

This port city, which began life as a naval base in 1889, played a major role in Japan's shipbuilding and steel-making industries. Explore Japan's naval and shipping history at the **Kure Maritime Museum** – often called the Yamato Museum due to a 1:10 scale model of the WWII battleship *Yamato*, produced in Kure. The next-door **JMSDF Kure Museum** showcases submarines and the role of the Japan Maritime Self-Defense Force.

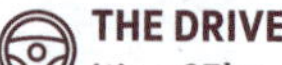

THE DRIVE
It's a 23km drive on to central Hiroshima, via the Hiroshima-Kure Road. Take the Yoshima Exit and continue 3km to the Peace Park.

06 HIROSHIMA (広島)

End your trip in Hiroshima City, an iconic symbol of hope for a peaceful world. Major points of interest include the **Peace Memorial Park** (containing the Peace Memorial Museum and A-bomb Dome) and the attractive **Shukkeien** garden.

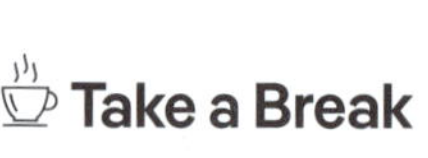

Take a Break

SHIMA CAFÉ KITATANI offers a welcoming space to enjoy a meal along the Tobishima Kaidō. The signature beef curry, slow-cooked to perfection, is infused with a hint of locally grown lemons, and the menu also features pizza topped with fresh vegetables, sweets and a range of drinks. It carries gift items, too. Open every day – uncommon along this route – the cafe is found just past the Toyohama Bridge as you drive onto Toyoshima Island.

SEAN PAVONE/SHUTTERSTOCK

Hiroshima

Ports of Call

During the Edo Period (1603–1868), both Sannose (Shimokamagari) and Mitarai (Osakishimojima) were important centres for sea trade. Envoys from Korea were welcomed and entertained in Sannose, fostering early diplomacy between the two nations. The exhibit about these visits in Shōtōen includes a historic UNESCO-listed scroll with detailed pictures. Mitarai flourished as a hub for cargo ships that anchored here to await favourable sailing conditions. Built in the early 18th century, the Wakaebisuya Teahouse was one of a number of establishments where courtesans entertained sailors. The building was restored and is now open to the public.

03

BEST FOR WATERFALLS

Visit several stunning cascades, including Kegon Falls – one of Japan's best three.

Romantic Road

DURATION	DISTANCE	GREAT FOR
2 days	203km	Hot springs, waterfalls, history & autumn foliage

BEST TIME TO GO	May to early November (particularly autumn)

AARONCHENPS2/SHUTTERSTOCK

Kegon Falls

Japan's Romantic Road stretches 350km from Ueda in Nagano Prefecture, across Gunma Prefecture and on to Utsunomiya in Tochigi Prefecture. You'll still pass through all three prefectures in this compact version, anchored by history-rich Nikkō and the mountain resort of Karuizawa, visiting waterfalls, lakes and a charming onsen town along the way. This route is stunning in autumn and the section between Nikkō and Kegon Falls gets congested. In order to beat the traffic, try to avoid weekends, and consider staying overnight in Nikkō to explore all it has to offer, then getting an early start the following morning.

Link Your Trip

08 Nagoya to Matsumoto

From Karuizawa, drive 70km west via Rte 254 to join Drive 8 from Matsumoto.

09 Matsumoto to Nozawa Onsen

From Matsumoto you can also pick up this drive to Nozawa Onsen.

01 NIKKŌ (日光)

Explore the historical treasures that make up Nikkō's collective World Heritage Sites, conveniently clustered within easy walking distance of each other. The most popular is the richly decorated **Tōshugu Shrine**, built in 1617 and the location for the mausoleum of Tokugawa Ieyasu, founder of the Tokugawa shogunate. Standing nearby is **Taiyuin**, the final resting place of his grandson, Iemitsu. The other major sites, both dating back to the 8th century, are **Futarasan Shrine** and **Rinnonji Temple**. Don't miss a photo stop at the vermilion **Shinkyō Bridge**, too.

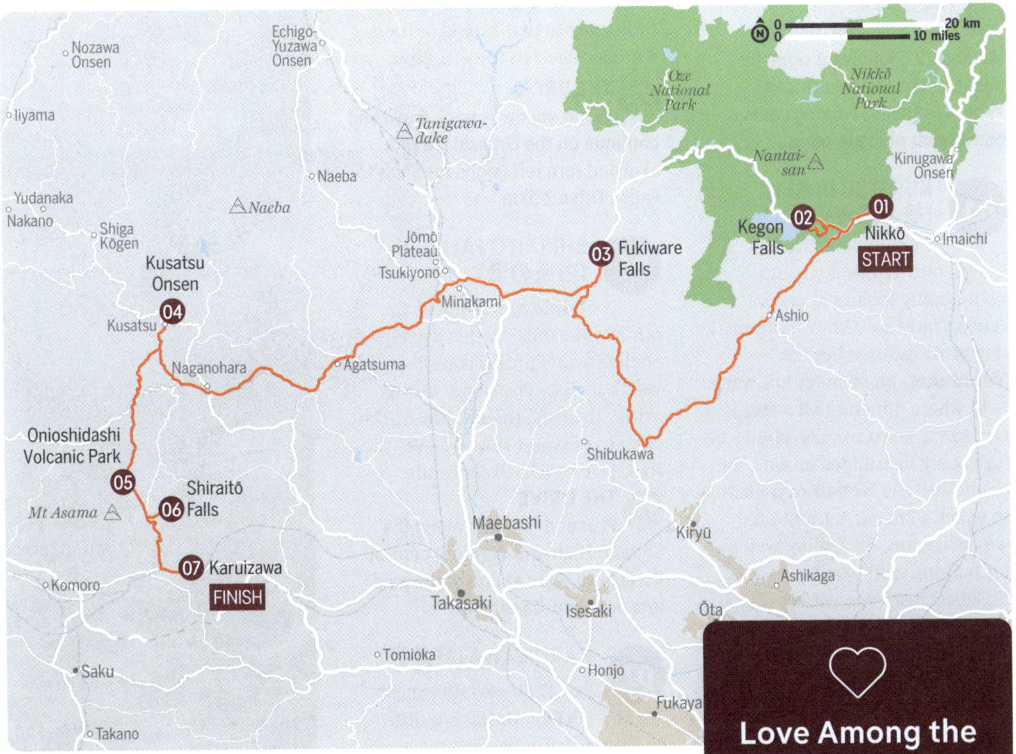

THE DRIVE
From central Nikkō, follow Rte 120 west for 16km, then turn right onto the Lake Chuzenji access road and drive 3km to the car park at the waterfall. You'll be driving through the upward section of a pair of famous winding roads known as the Irohazaka Slope. Take extra care as you navigate the numerous hair-pin bends on this exciting section!

KEGON FALLS (華厳の滝)

Cascading down 100m, this magnificent waterfall is ranked among the top three in Japan. Take a look from the free observation deck at the top, then descend to the base in the paid elevator for an entirely different perspective. Tranquil **Lake Chuzenji** is nearby.

THE DRIVE
Continue on Rte 120 for 55km. (Note that Rte 120 is a mountain road, usually closed from December to March. An alternative route is to travel 89km via Rtes 122 and 62.)

03 FUKIWARE FALLS (吹割れの滝)

Enjoy exploring these dynamic waterfalls from the path that runs along the gorge, as well as from atop the swing bridge. (Closed from mid-December to late March.)

Love Among the Cabbage Fields

The hamlet of **Tsumagoi** is arguably the most passion-filled stop on the Romantic Road. The name means 'missing one's wife', based on a legendary prince who was in the area when he got news of his beloved wife's death. Nowadays, Tsumagoi is Japan's leading producer of cabbages, which doesn't evoke an image of romance. However, since 2006, the cabbage fields at the **Aisai-no-Oka** (Beloved Wife's Hill) have hosted a quirky event in which shy husbands pluck up the courage to shout out their love. Aisai-no-Oka is located on Rte 406, 8km past the turnoff for Onioshidashi.

THE DRIVE
Drive 80km via Rtes 120, 145 and 292, following signs for Kusatsu. The Kusatsu Onsen Yubatake Tourist Parking Lot is a convenient place to park.

04 KUSATSU ONSEN (草津温泉)

Immerse yourself in the friendly atmosphere and high-quality springs at one of Japan's most well-known onsen towns. At its heart lies the **Yubatake** – an open-air hot water field where mineral-rich water is cooled via seven wooden chutes before being distributed around the town. Visit the **Netsunoyu** nearby to watch *yumomi*, a traditional way of cooling the boiling water for bathing with wooden paddles. Kusatsu Onsen is a perfect place for an overnight stay on this drive.

THE DRIVE
Drive 5km on Rte 292, then turn right onto Rte 59 (signs for Tsumagoi). Travel 10km and turn right to join the Onioshi Hwy and drive 11km.

05 ONIOSHIDASHI VOLCANIC PARK (鬼押出し園)

Walk through the otherworldly Onioshidashi Park, with a landscape shaped by sediment deposited during the 1783 eruption of Mt Asama. Various flowering plants in spring and summer, and autumn foliage, bring colourful contrast to the lava landscape. At the centre of the park is a beautiful **temple** dedicated to those who perished in the eruption.

THE DRIVE
Wend your way back down and continue on the Onioshi Hwy for 6km and turn left (signs for Shiraitō Falls). Drive 2.5km.

06 SHIRAITŌ FALLS (白糸の滝)

While not as big as the other waterfalls on this drive, enchanting Shiraitō is well worth a visit. The name means 'white threads', inspired by a 70m curtain of water flowing over the rock face in silk-like strands.

THE DRIVE
Proceed for 14km along the Shiraitō Highland Way into central Karuizawa. Park at one of the paid lots near Kyu-Karuizawa.

07 KARUIZAWA (軽井沢)

Set at an elevation near 1000m, in the late 19th century Karuizawa became a popular retreat among foreign residents escaping Tokyo's sweltering summer. The stylish mountain resort makes a nice contrast to the traditional towns on this itinerary. The centre of town, **Kyu-Karuizawa**, is lined with bakeries, cafes and boutiques, and **Kumobaike**, a pretty pond with a mirror-like surface, is a 1.5km drive away. Enjoy the 160km drive back to Tokyo – or wherever your travels take you next.

Take a Break

Lying along the Shima River, the hot-spring town of Shima Onsen is an ideal choice for those seeking a relaxed stay surrounded by nature. Take a walk by the river to see the SHIMA POTHOLES, eight smooth holes that have formed in the riverbed, or admire views of two nearby lakes, Lake Shima and Lake Okushima. The waters of both lakes are a stunning cobalt hue that locals proudly call 'Shima blue'.

SHAWN.CCF/SHUTTERSTOCK

Kumobaike, Karuizawa

Let Him Be

Attracted by Karuizawa's relatively cool climate, a Canadian missionary named Alexander Croft Shaw built Japan's first summer residence there in the 1880s. Karuizawa became a popular spot among the affluent for vacation homes, including the family of musician and artist Yoko Ono. After Ono married ex-Beatle John Lennon, the couple spent four summers in Karuizawa. They stayed at the Manpei, established in 1894 as one of Japan's first Western-style hotels. Away from the glare of the media, Lennon is said to have enjoyed his annual visits to Karuizawa up until his death in 1980.

0 50 km
0 25 miles
N
Suwa-ko
Chino
Fukaya
Kumagaya
Hokota
Tsuchiura
Kasumiga-ura
Tone Gawa
Kashima
Chichibu
Kobushi-ga-take
Chichibu-Tama-Kai National Park
Kobuchizawa
Senjō-ga-take
Nirasaki
Kōfu
Enzan
Ōtsuki
Ōme
Kawagoe
Saitama
Koshigaya
Kashiwa
Kawaguchi
Narita
Sakura
Chōshi
Tokyo
Funabashi
Hachioji
Chōfu
Yokoshiba
Chiba
Tōgane
Minami Alps National Park
Sagamihara
Kawasaki
Tokyo Bay
07
Fuji-Yoshida
Lake Yamanaka
Yamato
Atsugi
Yokohama
Mobara
Fuji-Hakone-Izu National Park
Mt Fuji
Minobu
Hadano
Chigasaki
Fujisawa
Kisarazu
Hiratsuka
Kamakura
Enoshima
Gotemba
Bōsō Peninsula
Fujinomiya
04
Odawara
Hakone
Yokosuka
Ōhara
Lake Ashi
Miura Peninsula
Fuji
Mishima
05
Katsuura
Numazu
Atami
Kamogawa
Shimizu
Shizuoka
Sagami-wan
Tateyama
Itō
Izu Peninsula
Yaizu
Shimada
Suruga-wan
Inatori
Izuōshima
PACIFIC OCEAN
06
Shimoda
Toshima

ANDREAS_FOTOS/SHUTTERSTOCK

Torii, Hakone (p38)

Around Tokyo

04 Hakone

Historical mountain town long famous for its onsen (natural hot spring) baths, plus wide-ranging gastronomical options including a storied 400-year-old teahouse. **p38**

05 Chiba's Bōsō Peninsula

Coastal lighthouses and shrines, dramatic seascapes and endless stretches of swimming and surfing beaches line this palm-tree-fringed peninsular drive. **p42**

06 Izu Peninsula

More onsen bathing, plus scenic hiking trails, copious seafood, fantastic diving and snorkelling and a collection of idyllic offshore islands. **p46**

07 Fuji Five Lakes

Views of deeply sacred Mt Fuji from multiple vantage points await at these volcanically formed lakes, along with camping, kayaking, bird-watching, museums and cafes. **p50**

Explore

Around Tokyo

Tokyo (東京), the largest metropolitan city across the globe and also one of its most dynamic, has to be experienced to be believed. Meanwhile, surrounding the capital's pulsing urban centres are regions featuring a dramatically slower pace of life. This collection of drives highlights several such areas right in the capital's proverbial backyard, where you'll discover spectacular beaches, unique onsen (hot springs) and untamed nature that rivals more remote rural locales across the country. Despite being Tokyo-adjacent, some of these regions see few international tourists; others, meanwhile, are oversaturated. In either case, a few Japanese phrases and a respectful, friendly attitude will go a long way.

Tokyo

Before (or after) embarking on these drives, be sure to explore the highlights of the metropolis in neighbourhoods such as Shibuya and Harajuku for hip youth culture, Omotesando and Aoyama for high-end shopping and art galleries, Asakusa and Ueno for temples and vibrant street culture, Kuramae for atmospheric cafes and artisan ateliers, and Odaiba/Tokyo Bay for scenic coastal views and art installations.

Several districts offer convenient access to the Bōsō Peninsula drive in Chiba Prefecture via the Tokyo Bay Aqua-Line, making them good stopover hubs. These include the Tokyo Station area, where you'll find numerous hotels and car-rental services. The main station-side neighbourhoods are Marunouchi, a business district also known for its upscale boutique shops, and bustling Yaesu, featuring eateries galore. Adjacent Nihonbashi has similar conveniences, along with numerous historical buildings renovated to find new life as hip eateries and bars – particularly in its financial subdistrict of Kabutocho (don't miss Caveman restaurant for eclectic dining in stylish surrounds). Nihonbashi also features an intriguing bit of transport-related history: the five highways built during the Edo era in the early 1600s, which fanned out in various directions across the country, all originated here – making the area a vital merchant centre. A major reconstruction project is presently underway to restore the area's majestic Nihonbashi Bridge to its previous splendour

WHEN TO GO

Spring and autumn have ideal weather and natural grandeur (cherry blossoms and autumn colours, respectively), although this can be offset by massive crowding, particularly on weekends and national holidays. Summer brings the rainy season from mid-June to mid-July, followed by brutal heat that can last until October. Winter sees fewer tourists and glorious wildflowers (bring tyre chains).

by 2041 by completely removing its unsightly overhead highway system, which was hastily erected before the 1964 Olympics.

Prior to embarking on the Fuji Five Lakes drive, consider a stay in one of the commuter cities along the western edge of Tokyo, such as Tachikawa or Hachioji. Both are convenient for accessing the E20 Chuo Expressway heading toward Yamanashi Prefecture, and are thriving urban centres with numerous options for car-rental agencies, shopping outlets and accommodation (particularly around the train stations). In Tachikawa, the Green Springs shopping complex offers numerous restaurants and an outdoor evening cinema in summertime (including kid-friendly films, making this a great spot for those travelling with little ones).

Odawara

Odawara (小田原), a historic castle town in Kanagawa Prefecture, makes a good base for setting off toward Hakone and Izu Peninsula, as it is the starting point for both drives. Although quieter than many Tokyo districts, it still has everything necessary for overnight stays, car rentals and any pre-departure shopping needs (again, the areas in and near the train station tend to offer the most options).

TRANSPORT

Tokyo is serviced by two international airports: Narita in northern Chiba Prefecture, and Haneda, located near Tokyo Bay. There is also shinkansen (bullet train) and express train service connecting the capital with cities throughout the country, as well as overnight buses – a cheaper alternative that can be surprisingly comfortable if reclining seats are booked in advance.

WHAT'S ON

Among Tokyo's packed year-round festival calendar, summer is particularly replete with good options including the following:

Sumidagawa Fireworks Festival
A colourful melange of riverside fireworks at the foot of Tokyo Tower on the last Saturday in July.

Koenji Awa-odori
Lively event in this western Tokyo neighbourhood featuring over 10,000 street dancers in the late August O-Bon season, when departed spirits are said to return to the earthly plane to visit their loved ones.

Resources

Metropolis Japan *(metropolisjapan.com)* English-language magazine.

Time Out Tokyo *(timeout.com/tokyo)* Tokyo entertainment, events and travel.

Tokyo Weekender *(tokyoweekender.com)* Bi-monthly English-language lifestyle magazine, also online.

WHERE TO STAY

Wherever possible, aim to stay in a ryokan (traditional inn) for the unique experiences it affords, including sleeping in a fluffy futon atop fragrant tatami-mat flooring. Although far easier to find outside the metropolis, one centrally located option in Tokyo is the pleasant Fukudaya in Shinsen (just adjacent to Shibuya). Another option, which will leave you incredulous that you are still within Tokyo's borders, is the Kabutoya Inn in Hinohara, located in the far western corner of the metropolis. Featuring a thick, steep thatched roof and rooms with sunken hearths, and surrounded by lush trees and birdsong, this ryokan is the real deal.

04

BEST FOR ONSEN

Do not miss a dip in the healing waters of local hot spring pools such as the atmospheric Tenzan Onsen.

RED PAGODA/SHUTTERSTOCK

Odawara Castle

Hakone

DURATION	DISTANCE	GREAT FOR
2–3 days	50km	Onsen, history & nature
BEST TIME TO GO	Year-round	

Comprising a collection of onsen tucked along a volcanic mountain range, the beloved resort town of Hakone (箱根) draws year-round visitors for its unique combination of natural hot spring waters, scenic hiking trails, unique museums and burgeoning cafe culture. The region features landmarks such as a teahouse and cobblestone hiking trail that evoke the Edo era, when the area thrummed with foot traffic along the Old Tōkaidō Hwy between Kyoto and Edo (present-day Tokyo). Be vigilant when driving; streets can be very narrow, and pedestrians and cyclists often share the road. Studless tyres and chains are essential in winter.

Link Your Trip

06 Izu Peninsula

After completing the loop drive, take Rte 1 toward the coast to link up with Drive 6.

05 Chiba's Bōsō Peninsula

Take the 40 minute car ferry from Kurihama on the Miura Peninsula to Tateyama for Drive 5.

01 ODAWARA (小田原)

The glory days of this castle town spanned the Sengoku and Edo eras (15th–19th centuries). Destroyed via an early Meiji era (1870s) governmental edict, today's reconstructed **castle grounds** offer vibrant seasonal flowers. Nearby, **Kamaboko-dori** is lined with shops selling fish cake loaves, a local speciality.

THE DRIVE
From Ohoribata St along the castle's eastern edge, take Rte 1. Veer right onto Rte 723. The museum is shortly off to the right.

02 HAKONE OPEN-AIR MUSEUM (箱根彫刻の森美術館)

Alfresco sculptures created by global artists line the meandering paths of this delightful museum, along with a forested **foot bath**. Indoor installations include a circular staircase framed by kaleidoscopic stained glass, and a permanent Pablo Picasso collection.

THE DRIVE
Continue along Rte 723, turning left after the Hakone Yutowa Hotel.

03 GŌRA (強羅)

This small mountainous village boasts atmospheric hotels, *onsen ryokan* (traditional hot-spring inns), gardens and cafes. Some establishments are open to day-bathers, including **Merveille Hakone Gōra**. Greenery awaits at the **POLA Museum of Art**, featuring 10,000 multi-genre works.

THE DRIVE
Take Rte 734, which zigzags for 3.5km. Veer left onto Rte 735 toward Ōwakudani. The car park closes around 4pm; check the strictly maintained seasonal hours.

View from on High

Consider leaving the car behind for an afternoon in order to take advantage of additional local transportation modes via the 'Golden Route', which also allows you to take in stunning birds-eye vistas of the mountainous region. Begin by catching the Hakone Tōzan train line at Hakone-Yumoto station, and ride this to Gōra. Take a coffee break at the nearby airy, minimalist Coffee Camp, or indulge in an onsen bath. Transfer back at Gōra station to the cable car line, which crisscrosses the local mountains using a switchback system. At Sounzan station, transfer to a ropeway that travels over the impressive Ōwakudani crater.

04 ŌWAKUDANI (大涌谷)

Experience a living, breathing **volcano**, replete with billowing steam and sulphur-scented air. Activities here include hiking the **Ōwakudani Nature Trail** (advance online reservations required); riding a ropeway for picturesque birds-eye views; visiting the instructional **Hakone Geomuseum**; and enjoying *kurotamago* (black eggs boiled in volcanic onsen waters) – a local delicacy – at the **Tamago-Chaya Teahouse**.

THE DRIVE
Wend back up the crater along Rte 735. Turn right onto the zigzagging Ubago St, then a sharp left onto Rte 75 at the T-junction. Continue along the winding road; the Hakone Visitor Centre is on your left.

05 HAKONE VISITOR CENTRE (環境省箱根ビジターセンター)

Three **hiking trails** start here, leading respectively toward **Mt Kintoki**, **Lake Ashi** and the pampas-grass-laced **Sengokuhara Highland**. Also available is free-of-charge paraphernalia for **bird-watching** on the grounds.

THE DRIVE
Rte 75 snakes lakeside for around 9km; park just past the shrine.

06 HAKONE JINJA (箱根神社)

This shrine cuts a magnificent sight with its three crimson-red **torii** (gates), including one standing inside **Lake Ashi**. An on-site **fountain** is sculpted in the image of a nine-headed dragon that's enshrined here, which local lore says once threatened the area, and to whom is dedicated a yearly summertime fireworks festival.

THE DRIVE
Continue on Rte 75 to Motohakone-ko Pier, located around 1.3km past the shrine. Free parking.

07 HAKONE SIGHTSEEING CRUISE (箱根海賊船)

Glide along the waters of **Lake Ashi**, on whose surface you just might catch Mt Fuji's spectacular reflection. Boats are pirate-themed, promising a particularly fun excursion for kids.

THE DRIVE
From the lakeside Rte 1, turn right onto Rte 732 and continue winding downward, passing Otamaga Pond. The teahouse is on the left.

08 AMAZAKE TEA HOUSE (甘酒茶屋)

Feel history in this dimly lit, 400-year-old teahouse, featuring a rustically atmospheric hearth, which serves the same steaming *amazake* (fermented rice drink) that fortified Edo-era foot travellers traversing the Tōkaidō Hwy. Cash only. Experience a section of the historic **Hakone Hachiri Trail** along the cobblestone path running just behind the teahouse (sensible shoes required!). To walk a longer segment, park at nearby **Otamaga Pond** and catch the trail at the Kyu-kaido Ishidatami bus stop.

THE DRIVE
Turn left from the teahouse onto Rte 732, which curves downhill, for 3km.

09 HATAJUKU YOSEGI KAIKAN HALL (畑宿寄木会館)

On-site workshops here feature the local craft of *yosegi-zaiku* (marquetry), where wood segments are shaped into intricate mosaic patterns. Products and artworks featuring the artform are also available in shops throughout town.

THE DRIVE
Continue along Rte 732 toward Hakone-Yumoto for 3.8km.

10 TENZAN ONSEN (天山湯治郷)

The local practice of *tōji* (visiting onsen for several weeks as a medicinal cure for various health-related ailments) dates back to the Edo era. Tenzan honours this history by encouraging quiet, contemplative bathing in its atmospheric pools and dry/steam saunas, which are complemented by richly toned woods.

Take a Break

Local eateries include 808 MONSMARE, specialising in scrumptious wood-fired pizza (sister shop HAKONE DULCE STUDIO STELLA serves gelato in flaky, crispy cones). For breakfast, visit SAIEN, where *shōjin ryōri* (vegetarian Buddhist cuisine) is served by a monk. Consider staying at a unique inn such as the spacious, stylish ROHEN HAKONE YUMOTO (a renovated 100-year-old ryokan).

At HAKONE GŌRA PARK you'll find French-style gardens, tearooms, tropical plants and a crafthouse offering art-themed workshops. Caffeinate at NOMU HAKONE.

A Sobering History

Edo-era travellers walking the Tōkaidō Hwy between Hakone and Mishima regarded the terrain lying on the other side of the arduous mountain gorge as literally being in another world. The **Hakone Sekisho** (箱根関所; *sekisho* means checkpoint) was erected on the eastern edge of Lake Ashi – ostensibly for protecting potential weapons from being smuggled into Edo, but primarily to prevent the escape of feudal lords' wives, who were kept in the capital to prevent uprisings against the ruling Tokugawa shogunate. Today, the re-created checkpoint and on-site museum offer a glimpse back in time to what this 'crossing through worlds' might have felt like.

SATAO/SHUTTERSTOCK

Lake Ashi

05

BEST FOR BEACH VIBES

Surfers and sun-soakers alike are spoilt for choice; try crescent-shaped Onjuku Beach.

Chiba's Bōsō Peninsula

DURATION	DISTANCE	GREAT FOR
2–3 days	222km	Coastal views, surfing, onsen & organic farms

BEST TIME TO GO	Summer for beaches; winter to spring for flowers

LOVEPHOTOCHAN/SHUTTERSTOCK

Tateyama, Bōsō Peninsula

Unbeknownst even to many Tokyoites, who are prone to dismissing adjacent Chiba Prefecture as a mere offshoot of the capital, Chiba's Bōsō Peninsula (房総半島) offers a laid-back slice of the slow life alongside exquisite scenery. With its white-sand beaches and surf towns, unique cafes and organic farms, and numerous places of spiritual significance, this is an excellent destination to explore one of Japan's lesser-travelled regions – all easily accessible from Tokyo. Reaching peninsular Chiba used to involve snaking around the mouth of Tokyo Bay, but hours were shaved off the trip with the 1997 construction of the underwater Aqua-Line Expressway – an architectural marvel – linking Kawasaki with Kisarazu, about halfway down the peninsula.

Link Your Trip

04 Hakone

Take the car ferry from Tateyama to Kurihama on the Miura Peninsula, which offers easy access to Hakone.

06 Izu Peninsula

The Tateyama–Kurihama ferry also links you to the geothermal-rich Izu Peninsula.

01 KASAMORI-KANNON TEMPLE (笠森観音)

Built atop high stilts, this forested temple features wafting incense, panoramic 360-degree vistas from its wooden deck, **walking trails** lush with raw nature, and several inscribed stones – one etched with words from famed Edo-era poet Matsuo Bashō.

Visit a Working Organic Farm

This region is prime organic farm territory, and some welcome visitors. Located in Isumi is the **Peace and Permaculture Dojo** *(peaceandpermadojo.wixsite.com/home/english)*, which offers tours and experiences; and **Brown's Field** *(brownsfield-jp.com/english)*, which has a macrobiotic cafe and inn, and holds workshops. Both have full English-language capacity. In Minamiboso, two farms where a basic understanding of Japanese will be helpful are **Awa Retreat** *(awaretreat.com)*, which offers you-pick herb experiences and summer coastal sand bathing at its Herb Chikura Seaside Garden; and **Yamana House** *(yamanahouse.site)*, an Edo-era renovated *kominka* (folk house) run by a collective of young farmers and chefs, which hosts various farming/DIY-themed workshops. All farms require advance notice. Check websites for fees and details.

THE DRIVE Enjoy lush greenery as you head toward the southern stretch of the Kujukuri coastline via National Rte 409, linking up with coastal Rte 128.

02 TSURIGASAKI SURFING BEACH (釣りが崎海岸)

Surfers: grab your boards (or rent one at local shop **Wreaths**). This beach featured in the 2020 (well, 2021) Tokyo Olympics, and boasts prime waves. Everyone else: take your time exploring the relaxed surrounding beach town.

THE DRIVE Continue down Rte 128.

03 ONJUKU (御宿海岸)

Slow down to the ocean rhythms along crescent-shaped, white-sand Onjuku Beach. Swim, sunbathe and consider visiting the **monument** marking a 1600s Mexican shipwreck from which friendly international relations blossomed.

THE DRIVE Continue along coastal Rte 128 for 19km, veering onto the coastal access road just before JR Ubara train station.

04 UBARA BEACH (鵜原海岸)

At secluded Ubara Beach you'll find moss-covered rocks and the quietly atmospheric **Yasaka Jinja**, a shrine featuring a striking white *torii* (gate).

THE DRIVE Return to Rte 128 and follow it for nearly 19km; the inn is on the right. On-site parking available.

05 HŌRAIYA INN (蓬莱谷)

Soak in the steamy sodium chloride waters of this *onsen ryokan* alongside oceanfront views and sumptuous local cuisine. Peaceful energy reigns in **Kamogawa**, a fishing village and beach town that hosted Japan's first-ever surfing competition in the 1960s. Nearby, swim in the gentle waters off picturesque **Shirosaki Beach**.

THE DRIVE
Continue south, hugging the coast for 30km, then turn right on Rte 187. Bear left at the fork; the shrine is on the right.

06 TAKABE JINJA (高家神社)

Join hopeful chefs by paying your respects at Japan's only shrine worshipping the god of cooking. Its ceremonial calendar includes an impressive 1000-year-old knife ritual, held three times yearly.

THE DRIVE
Returning to Rte 187, turn right onto Rte 410 for 1.8km.

07 STRAWBERRY POT CAFÉ (ストローベリー・ポット・カフェ)

Swim or sunbathe at **Minami-Chikura Beach**, then visit this cafe run by an *ama san* (Japan's famed skin divers, often female, who catch local shellfish). Besides coffee and sweeping sea views, enjoy desserts featuring agar (seaweed-derived gelatin) during the May–September diving season. Closed on dive days; call first (0470-44-5552).

THE DRIVE
Continue down coastal Rte 410 to the peninsula's southernmost tip, enjoying dramatic scenes of ocean spray crashing against black rocks.

08 NOJIMAZAKI LIGHTHOUSE (野島崎灯台)

Ascend this government-designated historic monument for more ocean vistas, and visit its small on-site **museum**.

THE DRIVE
Continue winding around the peninsula via Rte 410, then left on coastal Rte 257 along a section of the Bōsō Flowerline (a route flanked by seasonal flowers year-round).

09 SUNOSAKI SHRINE (洲崎神社)

Brave the towering staircase for majestic ocean views at this shrine, built in 606 to protect Tokyo Bay and guard against maritime accidents. Find another **lighthouse** just northward.

THE DRIVE
Continue following the Bōsō Flowerline for 9km, then left (followed by a right) onto coastal Rte 250 (Kagamiura St) for 4km, and northwest onto Rte 302 for 2.4km. Turn left on the road after the barber shop on the left, and follow to the end.

10 HARAOKA PIER

One of Japan's few wooden piers, built in the 1920s, this spot is popular for its retro feel and photogenic setting.

THE DRIVE
Head north along coastal Rte 127 toward the Nokogiriyama Tozan Expressway (toll road).

11 MT NOKOGIRI

Jagged-edged Mt Nokogiri (literally, 'saw-toothed mountain') in Kyōnan offers a network of gentle **hiking trails**, plus a ropeway and impressive Tokyo Bay views. At its temple complex, **Nihonji-ji**, enormous statues of the Buddha and Hyaku-shaku Kannon (Buddhist Goddess of Mercy) are carved into the mountain face, while over 1500 intricate Buddhist statues sculpted during the late 1700s also dot the mountainside.

Take a Break

One cannot visit this region without indulging in freshly caught local seafood. Try the gleaming sashimi and spiny lobster tail at ISABAYA (いさばや), a laid-back coastal eatery in Isumi, run by a local fisheries cooperative. Enjoy cafe fare in Tateyama at oceanfront SEA DAYS at Hojo Beach, which has a working space and yoga/pilates studio, plus SUP rentals and superb Mt Fuji views. Or fuel up for a Mt Nokogiri hike at ROMI'S OCEAN, a unique burger joint in a converted school bus.

Where to Stay in Deep Chiba

An overnight stay in this region can be an excellent way to connect with local culture in a relaxed environment. Accommodation options in Minamiboso include the budget-friendly **Nemoto Marine Campground** along the peninsula's southern tip, which offers free camping from 20 July through 20 August. Midrange choices include spacious, airy cottage rentals at the nearby **Le Phare Shirahama**, as well as the **Sunset Beach Inn Kawana** further up the coast, known for its glisteningly fresh seafood. At the high end, there's the **Hotel Sunosaki Kazenosho**, offering stylish wooden oceanfront baths, and **Chikura Umi Base Camp**, a luxury glamping resort with exceedingly chic villas.

NISHI317/SHUTTERSTOCK

Haraoka Pier

06

BEST FOR WATER SPORTS

Enjoy marine sports of all types, including surfing at Shimoda's Shirahama Beach.

Izu Peninsula

DURATION	DISTANCE	GREAT FOR
3–4 days	255km	Seafood, ocean sports & nature

BEST TIME TO GO	Summer for beaches; winter to spring for flowers

SEAN PAVONE/SHUTTERSTOCK

Atami

Once an underwater volcanic landmass that drifted northward and joined Honshū Island some 600,000 years ago, today's Izu Peninsula (伊豆半島) is an explorer's playground. A designated UNESCO Global Geopark that's bubbling with geothermal waters, this is prime territory to experience Japan's famed onsen. Hiking, camping, sea kayaking, snorkelling and diving also abound along the long stretches of coastline, where local eateries offer the day's fresh catch. Fantastic surfing awaits on the peninsula's southeastern shores, while the lesser-visited western coast promises raw nature and dramatic sunsets. More adventuring and a quiet slice of tropical island life are found in the picturesque Izu islands (reached by ferry).

Link Your Trip

04 Hakone

Connect to circular Drive 4 from the ending point at Mishima Skywalk.

07 Fuji Five Lakes

Connect from Mishima Skywalk via Rtes 1/E1A and 138/E68, exiting the Fujiyoshida IC toward Lake Kawaguchi via Rte 707.

01 ODAWARA ART FOUNDATION'S ENOURA OBSERVATORY (小田原文化財団の江之浦測候所)

Contemplate Japan's artistic and architectural history amid majestic ocean views at this unique establishment encompassing an art gallery, outdoor stage, teahouse, strolling paths and more. Advance online reservations are required for visiting and parking. No children under 12.

Dive Deep with a Discover Izu Tour

Consider booking a tour with long-term Izu resident **Jimmy Nishida-Adams** *(discoverizu.com)*, whose extensive menu of creatively designed tours features various aspects of local history and culture. If preferred, Jimmy will also work with guests to craft their own customised tour based on specific interests and requests. In all cases, tours are dedicated to exploring authentic local Izu life. Groups of three or less can park their own car and head out in Jimmy's minivan; those with four or more can take their own vehicle and follow behind.

THE DRIVE

Heading southwest onto Rte 740, turn left onto Rte 739 and follow the peninsula.

02 MANAZURU PENINSULA NATURE PARK (県立真鶴半島自然公園)

Find fresh seafood along this lovely mini-peninsula, and ocean-front promenades at its forested nature park.

THE DRIVE

Take the toll-free, coastline-hugging Rte 135, passing numerous seafood shacks and *pachinko* (pinball) parlors. The Atami Beach Line (¥500 for normal-sized cars) leads into town after Yugawara Onsen.

03 ATAMI (熱海)

Emblematic of Japan's prosperous late-1980s economic 'bubble-era', Atami's heyday has long passed – but it is popular today for its retro feel and stationfront snacking opportunities. Catch early-blooming *sakura* (cherry blossoms; January–February) or vibrant fireworks displays (year-round).

THE DRIVE

Continue down coastal Rte 135, passing dilapidated resorts – a casualty of the bubble-era bust – plus numerous kitschy structures. A long tunnel leads to Itō City via the palm-fringed Orange Beach.

04 ITŌ (伊東)

Another historic onsen town whose attractions include a 10km **hiking trail**, suspension bridge and lighthouse/observation deck along the breath-taking **Jōgasaki Coast** – formed when lava met ocean following the 4000-year-old eruption of nearby **Mt Ōmuro**. A chairlift affords views of this now-extinct volcano's magnificent bowl-shaped, grass-covered peak. Also visit the nearby **Akazawa Onsen Hotel** for unparalleled ocean vistas.

THE DRIVE

Continue southward along Rte 135 amid panoramic seascapes and offshore views of the Izu islands.

KAWAZU (河津)

An annual riverside festival (February–March) celebrates this city's namesake, the early-blooming *kawazakura* cherry trees. Swim at scenic **Imaihama Beach**, and don't miss the inland **Kawazu Nanadaru** (Seven Waterfalls), accessible via a walkway wending through a plush forest. **Amagiso Onsen** features a collection of pools – some with stunning waterfall views, others in caves.

THE DRIVE
Continue along Rte 135 south. Approaching Shimoda, the Ogasaki Wing Parking Lot is a great lookout spot.

SHIMODA (下田)

Boasting glorious nature and fascinating history, Shimoda is a city to savour. Surfers, swimmers and sunseekers alike flock to its emerald-green waters and collection of white-sand beaches. The largest, **Shirahama Beach**, flaunts the striking red *torii* (shrine gate) of its **Shirahama Shrine**. Along the nearby **Suzaki Peninsula**, hike a coastal trail or swim at the secluded **Kujuppama Beach**. Visit photo-worthy **Ryugukutsu Cave** near Toji Beach. Near Shimoda Port, explore history along **Perry Road**, including the storied **Ryōsenji Temple** and its on-site **MoBS (Museum of Black Ship)**. Nearby, the 160-year-old **Kanaya Ryokan** inn boasts an impressive enormous wooden *sennin-buro* ('one-thousand-person bath').

THE DRIVE
Since petrol stations are sparse, fill up in Shimoda. From Rte 136, take Rte 16 to Nakagi.

07 HIRIZOHAMA BEACH (ヒリゾ浜)

Glittering schools of multicoloured fish await at this snorkeller's paradise, accessible from July to September via boat (no sailings on windy days). Beat the crowds by car camping at the pier – also a magnificent stargazing spot. Consider stopping at **Cape Irozaki** (the peninsula's southernmost tip) for a **shrine**, lighthouse and dramatic sea views.

THE DRIVE
Continue winding along coastal Rte 136. Along the way, find unique scenery at the Ishibu Rice Terraces, and Edo-era merchant buildings in pleasant, stroll-worthy Matsuzaki.

08 DŌGASHIMA (堂ヶ島)

Experience the slow life via a coastal hike and/or sightseeing cruise at Dōgashima, featuring **onsen** baths, ocean-framed sunsets and rare volcanic **rock formations**, and plentiful local seafood.

THE DRIVE
Continue up Rte 136, taking Rte 17 in Toi (a former gold-mining town also worth visiting), then head inland from the coast via the snaking Rte 18.

09 SHŪZENJI ONSEN (修善寺温泉)

This charming onsen resort town features a bamboo forest path, **Shūzenji** Zen Buddhist temple, and numerous ryokan.

THE DRIVE
From Rte 18, take Rte 136 and connect to the E70 at the Kannami-Tsukamoto IC. Exit at the Mishima-Tsukahara IC and follow Rte 1 toward Hakone.

MISHIMA SKYWALK (三島スカイウォーク)

Take in sweeping views of the peninsula (and Mt Fuji) via Japan's longest pedestrian suspension bridge. Advance online reservations required.

Take a Break

Japan is famous for its *michinoeki* (roadside stations), and KAIKOKU SHIMODA MINATO ROADSIDE STATION, fronting Shimoda Port, is particularly outstanding. In addition to the usual shelves of local products and car park car camping, this one has a staffed information desk packed with pamphlets on local surfing, sea kayaking, diving and more, plus a small museum that recounts the fascinating local geography and history. Also on-site is a fish market, a spacious outdoor deck, seafood restaurants, and the launch point for *kurobune* (black ship) sailing cruises.

Ferrying out to the Islands

Driving along Rte 135 offers spectacular views of the nine Izu islands; visit them for hiking, free camping, snorkelling, diving, onsen, seafood and lush nature. The islands include **Izu Ōshima** (the largest), home to the active volcano Mt Mihara, plus horse riding and striking wintertime camellia flowers. **Niijima** is famous for its fantastic surfing, glass art museum, and unique local sculptures crafted from volcanic pumice stone; while **Kozushima** is said to be dotted with mystical power spots. All island ferry services from the mainland are for foot passengers only except the Shimoda-Kozushima route, which accommodates vehicles (you can ferry out to other islands from there).

K THITIPONG/SHUTTERSTOCK

Mishima Skywalk

07

BEST FOR VIEWS

Magnificent views from Arakurayama Sengen Park's towering observation deck.

Fuji Five Lakes

DURATION	DISTANCE	GREAT FOR
2–3 days	106km	Nature, spirituality, museums & cafes
BEST TIME TO GO	Year-round	

FLORIAN AUGUSTIN/SHUTTERSTOCK

Mt Fuji view, Lake Yamanaka

Mt Fuji (富士山) is more than a mountain; it is a cultural icon. An active volcano said to house the goddess who placates eruptions, Fujisan is deeply sacred to Japan's people. Religious pilgrims have been summiting the mountain for centuries, with secular outdoor enthusiasts joining them more recently. Mt Fuji flaunts a perfect cone that's often encircled by mystical cloud formations, reflecting the subtle chromatic shifts of the changing seasons and hour of day. The mountain's 2013 UNESCO World Heritage designation encompassed the Fuji Five Lakes (富士五湖), which offer a plethora of outdoor activities alongside numerous shrines and museums.

Link Your Trip

06 Izu Peninsula

Head 50km south to join the Izu Peninsula drive at Mishima.

04 Hakone

From Lake Yamanaka, it's about an hour's drive along Route 138 to Hakone.

01 YAMANAKA-KO PANORAMA-DAI (山中湖パノラマ台)

From Tokyo begin at **Lake Yamanaka**, the furthest eastward point on the trip, accessible from the north (Chuo Expressway to Higashi Fujigoko Rd via Ōtsuki and Kawaguchiko IC) or south (Tōmei Expressway to Rte 138 via Gotemba and Subashiri IC). Get your bearings at this observation point's sweeping views of both the lake and **Mt Fuji**. Stop for coffee and pie at the elegant **Paper Moon** cafe (no children under 10). Alternatively, take the kids for a splash on the 20-minute hippo-themed **Yamanakako no Kaba** amphibious bus cruise.

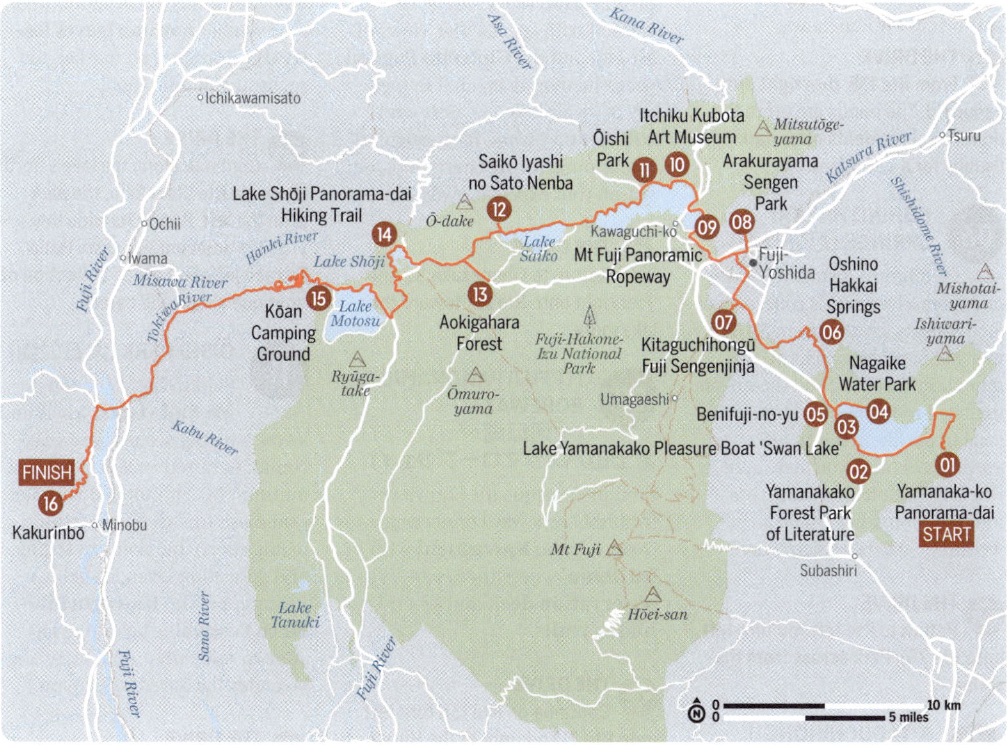

THE DRIVE
From the observation point follow Rte 730, take two left turns onto Rtes 729 and 413, following the lake's south shore (which becomes Rte 138).

02 YAMANAKAKO FOREST PARK OF LITERATURE (山中湖文学の森公園)

Several **literary museums** are housed in this complex, along with outdoor **forested paths** lined with poetry-inscribed stone monuments.

THE DRIVE
Continue following Rte 138 lakeside for 2.5km.

03 LAKE YAMANAKAKO PLEASURE BOAT 'SWAN LAKE' (遊覧船 白鳥の湖号)

Another lake cruise departs here (this one in swan-shaped vessels). In winter, enjoy crunching through snow while taking a lakeside walk and observing real-life whooper swans and coots, some wintering all the way from Siberia. This is a particularly otherworldly scene at dusk on the semi-frozen lake.

THE DRIVE
Veer right along the lake's north shore via Rte 729 (Marimo St).

04 NAGAIKE WATER PARK (長池親水公園)

Join the photographers jostling to capture superb views of **Mt Fuji's lake reflection** – including the ultimate 'double diamond Fuji' phenomenon at sunset. Winter is again optimal; watch for the late February evening **ice candle festival**.

THE DRIVE
Backtracking along Rte 729, take a sharp right onto Rte 138, turn left after 650m, then right.

05 BENIFUJI-NO-YU (紅富士の湯)

Take a hot-spring break at this pleasant **onsen** featuring outdoor pools, dry/mist saunas, and prime Mt Fuji views.

THE DRIVE
From Rte 138, turn right onto Fanuc Rd. The ponds are off to the right (local residents offer parking, usually for a ¥300 fee).

06 OSHINO HAKKAI SPRINGS (忍野八海)

Pilgrims historically purified themselves in this collection of eight **ponds**, created from Mt Fuji meltwater, prior to tackling the mountain. Stroll around the on-site thatched-roof houses and sample local treats like green-tinted *kusa mochi* (mugwort-flavoured rice cakes). Note that numerous tour buses stop here; mornings/weekdays may be less crowded.

THE DRIVE
Return to Rte 138 and turn left onto Rte 701. Park across from the shrine.

07 KITAGUCHIHONGŪ FUJI SENGENJINJA (北口本宮富士宣言神社)

For centuries, pilgrims ascending Mt Fuji have visited this sacred **forested shrine** to ask the gods for safe passage. It features a series of striking *torii* (shrine gates), along with an impressive fire festival held every 26–27 August.

THE DRIVE
Take Rte 139 for 3km, then turn left at the Akebonochō intersection. Turn right at Ohimezaka St, and left just before the Fujikyu railway line. Follow the road up to the park.

08 ARAKURAYAMA SENGEN PARK (新倉山浅間公園)

Climb a 400-step staircase (or parallel sloping road) to the **observation deck** and be rewarded with spectacular views of Mt Fuji and the **Chūreitō Pagoda** peace memorial, erected in memory of locals killed in 19th- and 20th-century wars. It's particularly stunning during cherry blossom season (but expect crowds).

THE DRIVE
Return to Ohimezaka St, and veer right onto Rte 137 toward the lakeshore.

09 MT FUJI PANORAMIC ROPEWAY (〜河口湖〜富士山パノラマロープウェイ)

Find picturesque Mt Fuji views from this ropeway connecting eastern **Lake Kawaguchi** with **Mt Tenjo**, where there's an **observation deck** and several **hiking trails**.

THE DRIVE
Continue on Rte 137, turn left onto Rte 21 and right at the Hirose intersection, then an immediate left. The area is crowded at festival time; find nearby parking such as the Momiji Tunnel #1 Parking Lot (もみじ回廊第一駐車場) or Asama Shrine (河口湖浅間神社).

10 ITCHIKU KUBOTA ART MUSEUM (久保田一竹美術館)

Fantastical architecture, exquisitely dyed textiles and a tranquil **garden** await at this unique museum. Depending upon time and interest, additional nearby museums worth visiting include the **Kawaguchiko Museum of Art** (showcasing Mt Fuji–themed works) and **Kawaguchiko Craft Park** (offering hands-on art workshops). **Momiji Tunnel** is an attractive corridor of maple trees along the lake's north shore, where a November **autumn leaves festival** features a craft market and nighttime illumination.

THE DRIVE
Continue along the lake's north shore via Rte 21 for 2km; the park is on the left. Park in its wide lot, or at the adjacent Fuji Ōishi Hana Terrace (offering a nice collection of boutique shops and cafes).

11 ŌISHI PARK (大石公園)

Said to boast the top **Mt Fuji vistas**, you'll find swoon-worthy scenes here year-round: fiery-red *kochia* bushes in autumn; Mt Fuji topped with her grandiose frosty cone in winter; iconic cherry blossoms in spring; and sprawling lavender fields in summer. The **Kawaguchiko Herb Festival** is held here late June to mid-July – don't miss the lavender-flavoured soft cream.

THE DRIVE
Turn left onto Rte 21 to rejoin the Kohoku View Line. Take the right fork toward Lake Saiko, hugging its north shore and following the signage to turn right.

12 SAIKŌ IYASHI NO SATO NENBA (西湖いやしの里根場)

Taglined the 'Healing Village', and recalling the nearby hamlets of times past, this collection of lovely restored traditional thatched-roof structures in a bucolic natural setting features local foods, a teahouse and craft-themed workshops.

THE DRIVE
Heading southeast, turn right onto Rte 21, then left on Rte 139 to reach the Ice and Wind Caves

Climbing the Sacred Mountain

If you wish to combine your drive with a Mt Fuji climb, the **Yoshida Trail** is accessible from the Fuji Five Lakes region (and is open from 1 July to 10 September). Parking is available at the Fujisan Parking Lot. Before your climb, visit the nearby **Fujisan World Heritage Centre**, where you'll find exhibits and important information about weather, safety and climbing conditions. Note that warm clothing and gloves are a must; it's also strongly advised to rest at a mountain hut. Advance reservations are required and huts tend to fill up quickly, so book early.

JAMOO/SHUTTERSTOCK

Yoshida Trail

SNOTWO/SHUTTERSTOCK

Camping & Sacred Sites up on High

The tagline for **Retreat Camp Mahoroba**, situated above Lake Kawaguchi is 'Retreat yourself with Mt Fuji' – an apt description of this full-service campsite featuring sublime views of the mountain and environs. Numerous camping styles include forested tent sites, auto camping, yurts, dome tents, villas and a spacious wooden deck. Morning yoga, sauna and Jacuzzi also on offer. From here, hike (or drive, minding the narrow road) to **Tenkū no Torii** ('Sky-High Shrine Gate'), affiliated with the nearby **Kawaguchi Asama Shrine**, which frames Mt Fuji to striking effect (¥100 fee for photos).

Mt Fuji view, Lake Kawaguchi (p52)

(both have parking). The caves are also connected via forested walking trails.

13 AOKIGAHARA FOREST (青木ヶ原樹海)

Known as *jūkai* ('sea of trees'), this thick primeval forest bloomed atop volcanic lava from Mt Fuji's Jōgan eruption of 864–866 (which also formed Lakes Saiko, Shōji and Motosu). Said to house *yūrei* (agitated spirits), the forest offers interesting walking terrain – stay strictly on the **marked trails** to avoid getting lost amid the density. Several **caves** also formed here from lava tubes of the same eruption, each with its own distinctive topography: the **Bat**, **Fūgaku Wind**, **Narusawa Ice** and **Dragon Caves**. Remember the temperature drop, and dress accordingly!

THE DRIVE
Backtracking and continuing via Rte 139, turn right onto Rte 358, then left onto Rte 706 to follow Lake Shōji's northern shore. The trailhead is at Tatego-hama Beach near Bus Stop 88.

14 LAKE SHŌJI PANORAMA-DAI HIKING TRAIL (パノラマ台)

This roughly two-hour (5.5km) **hike** affords lofty views of Mt Fuji, Lakes Shōji and Motosu, and the Aokigahara Forest.

THE DRIVE
From Rte 706, turn right onto Rte 139, then another right onto Rte 300, and follow Lake Motosu's north shore to the campsite.

15 KŌAN CAMPING GROUND (浩庵)

Among the lakes' numerous camping and glamping sites is this popular campground fronting **Lake Motosu**. It features two tent spaces (one lakefront, one forested), plus cottages (advance reservations required; spots fill up quickly). Also on-site are **kayak/canoe/SUP rentals** to glide on the lake's clear, placid waters. Fun fact: the Mt Fuji image appearing on the old ¥1000 note (still in circulation) was photographed from this spot.

THE DRIVE
Continue past the lake on Rte 300, crossing the Fuji River then turning left onto Rte 52 and right onto the winding Rte 805.

16 KAKURINBŌ (覚林坊)

Finish your visit with a unique stay at this historic **Buddhist temple**, including an onsite **garden** and vegetarian meals. Reservations required.

Take a Break

Caffeinate along Lake Kawaguchi at bright San Francisco–style CISCO COFFEE (シスコ・コーヒー) with decadent cakes and Mt Fuji gazing, or atmospheric L'ESSENCE PATISSERIE, with a lineup of French-inspired desserts and coffee. Consider a stay at stylish KAGELOW MT FUJI HOSTEL (陽炎) whose dormitory and private Japanese-style rooms include fragrant tatami and warm woods. Sample the regional speciality of *hōtō* at MOMIJI-TEI (もみじ亭) – these thick, flat noodles are served in a rich, earthy broth, accented with root vegetables. Also try the *goma* (sesame) tofu and soft-serve ice cream.

Also Try...

TAKEPH/SHUTTERSTOCK

Western Tokyo to Yamanashi Wine Country

DURATION	DISTANCE
2–3 days	104km

This 100km drive takes you through deep greenery from Tokyo's far western Tama region into the famed **wine country** of Yamanashi Prefecture (pictured). You'll pass the mighty **Tama** and **Hinohara rivers** and picturesque **Lake Okutama**, as well as sacred **Mt Mitake**. In **Ōme** is a collection of retro **movie theatres** and shops reminiscent of the Shōwa era, and the stylish **Botanica_Ome inn**. Nearby, crafts workshops featuring washi (traditional Japanese paper) are on offer at **Hinode Washi**, while further westward, near Okutama station, lies the laid-back **Vertere** craft beer brewery and taproom. Besides opportunities for camping, kayaking, river rafting and hiking, this drive offers access to numerous **onsen** before taking you to the **Kōshū Valley** – Japan's top winemaking region, featuring numerous local wineries.

Best of Saitama

DURATION	DISTANCE
2 days	100km

Start in **Kawagoe**, known for peaceful temples and shrines. In neighbouring **Ogawamachi** you'll find bucolic **organic farms** (plus unstaffed **veggie stands**; leave your coins in the box)! The local washi paper is included in the UNESCO Intangible Cultural Heritage designation – don't miss the incredibly artsy, aptly-named **Village of the Paper Lovers (紙すきのむら)** shop. Next, pass through the **Higashi-Chichibu** region toward tranquil Nagatoro to **kayak** its languid river and admire fiery autumn leaves. In nearby **Chichibu** are numerous atmospheric restored *kominka* (folk homes), including the **Nipponia Chichibu** inn. There are also numerous **sake breweries**, and one of Japan's top independent whisky brands, **Ichiro's Malt**. Finish in Hidaka by enjoying an organic lunch at the lovely **Alishan Café**.

NATTEE CHALERMTIRAGOOL/SHUTTERSTOCK

Nasu, Tochigi

DURATION	DISTANCE
2 days	64km

Begin in **Okushiobara** – deep onsen territory – featuring numerous secluded pools where sulphuric clouds billow up from the adjacent volcanic mountains. Next, stop at **N's Yard** for the eclectic works of modern artist Yoshitomo Nara; then visit the sleepy town of **Kuroiso**, which is in fact one of Japan's pioneering coffee culture towns (don't miss the Parisian-style **1988 Café Shozo**). Make your way toward the **Nasu Highlands**, where you might splash out for a night at the exceedingly stylish **Hoshino Resorts Risonare Nasu**. End the drive with more onsen at the 7th-century **Shika-no-yu** bathhouse (once frequented by samurai), or hike **Mt Chausu**. Kids will also love the **Minamigaoka Dairy Farm** and **Nasu Alpaca Farm**.

Miura Peninsula, Kanagawa

DURATION	DISTANCE
1–2 days	75km

Start in Kamakura, where must-see sights include **Kōtokuin Temple's** enormous bronze Daibutsu Buddha statue (pictured; local sights are best walked due to traffic); and a vibrant stretch of *uminoie* (beach shacks). Further south, a similar food/music scene reigns at **Blue Moon Hayama** along Isshiki Beach in summer, or at **Surfers Zushi** year-round. Continuing down the coast, scenic hikes include the **Koajiro Forest Trail**, and the craggy **Jōgashima Island Walking Trail** off the peninsula's southern tip. Local oceanfront cafes include the Hawaiian-themed **Kamehameha-daiō-no-nagisa** or, looping around the coast, French-inspired fare featuring local ingredients at **Beachend Cafe**. Take the Kurihama–Tateyama ferry for Drive 5 (p42); or continue northward for contemporary works at the architecturally stunning **Yokosuka Museum of Art**.

0
50 km
0
25 miles
11
Suzu
Noto Peninsula
Anamizu
Noto-jima
Nanao
Sea of Japan
Hakui
Himi
Toyama-wan
Kurobe
Itoigawa
Jōetsu
Kashiwazaki
Tokamachi
Tsunan
Iiyama
Nakano
Nagano
Kusatsu
Takaoka
Toyama
Shirouma-dake
O-yama
Kanazawa
09
Chūbusangaku National Park
Komatsu
Ueda
Asama-yama
Karuizawa
Yariga-take
Hotaka-dake
Haku-san National Park
Haku-san
10
Matsumoto
Saku
Fukui
Takayama
Shiojiri
Norikura-dake
Chino
Kobushi-ga-take
Shiratori
Ontake-san
Ina
Kiso-komagatake
Chichibu-Tama-Kai National Park
Senjō-ga-take
Tsuruga
08
Kōfu
Mino
Minami Alps National Park
Nakatsugawa
Iida
Nagahama
Sekigahara
Gifu
Lake Biwa
Ōgaki
Tajimi
Fuji-Hakone-Izu National Park
Mt Fuji
Hikone
Nagoya
Kuwana
Toyota
Fuji
Yokkaichi
Okazaki
Shizuoka
Tokoname
Handa
Suzuka
Yaizu
Suruga-wan
Shimada
Ise-wan
Tsu
Toyohashi
Hamamatsu
Atsumi Peninsula
Ise

TAKASHI IMAGES/SHUTTERSTOCK

Matsumoto Castle (p66)

Central Honshū

Explore

Central Honshū

Known to the Japanese as Chūbu (中部), Central Honshū is the nation's heartland, stretching out between the sprawling metropolises of Greater Tokyo and Kansai. While most of Honshū's mountain ranges run parallel to the coastlines, in Chūbu, the Itoigawa–Shizuoka Tectonic Line runs north–south, from the Sea of Japan to the Pacific Ocean, and has produced the country's highest mountain ranges – the North, Central and Southern Alps. Expect magnificent alpine vistas, exciting resorts, world-class skiing and hiking, onsen (hot springs), ancient towns and vibrant cities that are a joy to explore with your own wheels. Hit the road to visit places well off the beaten track.

Nagoya

Given its handy location on the Tōkaidō shinkansen, Nagoya (名古屋), Japan's fourth-largest city, is a good spot from which to head out into the mountains of Chūbu. It's much more than just a transport hub though, featuring plenty of traditional culture among the neon-lit buzz of what is one of Japan's most modern (yet laid-back) industrialised cities. The city is known for its showpiece castle, Nagoya-jō, dating from 1615; historic Atsuta-jingū, one of Japan's most sacred Shintō shrines; and the sublime Tokugawa Art Museum.

Kanazawa

The array of cultural attractions in Kanazawa (金沢) makes the city the drawcard of the Hokuriku region and a rival to Kyoto as the historical jewel of mainland Japan. Best known for Kenroku-en, a castle garden dating from the 17th century, it also boasts beautifully preserved samurai and geisha (known locally as *geiko*) districts, attractive temples, a wealth of museums and a wonderful market. These days, Kanazawa is linked to Tokyo by the Hokuriku shinkansen (via Nagano City); construction is well under way for the continuation of the shinkansen line through to Kyoto and Osaka.

Matsumoto

This exciting city sits in a fertile valley, with the magnificent North Alps, in all their splendour, to the west. Matsumoto (松本) is an attractive,

WHEN TO GO

There will be plenty of snow in the high mountains between December and April, not so much in the valleys. For snow sports enthusiasts, the best months are January to March; cherry blossoms will be out in April and autumn foliage in October. Summer is relatively cool in the mountains, compared to the humidity of the coastline.

cosmopolitan place loved by both residents and admirers around the globe who come to enjoy its superb castle, pretty streets, galleries, cafes and endearing vistas. There seems to be some extra enthusiasm for life here, with a youngish population that includes those who have forsaken the massive cities for this regional beauty. The mountains are close, the air is fresh and the rivers are invigoratingly cold. Matsumoto makes a great stepping-stone for exploring Chūbu; come here by train and pick up a rental car, or drive here...but don't miss Matsumoto.

Nagano

The mountain-ringed prefectural capital of Nagano City (長野) has long been a place of pilgrimage, evolving around its drawcard temple, the magnificent Zenkō-ji. Millions visit each year, with many also seeing the city as a gateway to the mountains, both in and out of the snowy months. The shinkansen line from Tokyo to Nagano was opened with great fanfare in time for Nagano to host the 1998 Winter Olympics and snow sports facilities and resorts in the area are top-class. There's a friendly, small-town feel here and so much of interest to do in the surrounding countryside.

TRANSPORT

In mountainous Chūbu, there's excellent road infrastructure in the river valleys, connecting inland towns and cities such as Nagano, Matsumoto and Takayama with those on the coast. While it's easy to rent a car in Tokyo, Nagoya or Kyoto and drive into and through Central Honshū, arriving by train and renting in regional cities is also a good option.

WHAT'S ON

Japan's Summer Vacation
Towns and resorts host fireworks festivals in July and August, while many ski-resort areas attract summer visitors with music festivals.

Takayama Matsuri
One of Japan's great festivals is in two parts. On 14 and 15 April there's the Sannō Matsuri, when decorated *yatai* (floats) are paraded through town. During Hachiman Matsuri, on 9 and 10 October, the colourful floats are decked out with lanterns.

Resources

Go Nagano *(go-nagano.net)* The prefectures's official tourism site.

Visit Toyama *(vIslt-toyama-japan.com)* The official Toyama tourism website.

Ishikawa Travel *(ishikawatravel.jp)* Information on Ishikawa Prefecture.

Visit Gifu *(visitgifu.com)* All you need to know on Gifu Prefecture.

Yamanashi Tourism *(yamanashi-kankou.jp)* The prefecture's tourist info site.

Visit Nagoya *(nagoya-info.jp)* Nagoya City information website.

WHERE TO STAY

There's a wide range of options when it comes to accommodation in Chūbu. Some of Japan's finest *onsen ryokan* (traditional hot spring inns) are found in the hollows of this densely forested alpine region and along the banks of its many rivers. In cities, modern, practical hotels offer midrange comforts, while there are great bargains to be had in resort areas outside the ski season. This is also the land of remote camping and mountain huts. Chūbu is a popular destination for Japanese in the summer holidays (late July to the end of August), so book ahead.

08

BEST FOR CULTURE

Narai's remarkably well-preserved Edo-era streetscape is enthralling.

Nagoya to Matsumoto

DURATION	DISTANCE	GREAT FOR
3–4 days	250km	History, scenery & traditional crafts
BEST TIME TO GO	April to November	

NOPPASIN WONGCHUM/SHUTTERSTOCK

Nagoya

There's plenty of history and culture on this drive into the mountains of Central Honshū from Japan's fourth-largest city, Nagoya. Check out one of the country's oldest surviving wooden castles in Inuyama before heading to Seki, a town with a long sword and knife-forging history. Follow the Nakasendō, the old 'central mountain route' of the Edo period through the Kiso Valley, stopping at gorgeous, restored post towns such as Magome, Tsumago, Kiso-Fukushima and Narai. There are top short walk opportunities along the way connecting these small towns. Finish up in the much-loved city of Matsumoto, ready to explore further from there.

Link Your Trip

09 Matsumoto to Nozawa Onsen
Head north and east to Hakuba and Nagano City.

10 Matsumoto to Kanazawa
Drive through the North Alps, then on to the Sea of Japan coast.

01 NAGOYA (名古屋)

Japan's fourth-largest city is on the Tōkaidō shinkansen line, between Tokyo and Kyoto; check out its famous castle **Nagoya-jō**, historic shrine **Atsuta-jingū** and **Tokugawa Art Museum** before you leave.

THE DRIVE
It's a 25km drive directly north of Nagoya to Inuyama.

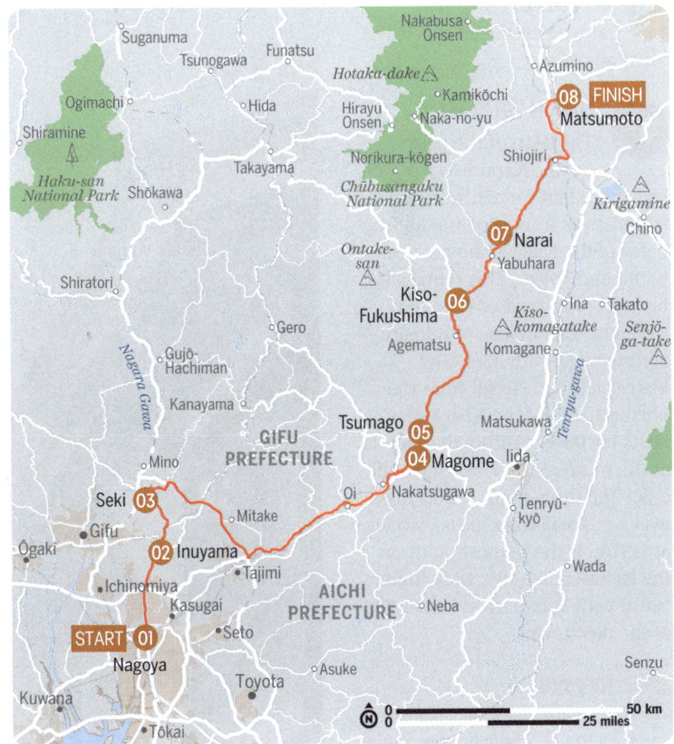

Nakasendō

During much of the Edo period (1603–1868), the Tokugawa shogunate maintained control and 'encouraged loyalty' by ordering the regional *daimyō* (feudal lords) to spend alternate years in Edo (now Tokyo) and requiring them to keep their family in Edo permanently, effectively as hostages. This meant a lot of travel, and the Gokaidō (Five Highways) were developed to link Edo with the outer provinces. The Tōkaidō ('eastern sea route') and Nakasendō ('central mountain route') linked Edo with Kyoto. Many travelled the Nakasendō as it required fewer dangerous river crossings when compared to the coastal Tōkaidō. The Nakasendō had 69 'stations' on its 534km route.

02 INUYAMA (犬山)

This historic town's main drawcard is its castle, **Inuyama-jō**, a designated National Treasure. One of Japan's oldest surviving wooden castles, dating back to 1537, it has undergone extensive renovation. The atmospheric walk up to the riverside castle passes through over 20 red *torii* (gates) and Shintō shrines before arriving at the four-level *donjon* (main keep). Inuyama's interesting Edo-era **old town** is at the base of the castle.

THE DRIVE
Head north for another 18km to Seki.

03 SEKI (関)

Famed across Japan for producing prized swords for millennia, Seki is where samurai would get their trusty blades made by master swordsmiths. Today, Seki is at the forefront of Japan's artisan knife industry, with makers using traditional techniques passed on through generations. Drop in to the **Seki Traditional Swordsmith Museum** and **G.Sakai Knife Museum**, where you can forge your own blade with a signature engraving.

THE DRIVE
It's an 83km drive east to Magome at the southern end of the Kiso Valley.

04 MAGOME (馬籠)

The small village of Magome was number 43 of the 69 post towns of the Nakasendō – they were numbered from Nihonbashi in Tokyo through to Sanjō Ōhashi in Kyoto. There's no better way to get a taste of rural, old-world Japan than the 7.8km **hike** from Magome to Tsumago, but as you're driving, it may be easier just to drop in to these historic, small villages. Magome's highlight is the steep, cobblestoned, pedestrian street that was the **old walking route**; the rustic shopfronts, guesthouses, museums, cafes and mountain views will keep your finger on the shutter.

THE DRIVE
Take Rte 7 for 8km up and over Magome Pass to get to Tsumago. The road basically follows the same course as the hiking trail, so keep your eyes open for walkers.

05 TSUMAGO (妻籠)

Arriving in Tsumago, post town number 42, it genuinely feels like you've stepped back into the 17th century as you stroll the preserved pedestrian street lined with heritage buildings, museums and inns, where weary travellers would, and still do, spend the night. The dark-wood glory of Tsumago's lattice-fronted buildings is particularly beautiful at dawn and dusk, and film and TV crews are often spotted here.

THE DRIVE
It's a 39km drive up the narrow Kiso Valley on Rte 19.

06 KISO-FUKUSHIMA (木曽福島)

Fukushima was number 37 of the post towns and a barrier checkpoint, where officials could monitor traffic, inspect travel permits and look for illicit goods. These days it's the Kiso Valley's largest town (population 11,000) and a handy base for hikers heading to Ontake-san. **Ue-no-dan**, the old district, features Edo-era houses, lacquerware shops and sake breweries that offer tastings.

THE DRIVE
Carry on northeast up Rte 19 for another 21km.

07 NARAI (奈良井)

The 34th of the post towns, Narai was a welcome sight for aching-limbed travellers as it marked the halfway point of the Nakasendō between Kyoto and Tokyo. This remarkably well-preserved post town is a delight, a showcase of Edo-era architecture, with a lengthy historical main street. Near the northern end of the Kiso Valley, it hosts far fewer visitors than towns at the southern end. Walkers will enjoy the three-hour, 6.4km hike over the **Torii-tōge** (pass), which, at 1197m, is the highest point on the Nakasendō – this walk links Narai with Yabuhara, number 35 of the post towns.

THE DRIVE
Wend your way back down and take Rte 19, which breaks out of the Kiso Valley at Shiojiri, then head north from there to Matsumoto (39km in total).

08 MATSUMOTO (松本)

This much-loved city is the second largest in Nagano Prefecture and is home to one of Japan's most impressive original castles, Edo-era streetscapes, excellent art galleries and museums, and clean mountain air.

Take a Break

The old post town of Narai is an excellent place to overnight and feel like a traveller on the Edo-era Nakasendō. Right on the main street, MINSHUKU SHIMADA offers a traditional, authentic experience in a family-run inn; the *katsudon* (pork cutlet on rice) is superb at corner restaurant MATSUNAMI; TOKKURIYA is a local favourite for handmade soba in a stunning Edo-era inn; while SUGINOMORI is a sake brewery dating to 1793, where you can sample the goods at its nearby bar.

SEAN PAVONE/SHUTTERSTOCK

Narai

Sacred Ontake-San

As you head northeast up the Kiso Valley, the mountains on your right are the Central Alps, with **Kiso-Komagatake** (2956m) as the highest peak. Off to the west is **Ontake-san** (3067m), Japan's second-highest volcano after Mt Fuji. Ontake-san is a sacred summit with its own religion, Ontake-kyō – a Shintō sect based on mountain asceticism. It is accessible to hikers from July to mid-October thanks to the Ontake Ropeway, which zips you up to 2150m. This is a mighty mountain and a top climb, though it's an active volcano – in 2014, an eruption that took everyone by surprise tragically killed 63 hikers.

09

BEST FOR OUTDOORS

The Happō-One lifts whisk visitors up for great views in Hakuba.

Matsumoto to Nozawa Onsen

DURATION	DISTANCE	GREAT FOR
3–4 days	200km	Mountains, nature & wildlife

BEST TIME TO GO	
	Once the snow of winter has disappeared

THERAPHONG/SHUTTERSTOCK

Matsumoto Castle

Experience some of the most dramatic alpine vistas in Japan as you drive north from Matsumoto to the resort town of Hakuba. The mountains of the North Alps are truly spectacular. Carry on to visit the ancient shrine of Togakushi-jinja, followed by Zenkō-ji, a National Treasure temple in Nagano City that was founded in the 7th century. The Hokusai Museum in Obuse is well worth a visit, and if monkeys are on your mind, see them at the famous Jigokudani Monkey Park. You'd be remiss if you didn't spend a night or two in Nozawa Onsen, trying out a few of the *soto-yu* (locals' baths).

Link Your Trip

03 Romantic Road

Visit volcanoes, hot springs, lakes and waterfalls on this drive through the mountains.

08 Nagoya to Matsumoto

Drive to Matsumoto from Japan's fourth-largest city.

01 MATSUMOTO (松本)

It would be a shame to drive out of Matsumoto without checking out the highlights of this attractive cosmopolitan city. Don't miss **Matsumoto Castle** or the charming former merchant district of **Nakamachi**, with its *namako-kabe kura* (lattice-walled storehouses).

THE DRIVE

It's a 58km drive directly north, via Shinano-Ōmachi, passing gorgeous lakes such as Kisaki-ko and

Tateyama-Kurobe Alpine Route

This famed route (alpen-route.com) connects Shinano-Ōmachi, on the eastern side of the North Alps, with Toyama, on the western side, from mid-April to November. It's one of the top alpine draws in Japan, with travel possible in either direction. From **Shinano-Ōmachi**, which is 34km north of Matsumoto, drive northwest for 16km to the car park at **Ogisawa**. From there, you'll ride a trolley bus, walk across the **Kurobe Dam**, then continue by cable car, ropeway and trolley bus up to **Murodō** (2450m) at the foot of the Tateyama Peaks. A bus, cable car and train will then take you through to Toyama, or come back down to your car at Ogisawa.

Aoki-ko, with the North Alps on your left the whole way.

02 HAKUBA (白馬)

This vibrant resort, the site of various skiing events at the 1998 Winter Olympics, has long been a winter sports destination, but is now wholeheartedly embracing adventure tourism as well. These days, visitors are turning up in other seasons for walking, mountain biking, paragliding and other activities. Ride the three lifts at **Happō-One** up to 1830m for a wonderful hike up to the pond, **Happō-ike**, at 2060m. There are lots of accommodation and eating places in Hakuba, so consider spending a night or two here.

THE DRIVE
Head east for 42km, initially on Rte 406, then on Rte 36.

03 TOGAKUSHI (戸隠)

Home to one of the most important shrines in Japan, **Togakushi-jinja**, this spiritually significant place has long been a destination for Shintō worshippers. It's made up of five shrines connected by roads and walking trails through ancient cedar forests. Steep stone steps – 274 in total – lead up to **Hōkōsha**, the oldest of the shrines. And then there's something different… the thoroughly intriguing **Ninja Museum and Ninja House**.

THE DRIVE
Head southeast, down out of the mountains for 24km to the prefectural capital.

04 NAGANO CITY (長野)

The capital city of Nagano Prefecture (yes, it can get confusing!), Nagano City is a pretty place, surrounded by mountains, that has seen more than its fair share of visitors over the centuries. Nagano is a *monzen-machi* – a town that developed in front of the gates of a temple. That temple is **Zenkō-ji**, a national treasure founded in the 7th century; pilgrims have been visiting ever since. The 1.8km walk from Nagano

Station to Zenkō-ji shouldn't be missed. There's a lively eating and drinking district near the station and visitors can stay in a *shukubō* (temple lodging) at one of Zenkō-ji's 39 sub-temples. This is a great experience.

THE DRIVE
It's only 15km northeast in the valley to reach Obuse.

05 OBUSE (小布施)

This lovely little town, popular with Japanese day-trippers, is known for its chestnuts, sake breweries and the world-class **Hokusai Museum**. Hokusai (1760–1849), one of Japan's most famous *ukiyo-e* (woodblock print) artists – best known for his '36 Views of Mt Fuji' series – spent his final years here in Obuse and this museum is well worth a visit.

THE DRIVE
Head northeast for 18km, lastly heading east into the mountains on Rte 292 toward Shiga Kōgen.

06 JIGOKUDANI MONKEY PARK (地獄谷野猿公苑)

One of the world's most iconic wildlife images is of the 'snow monkeys' of Japan bathing in steaming **hot springs** surrounded by snow. It's mesmerising stuff, but you'll have to turn up when there's snow around to see it. Outside of winter, the monkeys, enticed by handouts, still come, but that photo won't be quite the same. It's a 30 to 40 minute walk on a forested trail from the car park to the hot pools.

THE DRIVE
Head back out to the main valley, then north on Rte 38 to Nozawa Onsen; 33km in total.

07 NOZAWA ONSEN (野沢温泉)

This charming hot springs village, backed by dense alpine forest, is an absolute joy. An extremely popular ski destination in winter, its warren of streets is home to a range of stylish restaurants, local stores, bars, a gin distillery, guesthouses and, of course, onsen. There are around 30 onsen in total, including 13 small public baths scattered about town known as *soto-yu*. Each *soto-yu* is maintained by a different part of the village as a bathing spot for locals, but visitors are welcome. Onsen water is still used by many for cooking, laundry and heating. A magical place!

Take a Break

Wasabi ice cream anyone? No better place to try this tongue-tingling condiment than at DAI-Ō WASABI-NŌJŌ, a wasabi farm and extravaganza 15km north of Matsumoto in Azumino. The wasabi is high class here due to pristine, clear flowing water from the North Alps. Stroll among the fields and wasabi plants, learn about the cultivation process (130 tonnes of wasabi are grown here annually), then hit the restaurant for a wasabi burger or stock up on delicacies such as wasabi wine at the souvenir shop.

SEAN PAVONE/SHUTTERSTOCK

Nozawa Onsen

Nozawa Onsen's Baths

There are 13 baths, known as *soto-yu* (外湯; open 6am-11pm), dotted about Nozawa Onsen. Historically, these are locals' bathing houses; many older houses still do not have a bath. While there's no one to collect money, the correct etiquette for non-locals is to put some coins in the donation box on the wall outside. Head through the correct door – to minimise mistakes, all the onsen have English signage on their doors for Men and Women. Each place has two tiny baths: *nuru-yu* (ぬる湯) is the not-so-hot bath, *atsu-yu* (あつ湯) is the hot one – scaldingly hot at some of the 13!

10

BEST FOR MOUNTAINS

Kamikōchi is surrounded by the high peaks of the North Alps.

Matsumoto to Kanazawa

DURATION	DISTANCE	GREAT FOR
5–7 days	260km	Mountains, nature & history
BEST TIME TO GO	May to November	

PSNI08/SHUTTERSTOCK

Kamikōchi

Head west from charming Matsumoto into the heart of the North Alps. While you can't drive yourself into Kamikōchi, it's a spot not to be missed; park up and take the return bus into this secluded mountain valley, before carrying on to Shin-Hotaka Onsen, a remote hot springs village with a ropeway up close to the peaks. Historical Takayama is on many visitors' bucket lists, while World Heritage–listed Shirakawa-gō and Gokayama present steep, gabled thatched-roof farmhouses you'll have seen in Japan's marketing images. Wonderful Kanazawa is home to one of Japan's 'Three Great Gardens' and is a joy to explore.

Link Your Trip

08 Nagoya to Matsumoto

Head northeast into the mountains from Japan's fourth-largest city.

11 Kanazawa to Hakuba

Explore the Noto Peninsula, then head around the North Alps.

01 MATSUMOTO (松本)

Don't head west into the mountains until you've checked out delightful Matsumoto (p66).

THE DRIVE

Stunning Kamikōchi is not to be missed, but be aware that you can't drive your car up the road into this secluded valley. From Matsumoto, drive west on Rte 158 for 35km to the Sawando parking areas; park here (¥700 per day) and take a bus (return adult/child ¥2800/1400)

into Kamikōchi. Access into Kamikōchi is closed over winter from 15 November to 22 April.

02 KAMIKŌCHI (上高地)

Mention this famous spot to Japanese outdoor enthusiasts and their eyes light up. They'll tell you that this is where it's at and where you should be. It's feasible to visit on a day trip, but best to stay overnight to savour the snow-capped peaks, bubbling brooks, wild monkeys and ancient forests. Kamikōchi is renowned for **walking** and **climbing**; you can summit some of Japan's highest peaks or enjoy a walk in the magnificent **Azusa River valley**.

The Alps?

In the late 19th century, British missionary Reverend Walter Weston toiled from peak to peak in the North Alps area and sparked Japanese interest in mountaineering as a sport accessible to all. This was a new idea in Japan as the high mountains were seen previously as the realm of religious ascetics. While Weston is honoured with an annual festival in Kamikōchi on the first Sunday in June, the 'Alps' title is attributed to Englishman William Gowland, who compared Japan's Alps to the European Alps in his Japan Guide of 1888. The name stuck and Japanese call their mountains the Japanese Alps too.

THE DRIVE
Back at your car at Sawando, continue west for 15km, through the tunnel to Hirayu Onsen; turn north on Rte 271, then right on Rte 475 for the 18km drive back into the high peaks at Shin-Hotaka Onsen.

03 SHIN-HOTAKA ONSEN (新穂高温泉)

Deliciously remote, this tiny **onsen village** is at the end of the road, literally. It's in a narrow valley under the high peaks, but you can get up there without breaking a sweat by taking the **Shin-Hotaka Ropeway** up to 2156m for stunning alpine views. Hikers may want to break into that sweat by walking up to **Nishiho-Doppyō**

LEOCHACHAUME24/SHUTTERSTOCK

Kenroku-en, Kanazawa

(2701m; four to five hours return) from the top of the ropeway. The village boasts some lovely *onsen ryokan*, such as **Yarimikan**, where you can stay, eat, bathe and relax in a traditional setting.

THE DRIVE Head back out to Hirayu Onsen (18km), then west on Rte 158 for 35km out to Takayama, on the western side of the North Alps.

TAKAYAMA (高山)

Officially known as Hida-Takayama, this city of 90,000 has one of Japan's most atmospheric townscapes, with **Meiji-era inns**, hillside temples and a pretty riverside setting. A 'little Kyoto', packed with cultural jewels of museums, galleries, sake breweries and ornate bridges, Takayama is a great place to park up for a night or two. The only drawback is that it has been 'discovered' and tourists can outnumber locals in the busy seasons.

THE DRIVE Head west on Rte 158 from Takayama, then take the E41 expressway northwest to Shirakawa-gō; it's a 50km journey all up.

SHIRAKAWA-GŌ (白川郷)

The World Heritage–listed villages of Shirakawa-gō in Gifu Prefecture

Take a Break

Takayama's wonderful historical neighbourhoods, with lovingly preserved Edo-era streetscapes, are great for taking a break from the road. If you overnight in town, make sure to visit the riverside MIYAGAWA ASA-ICHI (morning market), selling fresh produce, street food and handicrafts. ŌNOYA BREWERY has been making soy sauce and miso for over 250 years, while you can try up to 15 varietals at 10th generation HARADA SAKE BREWERY – their sake ice cream is divine! FUNASAKA SAKE BREWERY dates back to a remarkable 1688.

The Three Great...

Since the concept of 'The Three Great Views of Japan' (Nihon Sankei) was created in 1643, the Japanese have loved to come up with lists and rankings of celebrated spots around the country, such as the 'Three Great Gardens' (Nihon Sanmeien) and the 'Three Holy Mountains' (Nihon Sanreizan). This even got extended out to the '100 Famous Mountains' (Nihon Hyakumeizan) and even the 200 and 300 Famous Mountains. Get the picture? Kanazawa's lovely Kenroku-en is known throughout Japan as one of the 'Three Great Gardens', along with the Kōraku-en in Okayama and the Kairaku-en in Mito. Who's to argue?

and Gokayama in Toyama Prefecture are excellent reasons to head back into the mountains west of Takayama. Both villages are famous for their beautifully preserved **wooden farmhouses**, many dating back 300 years. The steep, gabled thatched-roof designs give them the name *gasshō-zukuri*, likening them to hands pressed in prayer. The design provides a spacious attic for cultivating silkworms and can withstand the heavy snowfalls of winter. Shirakawa-gō is a popular spot and can get swamped with tour buses and tourists. Visit early or late in the day, or better yet, stay overnight in a *gasshō-zukuri* inn (book well in advance).

THE DRIVE
Driving north for 30km from Shirakawa-gō on Rte 156 will bring you to Gokayama.

06 GOKAYAMA (五箇山)

In Toyama Prefecture, Gokayama is significantly less developed and less crowded than Shirakawa-gō, with smaller, more intimate villages. Don't miss **Suganuma** and **Ainokura**, where the *gasshō-zukuri* houses offer a mix of private dwellings, guesthouses, restaurants and museums. In Ainokura, **Matsuya** does tasty soba and set-lunch menus in a restored *gasshō-zukuri* house.

THE DRIVE
Gokayama has an interchange on the E41 expressway; hop on here and follow signage onto the E8 expressway for the 56km drive to Kanazawa.

07 KANAZAWA (金沢)

The main city of Ishikawa Prefecture, with a population of 470,000, Kanazawa is a rare beauty. Kenroku-en is considered one of Japan's top three gardens, built in 1643 as the private outer garden of Kanazawa castle, and there are samurai and teahouse districts to explore. Stay a night or two here.

11

BEST FOR SCENERY

The Kurobe Gorge Railway is an open-carriage scenic train up the gorge.

Kanazawa to Hakuba

DURATION	DISTANCE	GREAT FOR
4–6 days	500km	Scenery, seafood & mountains
BEST TIME TO GO	May to November	

LINEGOLD/GETTY IMAGES

Kurobe Gorge Railway (p76)

Head out on an adventure from Kanazawa, driving up the western coast of the Noto Peninsula, which was pummelled by an earthquake on New Year's Day 2024. Drive back down the peninsula's eastern coast to see one of Japan's 'Three Great Buddhas' in Takaoka. Toyama is known for its seafood and as a gateway for the Tateyama–Kurobe Alpine Route. If you like scenic rail journeys, they don't get any better than the extremely remote Kurobe Gorge Railway. Finally it's a great drive along the Sea of Japan coastline to Itoigawa, before heading inland to the popular resort town of Hakuba.

Link Your Trip

10 Matsumoto to Kanazawa

Get to Kanazawa by driving from Matsumoto.

09 Matsumoto to Nozawa Onsen

This drive finishes in Hakuba, early in Drive 9.

01 KANAZAWA (金沢)

Don't head out of this delightful city without checking out the highlights (p73).

THE DRIVE
Head out to the Sea of Japan coastline, then drive north on Rte 60 for 34km.

02 KITA-KE (喜多家)

A splendid moss garden leads to the superbly preserved 16-room historical home

Noto Peninsula Earthquake

Japan is no stranger to earthquakes, being on the Pacific Ring of Fire, right where tectonic plates meet. On New Year's Day 2024, a massive earthquake, the largest to hit Ishikawa Prefecture since 1885 and the strongest Japan had encountered since the 2011 Tōhoku earthquake, caused considerable damage to the Noto Peninsula and over 500 fatalities. The towns of Suzu, Wajima and Shika were particularly hard hit, a number of roads closed and a mind-boggling 4.4 sq km of land was uplifted and gained from the sea. Be aware that the Noto Peninsula is still on the mend, albeit slowly.

of the Kita family, a wealthy clan who administered more than 100 villages around the region during the 1800s.

THE DRIVE
You're at the base of the Noto Peninsula, on its western coast. Next comes a real treat, the Chirihama Beach Driveway, an 8km stretch of sand that is the only beach in Japan on which you can drive; traffic runs in both directions. Stick to coastal roads on the western coast of the peninsula as much as you can for the 100km drive to Wajima.

03 WAJIMA (輪島)

On your drive you'll pass lots of interesting places such as sea caves and coastal trails at the **Ganmon scenic area**. **Sōji-ji Soin**, dating from 1321, was the head of the Sōtō school of Zen but is now a branch temple. The largest town in the north of Noto, Wajima is in recovery mode after the devastating earthquake on New Year's Day 2024. A relaxed fishing port, it is known for its Wajima-nuri, a delicate lacquerware. The daily **asa-ichi** (morning market) dates back 1000 years, but that part of town was particularly hard hit in the earthquake and is being rebuilt.

THE DRIVE
Carry on out to the tip of the peninsula on coastal roads for 70km.

04 ROKKŌSAKI LIGHTHOUSE (禄剛埼灯台)

The photogenic sculpted **Shiroyone Senmaida Rice Terraces**, right by the sea, suffered cracking during the earthquake but are back in rice production. At the northeastern tip of the peninsula, the white-brick Rokkōsaki Lighthouse is renowned as a rare vantage point that offers views of both sunrise and sunset.

THE DRIVE
Head down the eastern coast of the Noto Peninsula for 133km, crossing into Toyama Prefecture.

TAKAOKA (高岡)

Here you'll find the wonderful **Takaoka Great Buddha**, one of the 'Three Great Buddhas' of Japan – the other two are at Nara's Tōdai-ji and Kamakura's Kōtokuin temples. This elegant 16m bronze statue was completed in 1933 after the original wooden version, erected in 1745, was damaged by fire.

THE DRIVE
It's a 20km drive southeast to the prefectural capital, Toyama City.

TOYAMA (富山)

This modern port city was heavily targeted during WWII, suffering the most damage of any city besides Hiroshima and Nagasaki. Much of the city you see today has been rebuilt, though one well preserved area is the historical **Iwase** district (the wharf precinct) where you'll find 19th-century **shipping warehouses** converted into museums, restaurants and bars. Toyama has its own station on the Hokuriku shinkansen line and is the western terminus for the highly recommended Tateyama-Kurobe Alpine Route (p67).

THE DRIVE
Head northeast out of Toyama for the 50km drive; at Kurobe, drive inland into the mountains following the Kurobe River to Unazuki.

KUROBE GORGE RAILWAY (黒部峡谷トロッコ電車)

The reason you've come to **Unazuki** is to ride the **Kurobe Gorge Railway** *(kurotetu.co.jp)*, an old, open-air trolley carriage that plods along a single-gauge line built to service the construction of the Kurobe Dam. This is one of Japan's most scenic rail journeys, winding 20km through lushly forested ravines while criss-crossing over 20 bridges and through 40 tunnels as you follow the clear waters of the **Kurobe River**. The 80-minute one-way journey runs seasonally from mid-April to late November; there are also enclosed carriages with windows.

THE DRIVE
Head back out of the valley, then northeast up the Sea of Japan coast. The quickest route is on the E8 expressway which spectacularly heads out over the sea on bridges in a couple of spots. It's 54km in total to Itoigawa. Get off the expressway at Itoigawa IC, then turn south and inland on Rte 148 for the 47km winding drive up the Himekawa Valley to Hakuba.

HAKUBA (白馬)

Take time to explore one of Japan's top resorts (p67).

Take a Break

Firefly squid, anyone? Drop into the HOTARU-IKA MUSEUM in Namerikawa, 19km northeast of Toyama, for a unique experience. Between March and June, thousands of bioluminescent firefly squid come together in a stunning electric-blue display out in Toyama Bay. If a 3am Firefly Squid Sightseeing Tour to see them by boat sounds too much, head to the museum (year-round) to learn more. Even better, try firefly squid sashimi, tempura, pasta and more in KOUSAI, the rooftop restaurant, with sweeping views over Toyama Bay.

KITINUT JINAPUCK/SHUTTERSTOCK

Murodō

North Alps Splendour

Views of the Tateyama mountains and the high peaks of northern parts of the North Alps are absolutely stunning from all around Toyama Bay and the eastern coast of the Noto Peninsula. If you want to go up there on the **Tateyama-Kurobe Alpine Route** *(alpen-route.com)*, drive out to **Tateyama Station** (32km southeast of Toyama City), then take the cable car up to **Bijōdaira** (977m), then the bus up to **Murodō** (2450m). This is a stunning trip; you can climb the Tateyama peaks (3015m) from Murodō in four to five hours (return) once the snows of winter have melted.

Also Try...

JAPAN'S FIREWORKS/SHUTTERSTOCK

Kanazawa to Hakusan

DURATION	DISTANCE
1¾ hours	68km

This drive almost directly south into the mountains from Kanazawa is primarily used by pilgrims and hikers heading to **Hakusan** (白山), one of Japan's 'Three Great Holy Mountains'. Access to the best hiking trail is from **Bettōdeai**, to the southwest of the highest peak, **Gozen-ga-mine** (2702m). The drive south from Kanazawa is on wonderful Rte 157, then from **Shiramine Onsen**, in the Tedori River valley, Rte 33 winds up into the high mountains. Coming back down after your hike, continue south on Rte 157 to Ono, in **Fukui Prefecture**, known for its castle and temples. You can then either head west to Fukui City or east to Takayama in Gifu Prefecture.

Nagoya to Lake Suwa

DURATION	DISTANCE
2–3 days	200km

The first bit of this route is the same as in Drive 8 (Nagoya to Matsumoto; p62), but from **Magome** this route heads east and follows the **Tenryū River valley** northeast to **Lake Suwa** (諏訪湖; pictured). This wide valley has an expressway the whole way, but it's much more fun to take your time and travel on local roads. Whereas the Kiso Valley runs up the western side of the Central Alps, the Tenryū Valley is on their eastern side. There is a marvellous opportunity at Komagane to take the **Komagatake Ropeway** up to 2612m, then climb **Kiso-Komagatake** (2956m), the highest peak in the Central Alps. Lake Suwa is 33km south of Matsumoto.

SEAN PAVONE/SHUTTERSTOCK

Fuji Five Lakes to Matsumoto

DURATION	DISTANCE
1 day	150km

If you've made the effort to check out Fuji Go-ko (the Five Lakes of Mt Fuji; 富士五湖), consider extending your journey and driving northwest, along the eastern side of the South Alps, to Matsumoto. While you can meet up with the E20 expressway from Tokyo near Kōfu, Rte 20 parallels the expressway, is free to drive and provides access to the South Alps if you'd like to head into the mountains for some short walks. Once you're in Matsumoto, you're set up to link to other drives in this chapter. You'll pass over the **Tenryū River**, emptying out of **Lake Suwa**, and the **Narai River**, which flows southwest down the **Kiso Valley**.

Nagoya to Takayama

DURATION	DISTANCE
1 day	150km

While this journey can mostly be done on the E41 expressway, it is an extremely enjoyable trip when driven on regional roads. Head north from Nagoya to **Inuyama**, then on Rte 41 up the **Hida River Valley**. It's a winding drive following the river, but satisfying, as you pass through small towns and villages in the valley. Best known is **Gero Onsen** (pictured), a famous hot springs resort, about an hour south of Takayama (高山). This whole area is particularly attractive with autumnal foliage. Link into Drive 10 (Matsumoto to Kanazawa; p70) once you get to Takayama, either continuing northwest to Kanazawa or east through the North Alps to Matsumoto.

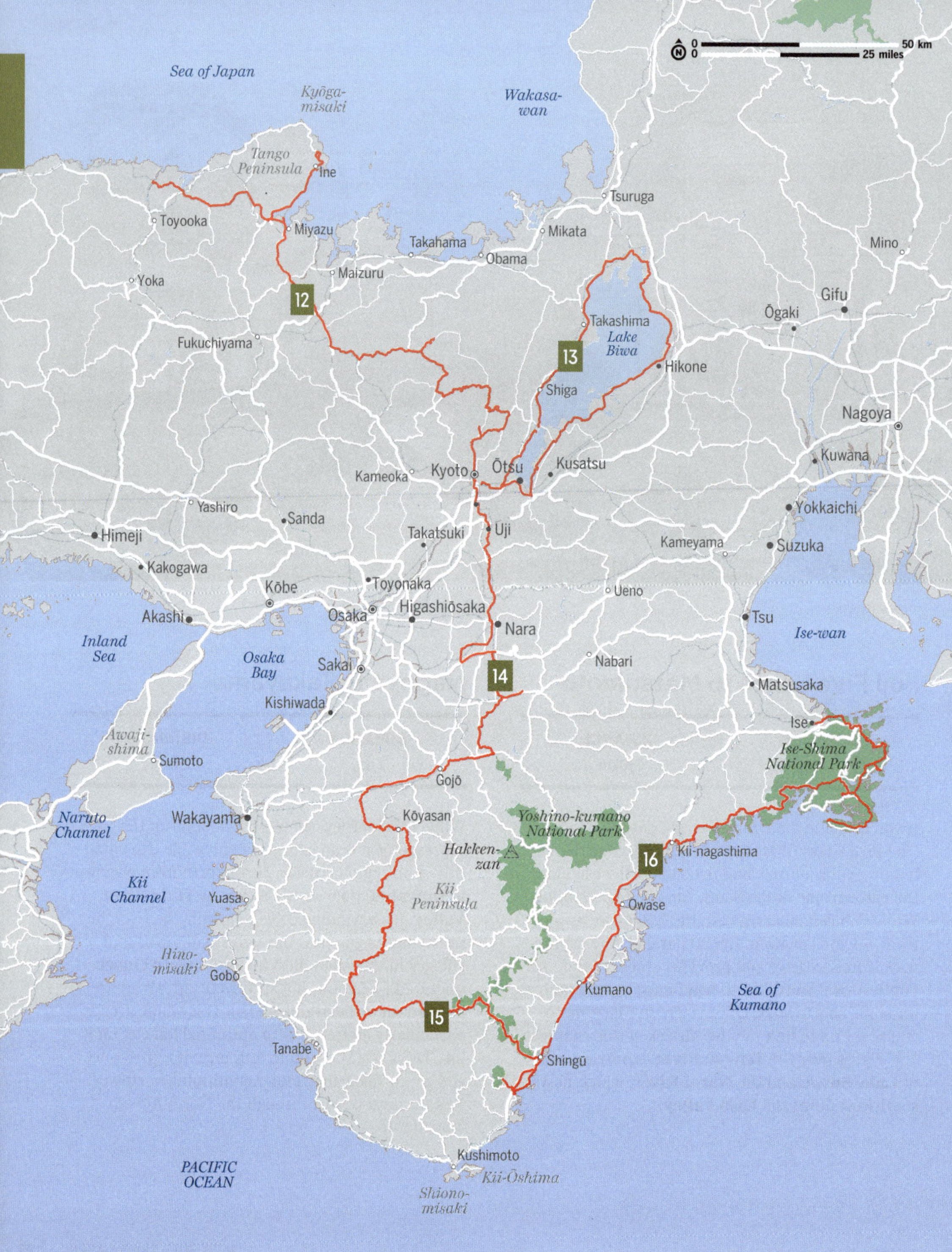

0
0
50 km
25 miles
Sea of Japan
Kyōga-misaki
Wakasa-wan
Tango Peninsula
Ine
Tsuruga
Toyooka
Miyazu
Mikata
Takahama
Obama
Mino
Yoka
Maizuru
12
Gifu
Ōgaki
Takashima
Lake Biwa
Fukuchiyama
13
Hikone
Shiga
Nagoya
Kuwana
Kameoka
Kyoto
Ōtsu
Kusatsu
Yashiro
Sanda
Yokkaichi
Himeji
Uji
Takatsuki
Kameyama
Suzuka
Kakogawa
Toyonaka
Kōbe
Ueno
Akashi
Osaka
Higashiōsaka
Tsu
Nara
Inland Sea
Osaka Bay
Ise-wan
Sakai
Nabari
14
Matsusaka
Kishiwada
Ise
Awaji-shima
Sumoto
Ise-Shima National Park
Gojō
Naruto Channel
Wakayama
Kōyasan
Yoshino-kumano National Park
Hakken-zan
Kii-nagashima
16
Kii Channel
Yuasa
Kii Peninsula
Owase
Hino-misaki
Gobō
Kumano
Sea of Kumano
15
Tanabe
Shingū
Kushimoto
PACIFIC OCEAN
Kii-Ōshima
Shiono-misaki

GUITAR PHOTOGRAPHER/SHUTTERSTOCK

Kyoto (p82)

Kansai

Explore

Kansai

Kansai (関西) is the heart of Japan, where much of modern-day Japanese culture originated. Two of its cities were once Japan's capitals – Kyoto and Nara – while electric Osaka and Kōbe embody the infectious work-hard, play-hard energy of a region more free and easy than Tokyo. Away from the urban whirl, Kansai shifts seamlessly into a lower gear. Down in the Kii Peninsula, the mountain pilgrimage sites of Kōya-san and the Kumano Kodō, along with sacred Ise-jingū, reveal Japan at its most spiritual. North, up on the Sea of Japan coast, lose yourself in rural backwaters along the rugged coastline.

Kyoto

Kyoto (京都) is old Japan writ large: atmospheric temples, sublime gardens, colourful shrines, traditional teahouses and intimate streetscapes where geisha (known as *geiko* locally) seemingly float. With more than 1000 Buddhist temples, over 400 Shintō shrines, and a whopping 17 World Heritage Sites, it is one of the world's most culturally rich cities, on the 'go-to' list of most visitors to Japan. Needless to say, Kyoto's popularity draws the crowds. The city also makes a great base or starting point for exploring the Kansai region by rental car, with intriguing destinations in all directions.

Osaka

If Kyoto was historically the city of the courtly nobility, and Tokyo the city of the samurai, then Osaka (大阪) was the city of the merchant class. Osakans take pride in shedding the conservatism found elsewhere in Japan, and this spirited city is a place where people are a bit brasher – the city's unofficial slogan is *kuidaore* ('eat until you drop') and it seems that everyone is always out for a good meal, and a good time. With a large number of cheaper business hotels, Osaka makes an economical base for Kansai explorations.

Nara

History in Nara Prefecture goes back further even than Kyoto, as it was here in the Yamato Basin that the forerunners of Japan's ruling Yamato dynasty consolidated power. They chose Nara (奈良) as their capital, and

WHEN TO GO

Most of the trips in this chapter can be driven year-round, although the mild weather of spring and autumn are ideal. Winters are cold, but the low-lying areas of Kansai see little snow. The heaviest snow falls in the mountains and on the Sea of Japan coast. Summer can be oppressively hot on the plains, marginally less so in the mountains.

although its time as capital was short (710–784 CE), its cultural legacy was enormous. It was here that Buddhism first flourished in Japan, and the city's fantastic repository of temples and Buddhist art attests to that fact. Stay a night or two to see the awesome Daibutsu (Great Buddha) at the Tōdai-ji, in one of the world's largest wooden halls; to visit the great shrine, Kasuga-taisha; and to enjoy the attention of the free-roaming deer in Nara Park.

Kōbe

Perched on a hillside sloping down to the sea, backed by the Rokkō range of mountains, Kōbe (神戸) is one of Japan's most attractive and cosmopolitan cities. It was a maritime gateway from the earliest days of trade with China and home to one of the first foreign settlements after Japan reopened to the world in the mid-19th century. Kōbe is compact, designed for walking, and is easily visited as a day trip from Osaka or Kyoto, or as a stopover en route to points west.

TRANSPORT

Kansai International Airport (KIX) is the main international point of entry for the region. There are also domestic airports, including Osaka Itami Airport and Kōbe Airport. Kyoto, Osaka (Shin-Osaka Station) and Kōbe (Shin-Kōbe Station) are on the shinkansen (bullet train) network, easily accessed from points east (such as Tokyo) or west (such as Hiroshima or Fukuoka).

WHAT'S ON

Barely a week goes by without a festival taking place somewhere in the main cities or out in the Kansai countryside.

Kōya-san Rōsoku Matsuri
Every 13 August, the Candle Festival sees 100,000 candles lit in remembrance of departed souls.

Gozan Okuribi
Huge fires are lit on five mountains around Kyoto every 16 August. The biggest is on Daimonji-yama.

Kisiwada Danjiri
In September and October, wooden floats careen around the streets pulled by whole neighbourhoods.

Resources

Another Kyoto *(kyototourism.org)* Kyoto Prefecture's tourism site.

Osaka Info *(en.osaka-info.jp)* Things to do in Osaka Prefecture.

Nara Travel *(visitnara.jp)* Nara Prefecture's tourism website.

Visit Wakayama *(visitwakayama.jp)* The official Wakayama travel site.

Visit Mie *(visitmie-japan.travel)* The prefecture's travel site.

Shiga.Biwako *(en.biwako-visitors.jp)* Shiga Prefecture's site.

Hyogo! Navi *(hyogo-tourism.jp)* Check out Hyogo Prefecture.

WHERE TO STAY

The big Kansai cities offer a huge range of places to sleep, from bunk beds in dorm rooms at hostels, to family-run *minshuku* (guesthouses), ryokan (traditional inns), business hotels, major hotels and even love hotels. There are a lot of options online. Demand for rooms is high in Kyoto at peak times, so budget accordingly. There are lovely *onsen ryokan* (traditional hot-spring inns) at places like Kinosaki Onsen, near the Sea of Japan coast, and on the Kii Peninsula. The mountaintop monastery complex of Kōya-san presents a wonderful opportunity to stay in *shukubō* (temple lodgings) and try *shōjin-ryōri* (vegetarian monk's meals).

12

BEST FOR SCENERY

Amanohashidate is one of the Three Great Views of Japan.

Kyoto to Kinosaki Onsen

BEEBOY/S/SHUTTERSTOCK

Amanohashidate (p86)

DURATION	DISTANCE	GREAT FOR
2–3 days	260km	Scenery, culture & onsen

BEST TIME TO GO	March to November

Head north for one of the premier onsen experiences to be had in Japan in the hot springs town of Kinosaki Onsen. There's a lot to see on the way too, including intriguing parts of rural Kyoto Prefecture and Amanohashidate, a 3.5km-long sandbar on the Sea of Japan coast that's renowned as one of the 'Three Great Views of Japan'. Local architecture is on display with thatched-roofed farmhouses in Miyama and *funaya* (boat houses) in Ine-chō on the Tango Peninsula. And, of course, it wouldn't be a Japanese experience without a few age-old temples and shrines to peruse along the way.

Link Your Trip

13 Kyoto – Lake Biwa Loop

Spend a day or two on this loop drive.

18 San'in–Shimane & Tottori

Encounter a sacred shrine, beautiful castle and amazing art museums.

KYOTO (京都)

If you're not coming back to Kyoto (p92), make sure you've seen all that you want to.

THE DRIVE
It's only a 15km drive north from central Kyoto.

KIBUNE (貴船)

A lovely, easy-to-follow mountain trail through old-growth forest connects **Kurama** and **Kibune**, two small villages in neighbouring valleys in the Kitayama mountains. Most walk from Kurama and end up in Kibune. The main attraction of the one-street community in the Kibune valley is gastronomic, with **kawadoko-style dining platforms** belonging to local restaurants completely covering the fast-flowing creek in summer, to take advantage of the natural cooling effect of the water. If you have time to explore, drive up both valleys, but if time is limited, visit Kibune.

THE DRIVE
Head east on Rte 40 for 11km.

ŌHARA (大原)

Since ancient times, Ōhara has been regarded as a holy site. The region provides a charming glimpse of rural Japan, along with the picturesque **Sanzen-in**, Jikkō-in and several other fine temples, and is perfect for strolling. At the **Jikkō-in**, check out instruments used in the *shōmyō* Buddhist chanting that is traditional in the area. Ōhara is most popular in autumn when the maple leaves change colour and the mountain views are spectacular; avoid weekends at that time.

THE DRIVE
It's a winding 64km drive through the mountains. Head north from Ōhara on Rte 367, then west on Rte 477, then north on Rte 162.

A Different Kansai

The northern reaches of Kansai are dramatically different from the densely populated urban areas to the south. Quiet hamlets such as Miyama are found in the mountains north of Kyoto city, and beyond lies the spectacular Sea of Japan coastline with rugged headlands, rocky islets and sandy beaches. Winter is much harsher on this northern coast, which is famous for its seafood, especially *zuwaigani* (snow crab). Crab season runs November to March, during which destinations such as Kinosaki Onsen are very popular. Summers are hot and there are popular beaches such as **Takeno-hama** at Takeno, on the coast near Kinosaki Onsen.

Take a Break

Near the southern end of the Amanohashidate sandbar, in the pine trees, HASHIDATE CHAYA is an enticing teahouse and restaurant with indoor tables and outdoor seats in the sand. Try *asari-don*, a dish of local boiled clams over rice, or *asari-udon* (clams with udon noodles). They also have shaved ice and soft-serve ice cream in summer when things can get hot. There are beach showers in the trees opposite if you want to take a dip on the white-sand beach.

04 MIYAMA (美山)

In the remote mountainous heartland of Kyoto Prefecture, Miyama is a scatter of rural hamlets in jade-green hillsides, joined up by quiet country lanes and dotted with sleepy temples and shrines. The star attraction is **Kayabuki-no-sato**, a hamlet of some 40 farmhouses notable for their traditional *kayabuki-yane* (thatched roofs) designed in the local Kyoto Kitayama style – a hipped roof with a peaked gable on top. Most are private residences or operate as cafes and guesthouses. You can see inside one that has maintained its rustic interior at the **Miyama Folk Museum**.

THE DRIVE More winding roads, initially west on Rte 12, then north on Rte 478 for a total of 76km to Miyazu, then Amanohashidate.

05 AMANOHASHIDATE (天橋立)

Meaning 'bridge to heaven', Amanohashidate is a 3.5km-long belt of sand that snakes across the azure waters of Miyazu Bay, with a pine-shaded path up the middle and an attractive white-sand **swimming beach**. Seen from viewpoints on either side in fine weather, it's hard to refute Amanohashidate's billing as one of the Nihon Sankei (Three Great Views of Japan). From the viewpoint atop the chairlift at **Amanohashidate View Land**, it's customary to bend over and peer at the sandbar from between your legs to see it as a flying dragon. Rent a bicycle and pedal the length of the sandbar and back for more fun.

THE DRIVE Follow Rte 178 up the eastern side of the Tango Peninsula for 24km.

06 INE-CHŌ (伊根町)

This fishing community is notable for its **traditional wooden houses** called *funaya* (literally 'boat houses'), built out over the water so that boats can moor underneath, with the living quarters up top. Ine has around 230 *funaya* stretched out around its bay; the best way to see them is from the water on a 25-minute trip with **Ine Bay Cruise** *(inewan-com; adult/child ¥1200/600)*. Funaya can also be booked online as short-term accommodation; book well in advance.

THE DRIVE Return down the eastern side of the peninsula, then head west on Rte 312 to Kinosaki Onsen; 63km in total.

07 KINOSAKI ONSEN (城崎温泉)

This is one of Japan's best places to sample the classic **onsen** experience. Overnight guests clip-clop around a willow-lined canal from bath to bath wearing *yukata* (light cotton kimonos) and *geta* (wooden sandals). Most ryokan and hotels in town have their own *uchi-yu* (bath for guests), but also provide guests with free tickets to seven popular **soto-yu** (public baths), which are scattered about town. Many of the town's houses, shops and restaurants retain their traditional charm and it's a lovely setting.

Tango Peninsula Detour

Tango-hantō juts into the Sea of Japan on the north coast of Kyoto Prefecture. Its serrated coast alternates between sandy beaches, gum-drop-shaped islands, bays, inlets and rocky headlands. If you're driving between Amanohashidate and Kinosaki Onsen, it's a worthy detour. After you've dropped into Ine-chō to see the *funaya* (boat houses), head around the coast to the **Nii rice terraces**, then carry on north to **Kyōga-misaki**, the northernmost point on the peninsula, with a historic lighthouse, steep clifftop walks and spectacular scenery. Heading west down the northern coast, **Ukawa Onsen Yoshino-no-sato** has big baths and sea views, while **Kotohiki-hama** is a gorgeous beach.

REI IMAGINE/SHUTTERSTOCK

Kinosaki Onsen

13

BEST FOR HISTORY

Hilltop Hikone Castle is a designated National Treasure.

Kyoto – Lake Biwa Loop

DURATION	DISTANCE	GREAT FOR
1–2 days	200km	Scenery, culture & history

BEST TIME TO GO	March to November

GOROSAN/SHUTTERSTOCK

Hikone-jō (p90)

Spend an extremely pleasant day or two exploring and driving around Biwa-ko, Japan's largest lake, east of Kyoto. It has lots of interesting things going on, mostly well off the crowded tourist trail, including a number of very picturesque, photogenic spots, plus the opportunity to ferry out to the sacred island in the lake, Chikubu-shima. Hikone has a lovely, original castle, while Nagahama and Ōmi-hachiman boast charming historic quarters. It's an easy drive clockwise around the lake, with plenty more of interest to stop and explore at your own whim.

Link Your Trip

12 Kyoto to Kinosaki Onsen

Explore rural Kyoto Prefecture and the Sea of Japan coastline.

14 Kyoto to Kōya-san

Head south to Nara, Kōya-san and the Kii Peninsula.

01 KYOTO (京都)

This drive is a loop so you'll be coming back to Kyoto (p92).

THE DRIVE

Head east on Rte 1 from central Kyoto to Ōtsu (12km); Mii-dera is here, if you're ready to try some *chikara-mochi* (p90). Get out onto Rte 558, which is lakeside, and head north for 15km.

Lake Biwa

Only 10km east of Kyoto at its southern end and Japan's largest freshwater lake, Biwa-ko is said to have been named during the Edo period (1603–1868) as its shape resembles that of a traditional short-necked, stringed instrument called the *biwa*. The lake is entirely within Shiga Prefecture, known as Ōmi Province before the prefectural system was established in 1868, and many places, such as Ōmi-hachiman, still incorporate Ōmi into their names. The main outlet is the Seta River at Biwa-ko's southern end, which becomes the Uji River, then the Yodo River and flows out through central Osaka into Osaka Bay.

02 UKIMI-DŌ (浮御堂)

This 'Floating Hall' is Biwa-ko's top photo spot, part of the small temple **Mangetsu-ji**. The hall is actually built on a jetty, but photographed from the right angle, appears to be floating above the lake. It became immortalised in one of the Ōmi Hakkei – 'The Eight Views of Ōmi' – by 19th-century master *ukiyo-e* (woodblock print) artist Utagawa Hiroshige. The present building is a 1937 reconstruction after the previous Ukimi-dō was damaged in a typhoon.

THE DRIVE Carry on driving up Rte 558 beside the lake for 10km, then follow signage inland to Biwako Valley Ropeway.

03 BIWAKO TERRACE (琵琶湖テラス)

Ride the **Biwako Valley Ropeway** *(biwako-valley.com; return adult/child ¥3500/1500)* up to Biwako Terrace, at 1108m above sea level – Biwa-ko sits at 86m in elevation. Views are absolutely stunning in all directions; there are a variety of eating options, hiking trails, playground facilities for kids, and in the winter, it all transforms into a **ski resort**.

THE DRIVE Get back on to Rte 558 and carry on north; stop for a photo at Shirahige-jinja, 13km up the coast, where you'll find a floating *torii* (shrine gate) out in the lake. Another 15km on will bring you to Imazu Port.

04 IMAZU (今津)

From the boat terminal, board a ferry to **Chikubu-shima**, the sacred island in the lake. Check out **Biwako Kisen** *(biwakokisen.co.jp; return adult/child ¥3000/1500)* for departure times from Imazu Port. Return journeys generally allow 80 minutes on the island. There are also departures from Nagahama Port, on the eastern side of Biwa-ko. The pint-sized island is believed to be sacred since ancient times and nowadays is considered one of the lake's 'power spots' – places with strong and mystical life force. On Chikubu-shima you'll find **Hōgon-ji**, a Buddhist temple dedicated to Benzaiten, the goddess of all that flows – water, music, art, wealth and so on.

THE DRIVE
It's a 48km drive around the northern end of Biwa-ko; use Rte 303, then turn south on Rte 44 to follow the eastern coast of the lake.

05 NAGAHAMA (長浜)

This old merchant town has a rebuilt lakeside castle, but the main reason for visiting is its charming historic quarter around **Kurokabe Sq**. Kurokabe means 'black walls', a nod to the stucco shopfront of **Kurokabe Glass House** (a former bank), which now showcases delightful artisanal glassware. Try the local dish, *yakisaba somen* (braised mackerel with thin white noodles).

THE DRIVE
Carry on down the eastern side of Biwa-ko for 15km.

06 HIKONE (彦根)

This small city is famous for its castle, which, unlike many, scraped through the feudal era intact. Standing proudly atop Hikone-yama, **Hikone-jō** was virtually lakeside when constructed, but due to land reclamation, now stands nearly 1km back from the water. It's not a huge castle, but it's original, attractive and considered a masterpiece. There's a nice museum and strolling garden within the grounds.

THE DRIVE
It's a 29km drive on Rte 25, lakeside.

07 ŌMI-HACHIMAN (近江八幡)

This small city was home to Musa-juku, the 66th of the 69 post stations on the Nakasendō (p63), the old 'central mountain route' of the Edo period, that linked Edo (now Tokyo) with Kyoto. Today, the city's old **merchant quarter** has a time-worn, lived-in vibe with some throwback Edo-era timber buildings along Shinmachi St and **Hachiman-bori**, a historic canal lined with cherry trees and often used as a setting for Japanese period dramas. **Haku'un-kan**, an atmospheric European-style school building dating to 1877, serves as the tourist office.

THE DRIVE
It's a 50km drive via Ōtsu to Kyoto; it'll be shorter time-wise if you jump on the E1 expressway.

Take a Break

For an extremely tasty local treat, head to the temple Mii-dera (三井寺), established in 672, near Ōtsu. Within the grounds, you'll find MII-DERA BENKEI CHIKARA-MOCHI, a place selling delectable matcha-flavoured rice cakes with soybean-flour flavouring. Benkei was a legendary warrior monk, renowned for his strength, and eating mochi is said to increase energy, stamina and power. All Japanese know Benkei's name – the shinbone is called *Benkei-no-nakidokoro*. It was the only place you could strike Benkei and make him cry.

Sekigahara Battlefield

Sekigahara Battlefield

Japanese history buffs will want to drive 20km east from Nagahama to Sekigahara, just over the prefectural border in Gifu, site of the largest and most important battle in Japanese feudal history. It was here in 1600 that the forces of Tokugawa Ieyasu defeated a coalition known as the Western Army, loyal to the Toyotomi clan. The battle ended the Sengoku (Warring States) period and created the Tokugawa shogunate, which governed Japan from Edo Castle (in what is now Tokyo) until 1868. Along with lots of battleground hot spots around present-day Sekigahara, check out the Gifu Sekigahara Battlefield Memorial Museum.

14

Kyoto to Kōya-san

DURATION	DISTANCE	GREAT FOR
3–5 days	180km	History, culture & religion

BEST TIME TO GO	March to November

There are so many interesting places to see on this drive south from Kyoto through Nara Prefecture that it could keep you intrigued for a week. Uji is renowned for its tea and the Byōdō-in (look on the back of the ¥10 coin). Nara City is an absolute delight, with free-roaming deer in Nara Park and the mesmerising Great Buddha at the temple Tōdai-ji. There's the opportunity for a ramble in the Nara countryside on the Yama-no-be-no-michi. You can also see ancient emperors' tombs at Asuka, check out cherry blossoms in Yoshino, and stay a night in a temple at the mountaintop monastery complex of Kōya-san.

Link Your Trip

13 Kyoto – Lake Biwa Loop

Check out Japan's largest lake before heading south.

15 Kōya-san to Nachi Grand Shrine

Carry on to the renowned Kumano Kodō.

01 KYOTO (京都)

Needless to say, don't head south out of Kyoto until you've seen all that you want to see. If you haven't been to **Fushimi Inari Taisha** yet, visit on your way south out of the city. You've definitely seen images of the countless red Shintō shrine gates here in Japan's tourism marketing. It's a spectacle not to be missed, one of the most impressive and memorable sights in the country. If you've got time,

BEST FOR CULTURE

Nara Park's Daibutsu (Big Buddha) and free-roaming deer are enchanting.

FOTOGRIN/SHUTTERSTOCK

Deer, Nara Park

the 6km loop trail up **Inari-san** is absolutely spectacular, featuring over 10,000 red *torii* gates, walkable in two to three hours.

THE DRIVE
Head south out of Kyoto on Rte 24, then Rte 241 to Uji; it's only a 14km drive.

02 UJI (宇治)

Almost a suburb of Kyoto these days, Uji City, located on the Uji River, is renowned throughout Japan for the **Hōō-dō** (Phoenix Hall) at the temple **Byōdō-in**, so revered that it's depicted on the back of the Japanese ¥10 coin. Overlooking a serene reflecting pond, this refurbished hall is a stunning sight. Also of renown are Uji's tea fields and tea production. Check it all out at **Fukujuen Uji Kōbō** (Fukujuen Tea Factory), just over the river from the Byōdō-in. Nearby, the **Tale of Genji Museum** offers a glimpse into the culture of the Heian era (794–1185) and the story of *The Tale of Genji*, considered to be the world's first novel. The last 10 chapters of the tale, written by the noblewoman, poet, and lady-in-waiting Murasaki Shikibu, are set in Uji.

THE DRIVE
Use toll-free Rte 24 to head south for the 28km drive to Nara. Points of interest in Nara are in the foothills in the east of the city.

03 NARA (奈良)

The first permanent capital of Japan during the Nara period (710–794), Nara is one of Japan's most rewarding destinations and you'll want to spend a night or two here on your journey. Not to be missed is the **Daibutsu** (Great Buddha; see p95), a 16m-high statue of bronze and gold, in the grand temple **Tōdai-ji** in the northern part of **Nara Park**. Strolling around in the park is an absolute joy, with some 1200 free-roaming deer, designated a National Treasure. Some have learned how to bow in return for *shika-senbei* (deer crackers). The deer are sacred to **Kasuga-taisha**, the head shrine

Take a Break

As a popular destination for both international and domestic visitors, Nara is packed with good restaurants, mostly near the train stations and in Naramachi. The covered arcade HIGASHI-MUKI SHŌTENGAI, between Kintetsu Nara Station and Sanjō-dōri, has a plethora of cafes, restaurants and bars. You'll find everything from udon, sushi and Italian to coffee-and-sandwich places. Look for the local specialty, *kakinoha-zushi* – individual pieces of mackerel or salmon sushi wrapped in persimmon leaf. Take it out of the leaf before eating.

of over 3000 Kasuga shrines across Japan, in the east of the park. Take time to explore Nara's marvellous museums and the historic **Naramachi** merchant quarter.

THE DRIVE
It's only a 20km drive southwest across the Nara plain to Hōryū-ji.

04 HŌRYŪ-JI (法隆寺)

Nara's outskirts are home to yet more big-league temples. Hōryū-ji was founded in 607 and has stayed true to its original blueprint, an image of how Nara might have looked some 1400 years ago shortly after Buddhism's arrival in Japan via Korea and China. A temple of two halves, Hōryū-ji features the **Sai-in** (West Temple), **Tō-in** (East Temple) and a beautiful five-storey **pagoda**.

THE DRIVE
Head back east across the flat Nara Plain on Rte 109, then Rte 25 for 12km to Tenri station. There's a surprising amount of agricultural production going on along the way.

05 YAMA-NO-BE-NO-MICHI (山辺の道)

For a fascinating ramble on your feet through the Nara countryside, head to **Tenri**, park at the station and go for a walk on the Yama-no-be-no-michi. Expect farming villages, 1400-year-old emperor's tombs, shrines and temples, family grave sites, honesty stalls selling fruit and vegetables, persimmon orchards, rice paddies, barking dogs and a rich aroma that makes this walk an extremely pleasant way to immerse yourself in historical and rural Japan. After viewing the imposing **Tomb of Emperor Suijin**, a massive keyhole-shaped mausoleum surrounded by moats, walk 800m west to Yanagimoto Station and take the train back north, two stops to your car at Tenri Station. The 6km walk will take two to three hours.

THE DRIVE
It's only 16km, first south on Rte 169, then east into the mountains up the Yamato River valley on Rte 165 to Hasedera. These are the upper reaches of the Yamato River that flows across the Nara Plain, through southern Osaka and out into Osaka Bay.

06 HASEDERA (長谷寺)

The thickly forested hills that rise up over the Nara Basin are home to some distinguished temples and shrines, well off the beaten track and all the more special for it. Hasedera, an 8th-century Buddhist temple, is notable for its 399-step **noborirō** (covered corridor), the ascent of which is itself a religious rite and act of self-purification. The **main hall** is perched up on the steep mountainside with inspiring views, while the grounds are renowned for 2500 hydrangeas, with peak blooming season around June.

THE DRIVE
It's another 16km drive, initially west and out of the river valley, then southwest to the Asuka Station area.

07 ASUKA (明日香)

With its rice paddies and rolling hills, Asuka is a picturesque pocket of rural Japan, the top dog long before Nara, with the archaeological evidence to prove it. Here you'll find some of Japan's best-preserved **kofun** (burial tombs), built for emperors and powerful nobles between the 3rd and 7th centuries. Plonked on a hillside plateau, **Ishibutai Kofun** is Japan's largest megalithic structure, no longer covered by its earthwork mound, which means you can go inside. Rent a bike by Asuka Station and explore the various *kofun* and ruins nearby.

THE DRIVE
Head directly south on Rte 169, then southeast on Rte 222 for a total of 14km to Yoshino. The township and valley are to the south of the Yoshino River.

08 YOSHINO (吉野)

Throughout April, the quiet mountain town of Yoshino transforms into Japan's most famous **cherry-blossom-viewing festival**, as hordes crowd the ridge to marvel at the spectacle for which Yoshino is renowned: the 30,000 cherry trees that paint the valley slopes a pale pink each spring. Seedlings were brought by pilgrims over the centuries; on the edge of the mystical Kii mountain range,

The Great Buddha

The awe-inspiring physical presence of the Daibutsu at the Tōdai-ji in Nara is not to be missed. One of the largest bronze Buddha images in the world, it is housed in the **Daibutsu-den**, among the largest wooden buildings on earth. Unveiled in 752, the Daibutsu is a towering 16m in height; as you circle the statue towards the back, you'll see a wooden column with a hole through its base. Popular belief maintains that those who can squeeze through the hole, which is the same size as one of the Great Buddha's nostrils, are assured of enlightenment. Helpful pushing and pulling is allowed!

DABOOST/SHUTTERSTOCK

The Daibutsu at the Tōdai-ji, Nara

CHECCO2/SHUTTERSTOCK

Stay at a Shukubō

Kōya-san presents a brilliant opportunity for visitors to stay at a Buddhist temple. The simplest *shukubō* (temple lodging) rooms are very basic, though some temples offer a private bathroom and others have gorgeous rooms with garden views. *Shukubō* have a fairly set routine. Check in by 5pm; most temples have evening prayers that guests can attend, followed by a *shōjin-ryōri* (vegetarian monk's cuisine) dinner. Communal bathing facilities are usually open until 10pm and guests are expected to retire early. Monks perform their daily morning prayers, which guests can observe, usually at 5am or 6am. A *shōjin-ryōri* breakfast follows, then an early checkout.

Shukubō, Kōya-san

Yoshino has long been revered by followers of Shugendō, a syncretic religion that combines elements of Buddhism, Shintōism and mountain worship. If you're planning on overnighting during cherry-blossom season, book well in advance. Yoshino is a tad sleepy at other times of the year, though still an interesting place to visit.

THE DRIVE
Head directly west down the busy Yoshino River valley for 26km to Hashimoto. The river becomes the Kinokawa and flows out into Wakayama Bay at Wakayama City. At Hashimoto, drive up into the mountains to the south on winding Rte 370 for 28km and pass through the huge *daimon* (gate) at the western entrance to Kōya-san.

09 KŌYA-SAN (高野山)

The mountaintop monastery town of Kōya-san is a living, breathing centre of Buddhist faith and one of contemporary Japan's most spiritual destinations. The town worships its 9th-century founder, the monk Kukai (posthumously known as Kōbō Daishi), believed to be in a state of eternal meditation in his forest tomb at the furthest reaches of Oku-no-in (inner sanctuary), surely the most intensely spiritual place in Japan. The temple **Kongōbu-ji** is the head temple of the Shingon school of Buddhism, with an estimated 10 million followers in Japan. Here you'll also find **Banryutei**, the largest rock garden in Japan. Kōbō Daishi was born on Shikoku and achieved enlightenment there; pilgrims have walked the 88 Sacred Temples of Shikoku Pilgrimage for 1200 years, trying to become enlightened by following in his footsteps. Eighty-eight Temple pilgrims traditionally come to Kōya-san to ask for Kōbō Daishi's support before leaving for Shikoku, then come again to thank him for that support on completion of their pilgrimage.

TOP TIP:

Take the Scenic Route

While you could cruise expressway E24 (Keinawa) south from Kyoto to Nara, then all the way to Wakayama, that would be a shame as you'd miss out on much of interest on this drive. We suggest staying off the expressway and using local roads.

Take a Break

Chances are you'll feel like a break after driving the winding road up to Kōya-san. Comfy little BON ON SHYA (梵恩舎) is a chilled cafe on the main street, generally open from 7am to 5pm. They serve a daily set-menu lunch, vegetarian dishes like tofu cheesecake, chocolate cake to die for and matcha tea, plus exceptional coffee from house-roasted beans. They also bake their own bread and run pottery and art exhibitions. The place feels as much like an art gallery as a cafe.

15

Kōya-san to Nachi Grand Shrine

BEST FOR CULTURE

The Kumano Sanzan are the three grand shrines of the Kumano Kodō.

NARONGSAK NAGADHANA/SHUTTERSTOCK

Nachi Grand Shrine (p100)

DURATION	DISTANCE	GREAT FOR
3–4 days	200km	History, culture & nature
BEST TIME TO GO	March to November	

This marvellous drive takes you from spiritual Kōya-san south into the heart of the Kii Peninsula and its World Heritage–listed ancient pilgrim trails, the Kumano Kodō. There are winding, mountainous roads, and this off-the-beaten-track adventure sees you visit remote Ryūjin Onsen and the Kumano Sanzan (three grand shrines of Kumano). You can also cook your own eggs at Yunomine Onsen, bathe riverside and in the river at Kawayu Onsen, take a short walk on historic spiritual trail, and view Japan's highest single-drop waterfall, Nachi-no-taki. An adventure well worth the effort.

Link Your Trip

14 Kyoto to Kōya-san

Carry on south into the Kii Peninsula following on from Drive 14.

16 Nachi Grand Shrine to Ise-jingū

Continue northeast up the Kii Peninsula Pacific coast.

01 KŌYA-SAN (高野山)

This drive continues on from Drive 14 (p92), which ends at the monastery town of Kōya-san.

THE DRIVE

It's a 50km drive south from Kōya-san on winding, ridgetop Rte 371, better known as the Kōya-Ryūjin Skyline Road. Opened in 1984, this scenic route was originally a toll road, but now it's free to drive and

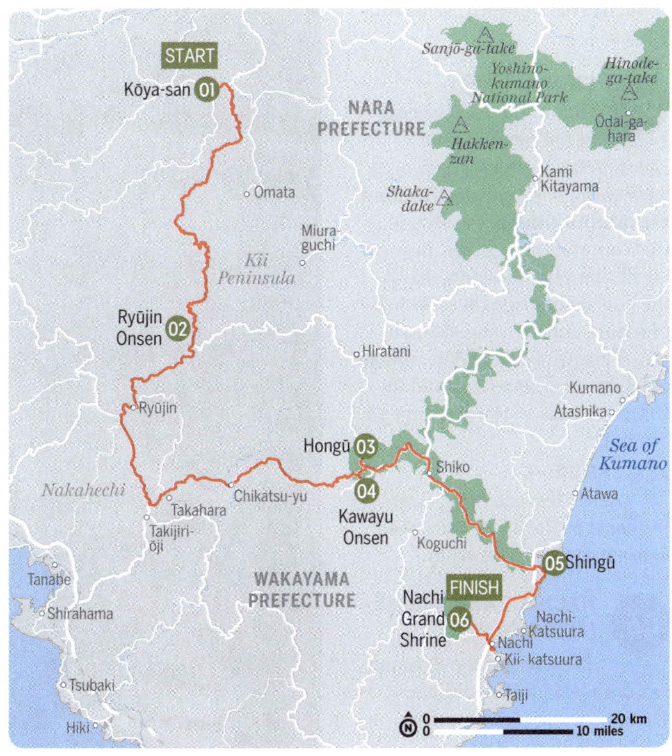

Kumano Kodō

An ancient network of trails dating back more than 1000 years, the Kumano Kodō pilgrim trails run all over the mountainous interior of the Kii Peninsula, linking the Three Grand Shrines, collectively called the **Kumano Sanzan** – Kumano Hongū-taisha, Kumano Hayatama-taisha and Kumano Nachi-taisha. In 2004, UNESCO declared the 'Sacred Sites and Pilgrimage Routes in the Kii Mountain Range' to be a World Heritage Site. These days, while many visitors come to walk the old trails, many of which have been restored, it's also feasible to visit **Kumano** and its main sites as part of an enjoyable road trip.

particularly attractive from mid-October with spectacular autumn foliage.

RYŪJIN ONSEN (龍神温泉)

Legend has it that Ryūjin Onsen was discovered by En-no-gyōja, the founder of Shugendō, a shamanistic religion of mixed origin focused on mountain worship. These days, the tiny onsen village, tucked into the upper reaches of the narrow Hidaka River valley, is a lovely, remote place to stay. The mineral-rich onsen waters, high in sodium bicarbonate are believed to be extremely nourishing to the skin, making Ryūjin Onsen one of Japan's Three Famous Bijin-no-yu – 'Hot Springs for Beautiful Women'. Stay at **Kamigoten**, a delightfully antique inn with riverside baths, originally built for the local lord.

THE DRIVE
It's a long, winding 65km drive through the mountains on Rtes 371, 198, then 311 to Hongū.

HONGŪ (本宮)

On the broad banks of the Kumano River, Hongū is the main hub of the **Kumano Kodō** and where you'll encounter **Kumano Hongū-taisha**, the first of the Three Great Shrines. **Ōtorii**, the world's largest shrine gate (34m high and 42m wide), marks the spot where the grand shrine originally sat, at the confluence of the Kumano and Otonashi Rivers, before it was partially destroyed in a flood in 1889. Surviving buildings were moved to the present site, about 400m north, on higher ground. It is an excellent example of Japanese shrine architecture, made of unpainted wood using traditional carpentry techniques with few nails, intricate joint work, and a cypress bark roof with signature *chigi* (cross-hatched beams).

THE DRIVE
There are three special onsen village areas within a short drive of

Hongū; it's only a 5km drive south, then west on Rte 311 to Watarase Onsen, with a large sprawling modern onsen complex next to the Yomura River. Then 2km north, atmospheric Yunomine Onsen is tucked in a narrow valley, while a short drive through the tunnel on Rte 241, to the south of Watarase Onsen, will bring you to Kawayu Onsen. All three have good accommodation options.

04 KAWAYU ONSEN (川湯温泉)

This riverside spot has its own geothermal marvel, with hot water percolating up through the gravel riverbank, meaning that you can make your own bathtub by digging out some of the stones and letting the hole fill with hot water. Cool off in the river, then do it all again. It's free; bring a bathing suit year-round. In winter, the riverside is turned into a giant *rotemburo* (outside bath) known as *Sennin-buro* (literally 1000-person bath).

THE DRIVE

It's a 35km drive southwest following the Kumano River valley out to the coast. In days of old, pilgrims took a boat down the river to Shingū, and these days, it's possible for visitors to do the same, departing from a roadside spot about halfway between Hongū and Shingū.

05 SHINGŪ (新宮)

Out on the Pacific coast, at the mouth of the Kumano River, Shingū (meaning 'new shrine') is home to **Kumano Hayatama-taisha**, the second of the Three Grand Shrines. Legend has it that Hayatama-no-okami, the god said to rule the workings of nature and, by extension, all life, is enshrined here. The orange pavilions and lanterns stand in sharp contrast to the greenery all around.

THE DRIVE

Head 12km southeast down the coast on Rte 42 to Nachi, then 8km northwest up the valley.

06 NACHI GRAND SHRINE (熊野那智大社)

The third of the Kumano Sanzan is inland from Nachi. This particularly atmospheric site is home to **Kumano Nachi-taisha**, the third shrine; **Nachi-no-taki**, the highest single-drop waterfall in Japan at 133m; and **Seiganto-ji**, the first temple in the Saigoku 33 Temples of Kannon Pilgrimage. Nachi's famous, otherworldly waterfall image incorporates the temple's three-storey pagoda in the foreground.

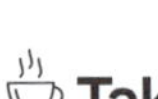

Take a Break

For something a bit different, head to Yunomine Onsen, near Hongū, to boil eggs in the public hot-spring cooking basin called YUZUTSU. It's down below the road, by the riverside, in the narrow valley and easy to use. Buy some eggs in the local shop, boil them in the hot water (Yunomine's spring comes out naturally at 93°C), then plunge the cooked eggs into the cold-running stream so they're ready to eat. Boiling your own eggs in the bubbling water is a tradition here.

CRISTI CROITORU/SHUTTERSTOCK

Kumano Kodō trail (p99)

Hongū Day Hike

During your road trip, for a pleasant 'taster' of walking an ancient Kumano Kodō trail, try this two- to three-hour hike (7.5km). From Hongū, catch a bus northwest into the mountains, to the trailhead at **Hosshinmon-ōji**, meaning 'gate of awakening of the aspiration to enlightenment', which marks the outer limits of the grand shrine, Kumano Hongū-taisha. From there it's a mostly gentle, flat and downhill walk on the Nakahechi Route back to Hongū and the grand shrine, on roads and mountain trails that pass through a mix of terraced tea fields, forests and a tiny village or two.

16

Nachi Grand Shrine to Ise-jingū

DURATION	DISTANCE	GREAT FOR
5–7 days	200km	Nature, families & history

BEST TIME TO GO	
	November to March for warm weather and a good chance of clear skies

BEST FOR SCENERY

Ise-Shima National Park is renowned for its coastline and islands.

BIRD_F/SHUTTERSTOCK

Meoto Iwa (p104)

A road less travelled these days, this drive basically follows the Kumano Kodō's old Iseji trail that connects the three grand shrines of Kumano with Japan's most sacred shrine, Ise-jingū. Head northeast up the Pacific coast of the Kii Peninsula from Nachi, before striking out east into beautiful Ise-Shima National Park on the Shima Peninsula, deemed so beautiful that it's even hosted a G7 Summit. Expect some spectacular scenery, an intriguing history of pearl cultivation, tasty seafood – especially if you visit an *ama* (women divers') hut for lunch – and finish up by exploring Ise-jingū and its surrounds.

Link Your Trip

15 Kōya-san to Nachi Grand Shrine
This drive is a continuation of Drive 15.

08 Nagoya to Matsumoto
From Ise-jingū, carry on north to Nagoya, then drive into Central Honshū.

01 NACHI (那智)

Nachi is home to three highlights – **Kumano Nachi-taisha** (Nachi Grand Shrine); **Nachi-no-taki**, the highest single-drop waterfall in Japan at 133m; and **Seiganto-ji**, the first temple in the Saigoku 33 Temples of Kannon Pilgrimage.

THE DRIVE
Head 8km back out to the Pacific coast; while you could drive to Ise-jingū in a tad over two hours by

driving northeast on the E42 and E23 expressways, that would defeat the purpose of getting out to see regional and rural Japan. Hop onto Rte 42 around the coast and drive 20km north, through Shingū.

02 KIHŌ SEA TURTLE AQUARIUM (ウミガメ水族館)

This nice little place offers a free **museum**, turtle rehabilitation centre and **aquarium** dedicated to the preservation of sea turtles found along this coast, especially the endangered loggerhead turtle.

THE DRIVE

To walk ancient bits of the Kumano Kodō's Iseji Route, which links Ise-jingū with the Kumano Sanzan, stop at Hadasu for the Ōbuki Pass track, or at Owase for the Magose Pass route. While flatter sections of the old trail have become sealed roads, many old stone trails over passes are still there. At Kii-Nagashima, head right on Rte 260 and eventually into Ise-Shima National Park; 140km in total.

03 ISE-SHIMA NP YOKOYAMA VISITOR CENTRE (横山ビジターセンター)

Drop in to this excellent visitor centre for everything you need to know about the national park. A short drive up the road is the **Yokoyama Observatory Deck**, with stunning views out over Ago Bay. For a splurge, consider overnighting at the **Shima Kankō Hotel**, where the G7 Summit was held in 2016, 5km south on the island **Kashiko-jima**.

THE DRIVE

It's all about the journey rather than the destination; follow Rte 260 for 25km as it curves all the way around Ago Bay and out to the beach Goza-Shirahama.

04 GOZA-SHIRAHAMA (御座白浜)

This pretty beach at the end of the peninsula is a pleasant place for a stroll and a break.

THE DRIVE

Head back along the southern side of the peninsula, then use Rte 128, crossing the Matoyawan Bridge before heading back out to the coast; 40km all up.

Ise-Shima National Park

If you've picked up some Japanese on your travels and figured out that *shima* means island, think again when you get to Ise-Shima (伊勢志摩). This isn't *shima* (島) as in island, but Shima (志摩) as in the name of the Shima Peninsula and Shima City. This large peninsula, which extends out into the Pacific Ocean, almost directly south of Nagoya City, thrives on tourism, with popular resort hotels and beaches – so impressive that the G7 Summit of 2016 was held here. Ise-Shima is also famed for its fresh seafood, particularly oysters, and pearl cultivation.

OSATSU AMA HUT OZEGO-SAN (海女小屋相差かまど)

Toba is home to about 1000 *ama* (literally 'sea women') who use weights to free-dive in the ocean to collect seafood such as *sazae* (turban shells), abalone, scallops and sea urchin. Some of the oldest active divers are in their 80s. An absolute highlight is to have a seafood lunch over a charcoal pit, most of it collected by *ama* that morning. Book online in English at osatsu.org.

THE DRIVE
Hop on the scenic Pearl Rd, featuring several observation decks to stop at on your way north; 40km.

MEOTO IWA (夫婦岩; WEDDED ROCKS)

This pair of natural rock pillars, just off the coast, are tied together by a *shimenawa* (twisted straw rope) and represent a married couple. The sacred rocks are a big draw for Japanese couples and more than a few engagement rings have been proffered in their vicinity. Facing Meoto Iwa from the shore, **Futami-Okitama Shrine** is famous for its frog sculptures.

THE DRIVE
It's 9km west to Ise-jingū.

ISE-JINGŪ (伊勢神宮)

Japan's most sacred Shintō shrine, Ise-jingū, dating back as early as the 4th century, is a paradox of old and new; the shrine halls are an example of ancient Japanese architecture, yet they are ritually rebuilt every 20 years and have been for 13 centuries. The current buildings will be rebuilt again in 2033. Ise-jingū is spread across two sites. **Gekū**, the outer shrine, enshrines Toyo'uke-no-Ōmikami, the god of food, clothing and housing, who is charged with providing food to the god Amaterasu-Ōmikami, the sun goddess who is enshrined in **Naikū**, the inner sanctuary. Amaterasu-Ōmikami is the ancestral goddess of the imperial family and the guardian deity of the Japanese nation. Several kilometres separate Gekū and Naikū, which are both set in sprawling, forested precincts.

Take a Break

OHARAI-MACHI, the historic pedestrian street approaching Naikū, the inner sanctuary of Ise-jingū, was developed in the Edo period (1603–1868) to provide visitors with food, drink and souvenirs. It's still doing that with beautifully restored storefronts that retain the atmosphere of centuries past. Wander down side alleys such as OKAGE-YOKOCHŌ, along the banks of the Isuzu River, then cross the lovely wooden bridge, UJI-BASHI, on your way to the inner sanctuary. Most restaurants open from 11am and shut around dusk.

AEYPIX/SHUTTERSTOCK

Pearl diver, near Mikimoto Pearl Island

Home of Cultivated Pearls

A sight that may surprise you around Ise-Shima National Park is the large number of pearl cultivation rafts floating offshore. In 1893, after many failures and near bankruptcy, local businessman Kōkichi Mikimoto became the first person to successfully cultivate pearls. He set up a pearl farm in Ago Bay, opened the first Mikimoto Pearl Store in 1899 in Ginza in Tokyo, expanded overseas by opening a store in London in 1913, and was eventually selected as one of Japan's 10 greatest inventors. Head to **Mikimoto Pearl Island** in Toba, with its museum, restaurant and store to learn more.

Also Try...

SCOTT MIRROR/SHUTTERSTOCK

Osaka to Himeji

DURATION	DISTANCE
1 day	100km

This drive sets you up to continue from **Himeji** (姫路) along the coastline of Western Honshū toward Okayama and Hiroshima. While it's feasible to drive on Rte 2 between Osaka and Kōbe, you may want to drive on the expressway to avoid the frustration of heavy traffic and countless traffic lights in the massive Kansai metropolis. After Kōbe, stick to Rte 2 on the coast for amazing views of the 3.9km-long **Akashi Kaikyō Ōhashi** (pictured) to Awaji-shima. The highlight of Himeji City is its soaring, 45m-tall white castle, **Himeji-jō**, constructed in 1609 and known as 'White Heron Castle'. It's a glorious sight, particularly in spring, when 1000 cherry trees erupt in the castle grounds.

Kōbe to Awaji-shima

DURATION	DISTANCE
1 day	90km

While **Awaji-shima** (淡路島) is an interesting destination in its own right, it makes a great stepping stone between the Kansai region and Shikoku, thanks to the 3.9km-long bridge **Akashi Kaikyō Ōhashi**, completed in 1998. It's a stunning drive above the water and you'll want to pull off at the **Awaji Service Area** once on the island for views back to the bridge and Honshū. At the southern end of the island, the 1.6km-long **Ōnaruto Bridge** connects Awaji-shima to Naruto on Shikoku. On the island, **Awajishima Anime Park**, at the northern end, is popular with anime lovers, while **Sumoto**, on the east coast, is a nice spot to overnight, with beaches and good accommodation options.

SEANPAVONEPHOTO/GETTY IMAGES

Osaka to Shirahama

DURATION	DISTANCE
1–2 days	160km

While many visitors to the Kii Peninsula come to walk and explore the old pilgrim trails of the Kumano Kodō, others head south to hit the beach and onsen at the resort area of **Shirahama** (白浜). Heading south out of Osaka, pass Kansai International Airport on its island out in Osaka Bay on the way to Wakayama City. **Wakayama Castle** (pictured) is perched high in the park in the middle of the city, with the port and ferries to Shikoku only a few kilometres west. A further 90km down the coast, Shirahama boasts a lovely white-sand beach, onsen and a good number of hotels and resort activities. It has long been an onsen destination for Japanese visitors.

Amanohashidate to Tsuruga

DURATION	DISTANCE
1 day	120km

For those who took Drive 12 (p84), this is a way back east along the Sea of Japan coastline to **Tsuruga** (敦賀), in Fukui Prefecture, that can lead on to driving back to Kyoto via Lake Biwa or onward northeast along the coast to **Kanazawa** in Central Honshū (p59). While you could drive on an expressway most of the way, it's much more interesting to drive smaller local roads via **Miyazu**, to **Maizuru**, then continue east to **Takahama**, with its lovely beaches, then on via **Obama** and Tsuruga. If you like pottering around in small backwaters, this is for you and you're unlikely to run into many international tourists once you've left Amanohashidate.

0 50 km
0 25 miles

Dōgo
Nishino-shima
Nakano-shima
Oki Islands
Chiburi-jima
Sea of Japan
Naka-umi
Sakaiminato
Matsue
Shinji-ko
Izumo
Yasugi
18
Daisen
Daisen-Oki National Park
Kurayoshi
Tottori
Chizu
Ōda
Gotsu
Hamada
Tsuyama
Sayo
Niimi
Miyoshi
Shōbara
Masuda
Okayama
Akō
Kurashiki
Nagato
Hagi
17
Hatsukaichi
Hiroshima
Mihara
Fukuyama
Onomichi
Shōdo-shima
Sea of Harima-nada
Miyajima
Kure
Ikuchi-jima
Inno-shima
Takamatsu
Inland Sea
Mine
Yamaguchi
Eta-jima
Ōmi-shima
Marugame
Iwakuni
Hakata-jima
Seto-nai-kai National Park
Shimonoseki
Kanmon Straits
Hōfu
Sea of Aki
Inland Sea
Ō-shima
Naruto
Ube
Yanai
Imabari
Sea of Hiuchi
Kitakyūshū
Kawanoe
Mima
Tokushima
Inland Sea
Niihama
Sea of Suo
Yashiro-shima
Matsuyama
Saijō
Yukuhashi
Iizuka
Tsurugi-san
Bungo-Takada
Ishizuchi-san
Sea of Iyo
Kunisaki

BEEBOYS/SHUTTERSTOCK

Akiyoshidō (p113)

Western Honshū

Explore

Western Honshū

Blending natural beauty with deep-rooted history and folklore, the five prefectures of Hiroshima, Okayama, Shimane, Tottori and Yamaguchi make up the captivating region of Western Honshū (西本州). The two drives featured in this section lead you through some of Japan's least-explored areas – Yamaguchi and the San'in region (Shimane and Tottori) – where the dramatic Sea of Japan coastline reveals breathtaking views. For two additional drives through Western Honshū, including Hiroshima, see Drive 1 (p22) and Drive 2 (p26), which take you island-hopping through the beautiful Inland Sea.

Hiroshima

The largest city in this region, Hiroshima (広島) is among the best-known of Japanese cities. Out of the devastation following the dropping of the atomic bomb in 1945, Hiroshima has made a remarkable recovery, transforming into a respected symbol of resilience with a strong commitment to peace education. The Hiroshima Peace Memorial Park is among its most famous attractions. Hiroshima is also known for its *okonomiyaki*, a savoury pancake cooked on a griddle, as well as its fresh oysters. The city is a good base for travelling to Yamaguchi and other points south.

Okayama

Okayama (岡山), the second-largest city in Western Honshū, is known for its cultural treasures, including its atmospheric black castle and Kōraku-en, one of Japan's three most celebrated landscape gardens. The Seto Ōhashi Bridge connects Okayama to Kagawa Prefecture, while its proximity to Hyōgo Prefecture makes it ideal if you are travelling to or from the Kansai region (p81).

Onomichi

While relatively small, Onomichi (尾道) has become an important tourism hub as the starting point of the Shimanami Kaidō, a cycling and driving route that connects Imabari in Kagawa Prefecture via a series of islands in the Inland Sea. The success of this route has helped Onomichi develop cyclist-friendly infrastructure and has led to the

WHEN TO GO

These drives can generally be enjoyed year-round, with spring (March to May) and autumn (September to November) being the most comfortable times to travel. Summer is ideal for enjoying marine activities along the Inland Sea island routes. Winter has the advantage of being less crowded, but the San'in region can experience heavy snow, so prepare accordingly.

expansion of other island routes. It also provides very easy access to the cities of Hiroshima, Kure, Takehara, Fukuyama and Kurashiki.

Matsue

The capital of Shimane Prefecture is often referred to as the 'City of Water', due to its proximity to two lakes and the Inland Sea. Founded in 1611 by Horio Yoshiharu, Matsue (松江) developed around its iconic Matsue Castle, one of only 12 with its original main tower intact. The city is also closely associated with Lafcadio Hearn, the writer who introduced Japanese folklore to English-speaking readers. The city serves as a gateway to San'in (the combined name for Shimane and Tottori), which is not connected by the bullet train. Matsue is a solid base for exploring the San'in region along the rugged coastline of the Sea of Japan.

TRANSPORT

Hiroshima City is the main gateway for the region, and the prefectures of Yamaguchi, Hiroshima and Okayama are all served by the bullet train. Yonago (Tottori) and Izumo (Shimane) airports provide good access by air from around Japan, while the Yakumo Limited Express connects Izumo, Matsue and Yonago with Okayama.

WHAT'S ON

Hadaka Matsuri
(Naked Festival) Clad in loincloths, thousands of men battle for a lucky stick at Okayama's Saidaiji temple each February.

Yabusame
In a ritual dating back 800 years, mounted archers compete in April in Tsuwano, Shimane Prefecture.

Yamaguchi Tanabata Lantern Festival
Thousands of red lanterns illuminate Yamaguchi City each August.

Tottori Shan-Shan Festival
Dancers parade through Tottori City with colourful paper umbrellas adorned with bells in August.

Saijō Sake Matsuri
Held in October in Higashihiroshima, this festival celebrates brewing heritage and offers sake tastings.

WHERE TO STAY

A wide range of accommodation is available. Cities offer Western-style business hotels and bigger centres have luxury options, while there are Japanese-style inns at the hot-spring towns scattered all over the region. Boutique hotels and guesthouses are popular for unique stays reflecting the local culture, particularly on the Inland Sea islands. Another small but growing trend sees traditional buildings being renovated into ambient accommodations, blending Japanese design aesthetic with modern comforts. Campsites (and glamping) are other options to consider, although not for winter.

Resources

Destination Chugoku *(www.japan.travel/en/destinations/chugoku)* JNTO site for this region.

Chugoku Region Tourism Guide *(into-you.jp)* Official regional tourism website.

San'in Tourism Organization *(sanin-tourism.com)* Official site for San'in tourism (Shimane and Tottori).

Japan Guide *(japan-guide.com/list/e1106.html)* In-depth travel articles with helpful tips by international residents.

17

BEST FOR CAVES

Akiyoshidō is one of Japan's largest limestone caves.

Yamaguchi Prefecture

DURATION	DISTANCE	GREAT FOR
2 days	165km	Diverse landscapes, photo ops, sea views & history
BEST TIME TO GO	Year-round	

BEEBOYS/SHUTTERSTOCK

Rurikōji Temple

Yamaguchi Prefecture richly rewards road trippers with diverse landscapes and photogenic spots. This route takes you through bucolic countryside with limestone caves and natural springs, along the coast of the Sea of Japan, and ends in the castle town of Hagi. The Motonosumi Inari Shrine became famous after making CNN's list of Japan's most beautiful spots. To avoid congestion on the narrow roads up to the shrine, consider staying overnight nearby and visit Motonosumi in the morning. One option is Nagato Yumoto Onsen, the prefecture's oldest hot spring town, with a range of accommodation lining the Otozure River.

Link Your Trip

02 Tobishima Kaidō

From Yamaguchi Station, proceed 130km to Hiroshima City to pick up this drive.

18 San'in-Shimane & Tottori

Travel 150km from Hagi to Iwami Ginzan to connect with this drive.

01 YAMAGUCHI (山口)

Begin your trip in the prefectural capital, and check out two noteworthy historical sites, both a short drive from Yamaguchi Station. Part of Kozan Park, **Rurikōji Temple** is known for its stunning five-storey pagoda, built in 1442. A few minutes' drive brings you to **Jōeji Temple** and **Sesshutei**, a beautiful Zen garden created around 500 years ago by Sesshū Tōyō, a celebrated artist and garden designer. Head back toward the station to continue on your way.

THE DRIVE
From Yamaguchi Station, drive 27km via the Yamaguchi bypass and then Rte 435 and onto Karst Rd, following signs for Akiyoshidō. Park in the paid lot by the information centre at the front entrance, or park for free at the Kurotani and Elevator entrances.

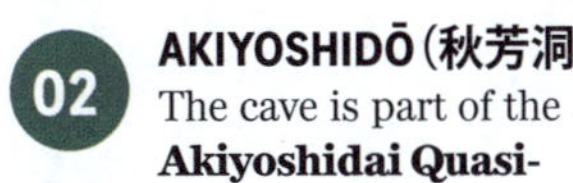

02 AKIYOSHIDŌ (秋芳洞)

The cave is part of the **Akiyoshidai Quasi-National Park**. Descend into a realm of pools, stalactites and stalagmites in one of Japan's largest limestone caverns, where the temperature remains 17°C year-round. After your subterranean visit, take the elevator back to the surface and walk over to the nearby **observation deck** for panoramic views of the surrounding plateau.

THE DRIVE
It's a pleasant 10km drive through the countryside via Rte 31 to the pond.

03 BEPPU BENTEN POND (別府弁天池)

Located within the grounds of a small shrine, the clear blue water of Beppu Benten Pond makes for a nice photo stop. Refill your water bottles with the natural spring water from the taps nearby.

THE DRIVE
Drive 19km along Rte 316, following signs for Nagato, then

Landscapes Shaped by Time

Yamaguchi's Akiyoshidai Plateau boasts impressive scenery, with the Akiyoshidō cave system below and the distinctive karst topography above. The plateau began as a coral reef some 300 million years ago, and the gradual dissolution of limestone by rain over the millennia created Japan's largest karst. Today, the plateau is covered in grass and dotted with swathes of limestone, with trails for hikers and cyclists. In a long-standing tradition, locals set fire to the grasslands every February to encourage new growth and maintain the ecosystem.

turn right onto Minori Rd and travel 31km via Rtes 191 and 276 toward the Tsunoshima Bridge, with the Sea of Japan on your right. Cross the bridge and drive 6km to the lighthouse.

TSUNOSHIMA LIGHTHOUSE PARK (角島灯台公園)

A popular photo attraction, the 1.8km **Tsunoshima Bridge** is a stunning sight. It takes you to **Tsunoshima Island**, with beaches, small shops and a historic lighthouse dating back to 1876. Now part of a scenic park with seasonal flowers, the lighthouse was one of 26 in Japan designed by Richard Henry Brunton, a Scottish engineer hired by the Japanese government. Climb up to the top for wonderful views, particularly at sunset. For nice shots of the bridge itself, park at the **Tsunoshima Bridge Observatory**, on the left just before you enter the bridge from the mainland.

THE DRIVE
From the lighthouse, retrace your journey, driving 9km on Rtes 276 and 191, continuing 22km with the sea on your left, then follow signs up the mountain for Motonosumi Inari Shrine. Drive with care on the narrow roads. There is plenty of parking but the approach can become congested. Consider staying overnight at the hot spring town of Nagato Yumoto Onsen and visiting the shrine first thing the next morning.

MOTONOSUMI INARI SHRINE (元乃隅神社)

With 123 vibrant red *torii* (gates) cascading down toward the sea, it's easy to see why this photogenic shrine has become very popular thanks to social media in recent years.

THE DRIVE
Continue on Rte 66 for 10km, then turn left onto Rte 191 and drive 31km to central Hagi. The car park at Hagi Central Park is handy for the attractions on this itinerary.

HAGI (萩)

Explore the rich Meiji-era heritage of this castle town. Though the actual castle is now in ruins, you can see well-preserved samurai homes when strolling through the atmospheric streets of the **Hagi Castle Town** neighbourhood. The **Hagi Meirin Gakusha**, a visitor centre and museum, showcases the city's educational and industrial heritage. The splendid wooden buildings housed the Meirin School from 1935 until 2014, when the school moved to new premises nearby.

Take a Break

ŌMINE SHUZŌ is a sake brewery cafe on the drive from Akiyoshidō, close to Beppu Benten Pond. The brewery has an interesting history. Founded in 1822, the business shut in 1955 and was dormant for half a century before being revived in 2010 with a fresh vision for the storied brand. Enjoy a coffee and some delicious cheesecake at the on-site cafe, and pick up sake brewed with locally grown rice and spring water from Benten Pond. Ōmine Shuzō is open daily.

TOBIUME/SHUTTERSTOCK

View from Tsunoshima Bridge Observatory

Secret Sailors to Senior Statesmen

Japan's Meiji era (1868–1912) brought rapid modernisation, and Hagi was ahead of the curve. In 1863, five promising local youths were sent to study at University College in London. Under Japan's seclusion policy, leaving the country was illegal until 1866, so they went disguised as British sailors. Known as the Chōshu Five, all went on to become influential politicians and industry leaders. Learn more about them and Hagi's industrial heritage at the Hagi Meirin Gakusha visitor centre. It also has information on the five UNESCO 'Sites of Japan's Meiji Industrial Revolution' locations around Hagi.

18

San'in–Shimane & Tottori

BEST FOR HISTORY

Izumo Taisha Grand Shrine is one of Japan's oldest and most storied Shintō sites.

PIOTF MILEWSKI/SHUTTERSTOCK

Procession, Izumo Taisha Grand Shrine

DURATION	DISTANCE	GREAT FOR
3 days	310km	History, traditional architecture, mythology, gardens & art

BEST TIME TO GO	Year-round, but the area may get some snow in winter

Shimane and Tottori are known as the San'in region and are among Japan's least populous prefectures – making them ideal for relaxed road trips. Follow the Sea of Japan along the San'in coast, and delve into Japan's mythology, folklore and history. Encounter one of Japan's most sacred shrines, a beautiful castle and amazing art museums. Explore atmospheric and well-preserved historic townscapes, romp on vast sand dunes, and get up close and personal with a bevy of quirky spirits. With its blend of cultural sites, scenic landscapes and traditional architecture, travelling around the San'in region is an enriching experience.

Link Your Trip

12 Kyoto to Kinosaki Onsen
Pick up this trip to Kyoto with a traditional onsen experience.

13 Kyoto–Lake Biwa Loop
Make a circuit of Lake Biwa from Kyoto, 299km southeast.

01 IWAMI GINZAN (石見銀山)

Established in the early 1500s, Iwami Ginzan in Ōda City was Japan's leading silver mine for almost 400 years. It's now a UNESCO site. Begin your visit at the comprehensive **World Heritage Centre** to learn about the area's rich history and receive guidance on navigating the area. Parking in the historic area can be tight, so take the bus to **Ōmori Town** to stroll along the narrow streets of wooden residences, small shops and temples, and soak in the atmosphere. You can explore an actual silver mine at the **Ryugenji Mabu Mine Shaft**; to get there, rent a bicycle or ride the golf cart service.

THE DRIVE
Take Rte 31 and drive 8km toward the coast, then merge onto the expressway (Rte 9) and drive 29km toward Izumo. Then follow Rtes 340 and 431 for 17km, following signs for Izumo Taisha. There are several large car parks around the shrine.

02 IZUMO (出雲)

Steeped in history and mythology, Izumo is home to **Izumo Taisha Grand Shrine**, one of Japan's oldest and most sacred Shintō shrines. While its founding date is unclear, the shrine appears prominently in ancient chronicles dating back to the 8th century and has connections with Japan's founding myths. Take your time soaking in every aspect of this impressive shrine, including the huge *shimenawa* (sacred straw rope) hanging on the **Haiden** (worship hall) and the 24m-tall **Honden** (main sanctuary; Japan's tallest shrine building). Learn more about the shrine's history and architecture at the adjacent **Shimane Museum of Ancient Izumo**.

THE DRIVE
Follow Rte 431 for 39km all the way to central Matsue, passing lovely Lake Shinji on the way. Park near the castle for easy access to attractions.

03 MATSUE (松江)

Shimane Prefecture's capital city, Matsue sits between the Sea of Japan and Lake Shinji. Its crown jewel is **Matsue Castle**, built in 1611 and one of Japan's 12 original castles that has survived with its main tower intact. You can wander around the grounds and see weapons and armour in the museum inside. However, skip a trip on the boats that travel through the surrounding canals, as they barely offer a glimpse of the castle. A short walk brings you to the city's

Take a Break

You might not expect to find authentic German-style bread in a small traditional mining town, but BÄCKEREI KONDITOREI HIDAKA is one of the most popular eateries in Iwami Ginzan. Run by a husband-and-wife team who trained in Germany, the business consists of a bakery, with a gelateria and cafe next door. You'll find them along the main street in Ōmori Town – just look for the line outside the bakery.

historic **samurai district** and the **Lafcadio Hearn Memorial Museum**, the former residence of the Greek-British writer and translator who helped introduce Japanese culture to the West.

THE DRIVE
With the lake on your right, follow Rte 37 for 5km and then turn left on to the expressway (Rte 9) toward Yonago. Take the Higashi-Izumo IC and continue 14km via Rtes 53 and 180 toward the Adachi Museum of Art.

04 ADACHI MUSEUM OF ART (足立美術館)

Founded in 1970 by local entrepreneur Adachi Zenkō, this museum blends award-winning garden design with Japanese paintings. The **gardens** can only be viewed from inside, beautifully framed by windows like living works of art. The museum houses nearly 1300 artworks, including a collection by Yokoyama Taikan, a leading artist of the early 20th century.

TOP TIP:

Sunset Views

Catch the sunset over Lake Shinji near central Matsue. Head to Shimane Art Museum (open until 30 minutes past sunset March to September; or until 6.30pm). Use the free car park on Rte 9, and take the underground walkway to the lake.

THE DRIVE
Follow Rte 180 for 9km, then turn left onto the expressway (Rte 9), following signs for Higashi-Izumo. Continue for 15km, via Rtes 153 and 260, crossing over two bridges to get to Daikon Island in the middle of Nakaumi Lake.

05 YUSHIEN (由志園)

Garden lovers will enjoy Yushien, which features an attractive collection of landscaped gardens and is noted for its 250 peony varieties, along with seasonal evening light-up events.

THE DRIVE
Drive 2km to the other side of the island to the Eshima Bridge.

06 ESHIMA BRIDGE (江島大橋)

This bridge, which marks the divide between Shimane Prefecture and neighbouring Tottori, has become an attraction in its own right. When viewed head-on from a distance, it appears alarmingly steep, although in reality, the gradient doesn't feel out of the ordinary when driving over it. The best place to see this optical illusion is from the Shimane side on **Daikon Island**. A telephoto lens is recommended to get the full effect.

THE DRIVE
Drive 7km over the bridge to the mainland and into Tottori Prefecture, toward Sakaiminato Station.

07 SAKAIMINATO (境港)

This is the hometown of manga artist Mizuki Shigeru, creator of the immensely popular *GeGeGe no Kitarō* series, but no prior knowledge of his work is necessary to enjoy this quirky little place. The manga draws inspiration from Japan's *yōkai* – supernatural beings and spirits rooted in Japanese folklore. Statues and images of these rather creepy yet endearing characters can be found everywhere on a stroll from Sakaiminato Station down Mizuki Shigeru Rd, where you'll also find a **museum** dedicated to the man behind the manga.

THE DRIVE
This section is the longest stretch in the itinerary. Travel 28km on Rte 431 then merge onto the expressway (Rte 9) and drive 27km along the coast. Turn onto Rte 151 and continue 14km to Kurayoshi. Park at the free lot near the city office or at the art museum.

08 KURAYOSHI (倉吉)

This charming small city is known for its traditional **storehouses** with white walls and red-tiled roofs along the Tama River in a small section of the central district. Once used for brewing and soy sauce production, many of them

Japan's Spiritual Home

Known as the 'land of the gods', Izumo is deeply woven into Japanese mythology and features prominently in the Kojiki, Japan's oldest existing historical record, completed in 712. Japan's ancient capital was in Yamato (now Nara Prefecture), and Izumo's northwest location aligned with the setting sun viewed from Yamato, showing the connection between this world and the afterlife. It was also believed that deities from across Japan gathered annually in Izumo. Izumo Taisha enshrines Ōkuninushi-no-Kami, a god of nation-building and relationships, and the shrine is popular for those seeking success in love and marriage.

MTAIRA/SHUTTERSTOCK

Haiden **(p117), Izumo Taisha Grand Shrine**

SEAN PAVONE/SHUTTERSTOCK

Mischievous, Magical & Macabre

Yōkai are supernatural creatures, ranging from playful spirits to frightening monsters. They evolved through storytelling, literature and art, often symbolising the forces of nature or human fears. Some are based on real animals, such as the shape-shifting *tanuki* (racoon dogs), while others take a human form, such as the *rokurokubi* (women who can stretch their necks to fantastic lengths). Even inanimate objects can become *yōkai*, including the mischievous *kasa-obake* – old-fashioned umbrellas that hop around on one leg. Manga artist Mizuki Shigeru helped introduce *yōkai* to new generations with his stories about Kitarō, a good-natured boy who lives among the creatures.

Tottori Sand Dunes

now house teashops, galleries, and local stores, making for some nice photo ops during a short stroll around town. A much more recent addition is the new **Tottori Prefectural Museum of Art**, about 1.5km from the historic quarter.

THE DRIVE
Head back toward the coast for 8km, and then turn right on the expressway (Rte 9), following the coast for 42km and taking the exit for Central Tottori. Park at the lot near the Tottori Sand Dunes Visitor Centre.

09 TOTTORI SAND DUNES (鳥取砂丘)

It may come as a surprise that Tottori boasts sand dunes stretching 16km along the Sea of Japan. Formed by river sediment, sea currents and wind over thousands of years, the golden slopes are up to 2km wide and 50m high in places. Climbing the dunes is fun, but often not as easy as it appears! They can get very hot in summer so climb with appropriate footwear and hydrate often. You can also take a short camel ride, go sandboarding and paragliding, or take the chairlift to an observation deck near the visitor centre. The nearby **Sand Museum** features incredible, large-scale sand sculptures based on an annual themed exhibition. (The museum shuts after the New Year holiday in January and re-opens at the end of April.)

THE DRIVE
Proceed 5km on Rte 265 and then turn onto Rte 29, following signs for Okayama/Himeji. Drive 5km, then merge onto the Chugoku Expressway and drive 28km, exiting at the Chizu IC. Continue 1.5km on Rte 53 to Ishitani Residence; park in the designated spot three minutes' walk away.

10 ISHITANI RESIDENCE (石谷家住宅)

Located in the unassuming town of Chizu, this splendid house remains something of a hidden gem in Tottori but is well worth the visit. The wealthy Ishitani family made their money in property and forestry. Starting in 1919, over the course of a decade Ishitani Denshirō rebuilt the family home. He incorporated Western-style elements into its traditional design to create the beautifully appointed residence, now designated as one of Japan's Important Cultural Properties. The complex includes storerooms with farming tools and a **cafe** with views of the lovely garden.

Take a Break

HAWAI ONSEN, a hot spring area on Lake Tōgō's western shore, is about 10km from Kurayoshi and a handy place to break your journey. Stay at a ryokan (traditional inn) and try fresh seafood and a bath with a lake view, or enjoy a relaxing dip in one of several free *ashi-no-yu* (foot baths) if you're just passing through. Contrary to expectations, Hawai Onsen has no connection to the US state – the name has been in use here for centuries.

Also Try...

FIIPHOTO/SHUTTERSTOCK

Yonago to Mt Daisen

DURATION	DISTANCE
1 day	22km

A day trip to majestic Mt Daisen (大山) can be combined with Drive 18 (p116) along the San'in Coast. Standing 1729m high, Daisen is particularly lovely in the autumn foliage season. Two major attractions are **Daisenji Temple**, located near the mountain's entrance, and **Ōgamiyama Shrine** further up. For information on the various hiking trails, stop by the **Daisen Town Tourist Information Centre** near the temple. One of the most popular is the **Daisendaki Waterfall** course, an easy one-hour hike to a picturesque two-tiered cascade, while the challenging climb up to the mountain's summit takes around three hours. Drive 22km from Yonago to reach the entrance to Mt Daisen.

Yamaguchi City to Iwakuni

DURATION	DISTANCE
1 day	95km

The castle town of **Iwakuni** (岩国) has interesting historic sites and museums clustered within easy walking distance. The best-known attraction is the iconic **Kintai Bridge** (pictured), with its five graceful arches. After crossing the bridge, take a ropeway up to **Iwakuni Castle** (a faithful replica of the original from 1604) for city views. Find out more about the former rulers of the region at the **Kikkawa Historical Museum**, and visit the **Kashiwabara Art Museum** to see a nice collection of samurai armour. Try bite-sized samples of local cuisine at **Honke Matsugane**, an information centre located in a former merchant's residence from the mid-19th century. From Iwakuni, it's a 45km drive to **Hiroshima City** (p28) on Drive 2.

GRASSFLOWERHEAD/SHUTTERSTOCK

Onomichi to Takehara

DURATION	DISTANCE
1 day	40km; plus 15min ferry ride

From **Onomichi** (尾道), take coastal Rte 185 to **Tadanoumi Port** and park in the terminal lot. Catch a ferry to **Ōkunoshima** (pictured), also called 'Rabbit Island' for its hundreds of free-roaming bunnies – probably descendants of class-room pets released there. You can buy vegetables for them at the convenience store near Tadanoumi Port. Incongruously for this bunny paradise, the island was a chemical weapons production site until 1945; learn more at the **museum**. Back on the mainland, head to the historical townscape of **Takehara** and see the well-preserved homes of merchants who prospered from the sake and salt trade. Don't miss **Saihōji**, an attractive temple with a viewing platform offering views of Takehara. **Kure** (p28) on Drive 2 is 52km from here.

Okayama & Tomonoura

DURATION	DISTANCE
1 day	75km

Explore Okayama Prefecture's capital city, home to **Kōraku-en**, one of Japan's top three traditional landscape gardens, and **Okayama Castle**, nicknamed the 'Crow Castle' for its striking black facade. Continue on to the **Kurashiki Bikan Historical Quarter** and take a boat trip through the canals that used to link the nearby port with white-walled warehouses, then have a break in one of the cafes. The nearby **Ōhara Museum of Art** includes an impressive collection of works by artists such as Gauguin, Monet and Matisse. Finish your day at **Tomonoura**, a peaceful fishing hamlet at the southern end of Fukuyama. Soak in the old-fashioned charm while strolling along the harbour or through the side streets. **Onomichi** on Drive 1 (p22) is 25km away.

0 50 km
0 25 miles
Fukushima
Ōma
22
Shimokita Peninsula
Tsugaru Strait
Mutsu
Tsugaru Peninsula
Mutsu-wan
Noheji
Goshogawara
Aomori
Ogawara-ko
21
Hirosaki
Sea of Japan
Hachinohe
Towada-ko
Ōdate
Kuji
Noshiro
Towada-Hachimantai National Park
Ōga Peninsula
Ōga
Iwate-san
Akita
Tazawa-ko
Semboku
Morioka
23
Miyako
Kakunodate
Hanamaki
Honjō
Kitakami
Tōno
Yokote
Kamaishi
Kitakami-gawa
Chōkai-san
Sanriku Fukko National Park
Ōfunato
Sakata
Ichinoseki
Kesennuma
Shinjō
Tsuruoka
Awa-shima
Gas-san
Ginzan Onsen
20
Ishinomaki
Bandai-Asahi National Park
Oshika Peninsula
Murakami
Yamagata
Sendai
Sado-ga-shima
Mt Zaō
Sendai-wan
Niigata
Shibata
Yonezawa
Sado Straits
Nakumura
Fukushima
PACIFIC OCEAN
Kitakata
Bandai-san
19
Sanjō
Aizu-Wakamatsu
Inawashiro-ko
Namie
Kashiwazaki
Nagaoka
Koriyama
Jōetsu
Shinano-gawa
Shirakawa
Iwaki
Oze National Park
Nikkō National Park
Tone Gawa
Naeba
Nantai-san
Otawara

KOUJI OKAFUJI/SHUTTERSTOCK

Shiriyazaki Lighthouse, Cape Shiriyakazi (p143)

Tōhoku

Explore

Tōhoku

Stretching across the northernmost part of Honshū, Tōhoku (東北) is a diverse region comprising Aomori, Iwate, Akita, Miyagi, Yamagata and Fukushima Prefectures. Although the bullet train provides easy access from Tokyo, Tōhoku remains somewhat undiscovered by international travellers. Brimming with natural beauty, Tōhoku's expansive landscapes, mountainous terrain and long coastlines make it well-suited for road trips. While each prefecture has distinct culture and traditions, the region is united by its harsh winters and rich agricultural heritage, with specialities that include rice, fruit, seafood and sake. Tōhoku occupies nearly one-fifth of Japan's total area, and getting from A to B often means travelling a long way.

Yamagata

Yamagata (山形市) was once a castle town under the rule of the Mogami family. The city retains historical sites such as Kajo Park, where remnants of Yamagata Castle can still be seen. The city is probably best known as a winter resort, with high-quality snow for skiers and snowboarders, as well as major attractions conveniently located within the city. These include Risshaku-ji (Yamadera Temple), a beautiful mountainside temple, and the resort town of Zaō Onsen, where the winter phenomenon of 'snow monsters' can be seen if the conditions are right.

Morioka

Iwate's central location in the middle of Tōhoku makes it an ideal base for exploring further afield. Every Japanese city or region has its own spin on a noodle dish, but Morioka (盛岡) has three, known collectively as the San Dai Men (Three Great Noodles of Morioka): *wanko soba, jajamen* and Morioka *reimen*. *Wanko soba* is a traditional Japanese dish, while *jajamen* and Morioka *reimen* have origins in China and North Korea, respectively. Strong community ties and family traditions have helped develop and sustain the San Dai Men brand in an area where rice did not grow well due to the colder climate – buckwheat and wheat flourished instead. *Wanko soba* is served in tiny bowls with bite-sized portions, and the entertainment value of the service is a major draw – you'll keep

WHEN TO GO

April to November is recommended for these Tōhoku drives; many scenic routes and tourism facilities close during the harsh winter. (The exception is Drive 20, which showcases winter attractions.) Generally, Tōhoku's cherry blossoms bloom from April to early May, and autumn foliage season is mid-October to November. Summer is less humid than Tokyo, with vibrant festivals in August.

getting refills until you manage to place the lid on your bowl. Another local food tradition is the Mikata morning market, which has served as the community's kitchen for decades, offering farm-fresh produce and homemade delicacies.

Aomori

Aomori (青森市) serves as a hub for exploring the northernmost part of Honshū – the last stop before reaching Hokkaidō. Aomori is famous for its Nebuta Matsuri, a vibrant summer festival featuring illuminated floats. Similar festivals take place throughout the prefecture in early August, with Aomori's event attracting around three million visitors annually. The Neputa Museum Wa Rasse and the Sannai Maruyama Archaeological Site, which showcase prehistoric culture, are two of the city's key attractions. For a taste of local culinary experiences, the A-Factory near Aomori Station offers regional specialities and restaurants, including house-produced cider – another popular product from Aomori, which is famous for its apples.

TRANSPORT

The bullet train is the easiest way to reach Tōhoku, and depending on your itinerary, combining your drives with judicious use of a JR East Pass may be useful. The pass costs ¥30,000 for unlimited travel on JR trains (and some private lines) for five consecutive days; available to foreign passport holders, including residents.

WHAT'S ON

Hirosaki Cherry Blossom Festival
Late April to early May is typically prime time for cherry blossoms and a festive atmosphere around this castle in Aomori.

Aomori Nebuta Matsuri
Massive illuminated floats are paraded through Aomori's streets with dancers and musicians in early August.

Akita Kantō Matsuri
Performers balance towering poles with lanterns on their palms, foreheads and shoulders in Akita City's summer festival.

Sendai Tanabata Matsuri
In early August, Sendai lights up with colourful decorations inspired by a legend of star-crossed lovers.

Aizu Matsuri
The samurai heritage of Fukushima's Aizu region is honoured in late September with parades and displays.

WHERE TO STAY

Larger cities offer accommodation to suit all budgets. Even low-end business hotels are usually clean and comfortable, often with free breakfasts, although rooms and showers can be cramped compared to hotels overseas. With many volcanoes and natural hot springs, there are charming onsen towns all over Tōhoku. Establishments range from the very traditional to newer hybrid styles offering a choice of Western or Japanese-style bedding along with the hot baths. Note that the evening meal is usually served at a set time at most ryokan (traditional inns), so plan your drives accordingly.

Resources

Destination Tohoku *(www.japan.travel/en/destinations/tohoku)* Information from Japan National Tourist Organization (JNTO).

Travel to Tohoku *(tohokukanko.jp)* The official website for tourism in Tōhoku.

A Different Side of Japan *(donnykimball.com/japan-area-guides)* Informative, engaging articles by a Japan-based travel writer.

19

BEST FOR SCENERY

The Bandai-Azuma Skyline alpine route is one of Japan's most scenic drives.

Aizu Bandai, Fukushima

DURATION	DISTANCE	GREAT FOR
2 days	128km	Nature, lakes, history, samurai & traditional architecture
BEST TIME TO GO	May to early November	

PATCHIYA WASITWORAPOL/SHUTTERSTOCK

Goshikinuma Ponds

The Aizu Bandai area of Fukushima is rich in natural beauty and fascinating history. This itinerary combines the best of both worlds. Although the driving distance is relatively short, you'll take scenic trails around a majestic mountain and among shimmering ponds and lakes. Then delve into history, visiting the samurai city of Aizu-Wakamatsu and a charming former post town. If you love spending time in nature, staying overnight in Japan's 'Lake District' of the Urabandai area near the Goshikinuma Ponds is ideal, while Japanese history and culture enthusiasts may prefer accommodation in Aizu-Wakamatsu.

Link Your Trip

20 Zaō & Ginzan Onsen

From Fukushima, take the Tōhoku Expressway for 86km to Yamagata to join Drive 20 in the green season.

03 Romantic Road

Drive about 2 hours south on the Tōhoku Expressway to reach Nikkō and the Romantic Road.

01 FUKUSHIMA STATION (福島駅)

Reached in 90 minutes from Tokyo by bullet train, Fukushima Station is an ideal starting point for this drive.

THE DRIVE

From Central Fukushima, drive 25km via Rte 70, following signs for the Bandai-Azuma Skyline, an alpine route through the Azuma Mountains. Stop at the observation platform for dynamic views of the **Fudōsawa Bridge**.

Honour & Tragedy in Aizu

Samurai were renowned for their values of loyalty, courage, courtesy and honour, and historians agree that the Aizu samurai exemplified these ideals to the fullest. The well-educated warriors were skilled in martial arts, horse-back riding, swordsmanship and calligraphy. Discover more about the proud history of the Aizu domain at Tsuruga Castle. Next to the Sazaedō Temple on Mt Iimori are the graves of the legendary Byakkotai (White Tiger Brigade), a unit of teenage samurai who met a tragic fate during the Bōshin War (1867–68), taking their own lives after being isolated from their comrades.

02 JŌDODAIRA VISITOR CENTRE (浄土平ビジターセンター)

The centre lies halfway along the **Bandai-Azuma Skyline**, serving as a gateway for the area's mountain trails. A good option for this itinerary is the one-hour trek around the crater of **Mt Azuma Kofuji**, a dormant volcano, starting and ending at the visitor centre. Short on time? Climb up to the crater's rim for great views, or stroll around the boardwalk on the **Jōdodaira wetlands trail**.

THE DRIVE
Continue 15km down the other end of the Skyline, turn right and follow Rte 115 for 2km, then right onto the **Bandai-Azuma Lake Line**, enjoying the lake vistas along the way. Drive 16km, following signs to the Goshikinuma Ponds and park at the Urabandai Visitor Centre. Located halfway along the Lake Line, the Nakatsugawa Valley Rest House offers views of a pretty gorge.

03 GOSHIKINUMA PONDS (五色沼)

The name of this scenic cluster of volcanic lakes, ponds and marshes means 'Five Coloured Ponds', but there are far more than five, with hues that shift with the seasons, weather and viewing angle. Walk the 4km-long ponds trail (about 80 minutes one way) then catch the bus back from the other end. The **Morohashi Museum of Modern Art**, featuring an impressive Salvador Dalí collection, is less than 1km up the road.

THE DRIVE
Take the scenic route toward Aizu-Wakamatsu, including a small section of lovely Inawashiro Lake. Drive 16km via Rte 459, turn left and drive 2km down to the lake, then turn right on Rte 49 (signs for Aizu-Wakamatsu) and drive 20km. Turn left onto Rte 64 (signs for Tajima) and drive 2km to Sazaedō. Time permitting on the way, stop by the Hideo Noguchi Memorial Hall, dedicated to Fukushima's

celebrated bacteriologist, on Rte 49.

04 SAZAEDŌ TEMPLE (さざえ堂)

This striking wooden temple features a highly unusual double-helix spiral ramp. Visitors move in a continuous one-way journey, crossing a bridge at the top without encountering people coming the opposite way. The monk Ikudo chose the ingenious design for a mini-version of the Saigoku 33 Kannon Pilgrimage. He installed 33 statues of Kannon (the Buddhist goddess of compassion), allowing visitors to pay respects to each one and complete the pilgrimage in a fraction of the usual time.

THE DRIVE
Drive 4km to the castle. Turn left onto the Shirakawa Kaidō, drive 1km and then turn left onto Rte 64.

05 TSURUGA CASTLE (鶴ヶ城)

Aizu-Wakamatsu's iconic white castle played a major role in the 1868 Battle of Aizu (part of the Bōshin War) between shogunate supporters and those favouring imperial rule. The Aizu samurai, loyal to the shogun, were besieged here for a month before surrendering. Carefully restored in 1965, the castle now houses a **museum** on the region's rich history and the top floor offers great city views.

THE DRIVE
Take Rte 121 for 23km, then turn right onto Rte 329 and drive 5km, following signs for Ōuchi-juku.

06 ŌUCHI-JUKU (大内宿)

Step back in time to Japan's Edō period (1603–1868) with a visit to one of its historic post towns, where travellers sought food and lodging during their journey. The main street of Ōuchi-juku is lined with beautifully preserved thatched-roof houses, offering an authentic glimpse into a bygone era. Many of the town's shops and restaurants are still run by families who have lived here for generations. It's 107km back to Fukushima Station from Ōuchi-juku.

Take a Break

Try traditional Aizu cuisine in ambient surroundings at MATSUYA. Founded in 1834 as a miso store, their specialty is *miso dengaku*, consisting of skewered vegetables and meat topped with a savoury miso paste and cooked over an open flame. Each skewer is prepared to order. Enjoy this and other local favourites for a hearty lunch, dished up with a side of warm hospitality. Matsuya is a few minutes' drive from Tsuruga Castle; parking available.

YU_PHOTO/SHUTTERSTOCK

Sazaedō Temple

Lucky Red Charms

You'll probably encounter images of *akabeko* – stylised red cows – during your travels. Originally crafted as children's toys made from papier-mâché, the animals are now beloved regional symbols. A legend from the early 9th century tells how a mysterious 'red' cow (probably brown in modern terminology) appeared during the building of a temple, working tirelessly as it led the workers and other cattle in their efforts. The red cow eventually came to represent good health and fortune. Try decorating your own *akabeko* at the Tsurugajō Kaikan near the castle or at Akabeko Land by Sazaedō Temple.

20

Zaō & Ginzan Onsen

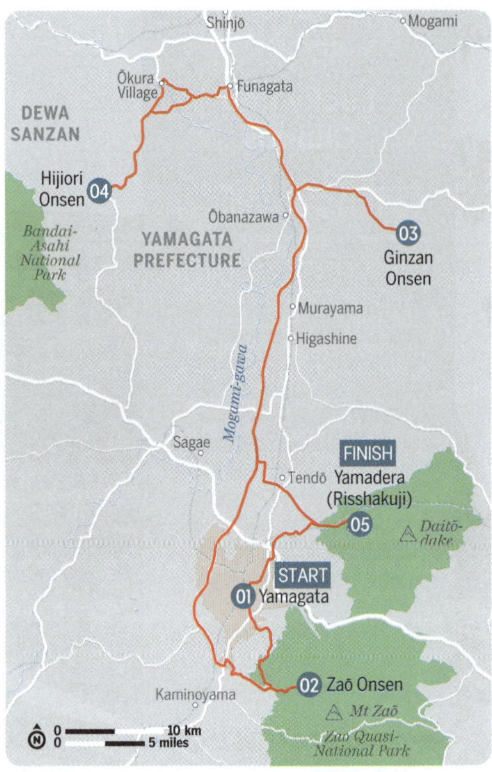

TABI-BUTA/SHUTTERSTOCK

DURATION	DISTANCE	GREAT FOR
2 days	240km	Hot springs, traditional town-scapes & snow activities

BEST TIME TO GO	December to early March to see snow, but it can be enjoyed in all seasons

Discover the magic of Yamagata in winter on this route, and see the sights that have enchanted the world on social media – the fairy-tale charm of Ginzan Onsen and 'snow monsters' on Mt Zaō, as well as a secluded hot-spring village and a mountaintop temple. Snow doesn't faze people here: roads are well maintained and rental cars come equipped with snow tyres and scrapers, but always drive to the conditions and use good judgement as you explore this winter wonderland. And if you're visiting in other seasons, see the tips opposite for adapting this itinerary.

Link Your Trip

19 Aizu Bandai, Fukushima

It's a little over 100km and two hours south along the expressway and Rte 121 to Fukushima. Some roads may be closed in winter.

21 Akita & Aomori Coast

It's about 3 hours north along the Tōhoku Chūō and Akita Expressways to Akita City.

01 YAMAGATA STATION (山形駅)

Your winter adventure starts at the prefectural transportation hub of Yamagata Station in Yamagata (p126), easily reached in less than three hours by bullet train from Tokyo. Take in some attractions in the centre. The evocative **Bunshōkan**, a former prefectural government building now open to the public, is a lovely example of Japan's early 20th-century Western-style architecture. **Yamagata**

Ginzan Onsen (p134)

BEST FOR SNOWSCAPES

Charming Ginzan Onsen is particularly lovely in winter.

Visiting in Other Seasons

Yamagata certainly looks good in snow, but while this itinerary has been tailored for a winter visit, almost everything on this drive can be enjoyed year-round. Although you won't get snow monsters in other seasons, you can instead see Ōkama, a stunning lake in the crater of Mt Zaō, with water that changes colour depending on the weather conditions. Take the Zaō Echo Line road (open from late April to early November) from Zaō Onsen up to the crater.

Creative City Centre Q1 offers cafes, small shops, art galleries and community events housed in a former elementary school.

THE DRIVE
Following signs for Zaō Onsen, drive 17km via Rte 53 (Nishi Zaō Kōgen Line) up to the Zaō Ropeway.

02 ZAŌ ONSEN (蔵王温泉)

One of the region's signature winter experiences is seeing the **juhyō** (snow monsters) on Mt Zaō. These are formed when water droplets freeze on the forested slopes, creating thick layers of frost and snow in otherworldly shapes. Take the **Zaō Ropeway** up the mountain where – weather permitting – you'll meet monsters. The *juhyō* begin forming in December and are usually at their peak in February; clear conditions are best for viewing. The ropeway cabins are enclosed, but dress warmly, as boarding lines may be long.

THE DRIVE
Drive 11km back along Rte 53, which turns into Rte 21 (Zaō Park Line), signs for Yamagata, then take the Tōhoku-Chuō Expressway for 52km toward Ōbanazawa. Exit at Ōbanazawa IC, turn right onto Rte 347 (signs for Ginzan Onsen) and drive 14km via Rtes 29 and 188. Leave your car at the Taishō Romankan visitor centre and take the shuttle into Ginzan Onsen.

03 GINZAN ONSEN (銀山温泉)

This picturesque and highly popular little hot-spring town features traditional ryokan and small shops along a river. It maintains a storybook charm, with cobblestone streets and gas lamps that come on around sunset. A couple of hours in Ginzan Onsen is usually more than enough for strolling through the compact town centre. Being particularly photogenic in snow, accommodation here can book out years in advance, so plan on staying elsewhere.

THE DRIVE
There are various options for onsen stays in Yamagata; the suggested route is for the Hijiori Onsen village. From the Taishō Romankan, travel 7km via Rtes 188 and 347 to the Tōhoku-Chuō Expressway. Drive 20km and exit at Funagata IC. Drive 10km to Ōkura Village, and turn left onto Rte 458 (signs for Hijiori Onsen). Continue 13km and look out for the giant *kokeshi* (colourful wooden dolls) as you approach the village.

04 HIJIORI ONSEN (肘折温泉)

Tucked away in a secluded part of Yamagata, Hijiori Onsen offers hot spring stays in family-owned ryokan serving fresh local produce. The original founding families continue to run the inns and shops, preserving a strong sense of community in this tranquil hamlet, which gets some of the region's biggest snowfall.

THE DRIVE
Retrace your route, driving 23km back to the Tōhoku-Chuō Expressway. Drive 43km and exit at Tendō IC. Drive 7km via Rte 111 to the temple, turn left onto Rte 19 and drive 5km.

05 YAMADERA (RISSHAKUJI) (山寺、立石寺)

Founded in 860, this mountain-top temple is officially named Risshakuji, but it's commonly known as Yamadera ('mountain temple'). The ascent via more than 1000 stone steps requires both physical and mental effort but the rewards are worth it. If the climb doesn't take your breath away, the views from **Godaidō Hall** at the top will. Yamadera looks magnificent decked out in snow, but winter conditions may make climbing challenging. Cleats or crampons are recommended for boots and trekking poles could come in handy. It's best not to climb solo or when black ice is present.

THE DRIVE
Return to Yamagata via Rte 19 for 18km, following signs for Central Yamagata.

Take a Break

SANBE is a small, family-run cafe a few minutes' drive down the mountain from Zaō Onsen. Its speciality is freshly made *igamochi*, a local sweet that has been produced in Zaō for more than a century. Made from locally grown rice, these soft rice cakes are filled with red bean paste and served on a bamboo leaf. Enjoy some *igamochi* with a cup of hot matcha tea. Sanbe also has ice cream, coffee and a variety of drinks.

Getting into Ginzan Onsen

Ginzan Onsen attracts throngs of tourists in winter. Since securing accommodation is akin to winning the lottery in this season, most visitors are day-trippers. Those who self-drive should park at the Taishō Romankan visitor centre and take a paid shuttle into town with other day visitors. To alleviate crowding, anyone not staying overnight needs a ticket for the privilege of being in the town between 5pm and 8pm (around the popular light-up time), or must leave by 5pm. This system is liable to change; check the latest rules when planning your visit.

OMJAI C/SHUTTERSTOCK

Yamadera (Risshakuji)

21

Akita & Aomori Coast

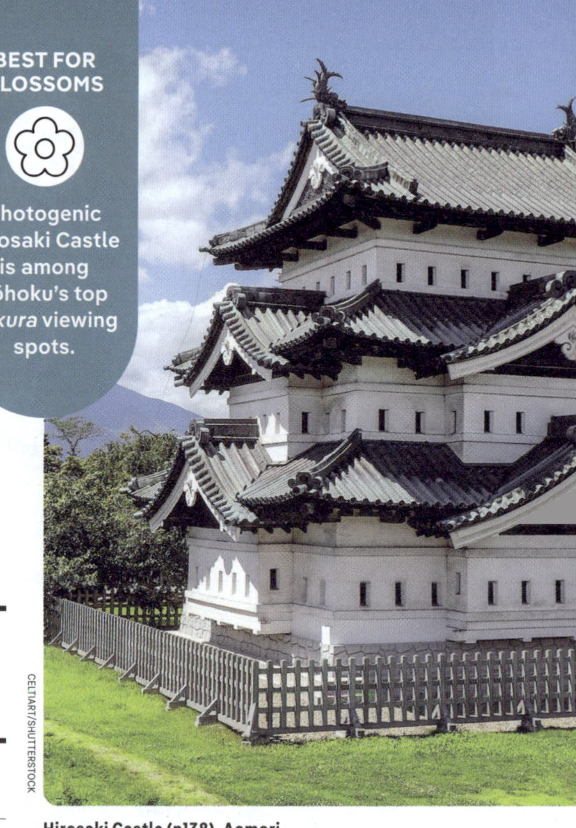

BEST FOR BLOSSOMS

Photogenic Hirosaki Castle is among Tōhoku's top *sakura* viewing spots.

DURATION	DISTANCE	GREAT FOR
3 days	321km	Nature, sea views, folklore & history

BEST TIME TO GO	May to early November

CELTIART/SHUTTERSTOCK

Hirosaki Castle (p138), Aomori

The Shirakami Sanchi mountain range (a UNESCO Natural World Heritage Site) sits on the border between Akita and Aomori. You'll be exploring parts of both prefectures on this drive, which includes an opportunity to walk through the beautiful Shirakami Sanchi beech forest. Work your way up the coast from Akita on scenic Rte 101, before turning inland to travel through Aomori's Tsugaru region. You'll encounter angry monsters and Japan's first people, and admire gravity-defying festival floats and one of Japan's most beloved castles, with photos ops galore. Free up space on your phone – you'll need it!

Link Your Trip

22 Around the Shimokita Peninsula

From Aomori City, drive 105km via Rte 279 to Mutsu for the Shimokita Peninsula.

23 Iwate Coast & Tōno

From Akita City, drive east on Rte 46 for 110km to Morioka to try Drive 23.

01 AKITA CITY (秋田市)

Before leaving Akita's prefectural capital, drop by the **Akarenga Folk Museum**, housed in a handsome red-brick building from 1912. The museum showcases the best of the region's arts and crafts, along with the part they have played in local history and culture. The museum is 1km from Akita Station.

THE DRIVE

Take the scenic route on the way to the Ōga Peninsula. From Akita Station drive 3.5km via Rte 26

Fooling the Fearsome Fellows

An Ōga legend tells of Namahage arriving from China 2000 years ago. They stole crops and abducted women, so angry villagers proposed a challenge: if the Namahage built 1000 stone steps in one night, they could take whatever they wanted. As the 999th step was laid, a villager mimicked a rooster's crow. Believing it was dawn and that they had lost, the embarrassed Namahage fled into the mountains. Time and energy permitting, visit atmospheric **Akagami-jinja Goshadō** and climb 999 steps to five shrine halls standing side by side; it's a 26km drive from the Namahage Museum.

and turn right onto Rte 7 (signs for Ōdate), then drive 8km. Turn right and continue 37km along the coast on Rtes 56 and 101 to the museum. The lovely peninsula is home to some decidedly unlovely characters – the Namahage ogres. You'll see two huge specimens standing guard outside the Ōga Tourism Information Centre at the entrance to the peninsula, providing a fun photo stop.

02 NAMAHAGE MUSEUM (なまはげ館)

Namahage are demon-like figures with red or blue faces. Dressed in straw capes, they visit Ōga's homes on New Year's Eve in pairs, causing a ruckus as they search for disobedient children or lazy adults. This custom was meant to instill hard work and discipline in residents, and it's an honour for local men to be chosen to play a Namahage – though these days, it's all in good fun. You can watch an exciting yet humorous reenactment of a Namahage visit (with multiple daily performances and English support) and check out the comprehensive displays at the museum to learn more about these ogres of Ōga.

THE DRIVE
Get back on Rte 101 and drive 30km. There are many opportunities to stop and admire the view along the coastal road; the suggested beach here is a particularly nice one.

03 KAMAYAHAMA BEACH (釜谷浜海水浴場)

Catch the sea breeze and enjoy a break at this spot tucked away in the city of **Mitane**. Considered one of Japan's best 100 beaches, Kamayahama offers summer swimming and great views of where you've been and where you're heading: the Ōga Peninsula and the Shirakami Mountains, respectively.

THE DRIVE
Drive 61km on Rte 101 (crossing the prefectural border into Aomori along the way) and turn right toward Juniko Lakes, part of the

Take a Break

Fukaura is known for stunning sunset spots, and one of the best is the beachside open-air bath at the KOGANEZAKI FUROFUSHI ONSEN hotel on Rte 101. The main bath is mixed-gender – once common in Japan but now increasingly rare – though modest bathers can rent or purchase a simple cover-up at the hotel. The facility also offers a smaller women-only outdoor bath and separate indoor baths for men and women. Day-trippers are welcome until 4pm, but an overnight stay is required for the sunset experience.

Shirakami Sanchi forest. Continue 5km to the car park.

04 JUNIKO LAKES (十二湖)

Although Juniko means 'Twelve Lakes', there are more than 30 bodies of water around here. An easy **loop trail** takes you through the forest and around several ponds in about 45 minutes, making for a perfect nature break in this itinerary. The star of the show is the cobalt-blue **Aoike Pond** near the start of the trail; the colour varies with the season, with April to August best for viewing. (No access December to March.)

THE DRIVE
Drive 5km back and turn right to rejoin Rte 101. Continue for 39km to the car park for Senjōjiki.

05 SENJŌJIKI COAST (千畳敷海岸)

Make a short stop to see the dynamic **rock formations** and **tidal pools** on this bedrock beach. The surrounding coastline was shaped by an earthquake in 1792. Senjōjiki means '1000 Mats', referencing the story of a feudal lord who spread out 1000 tatami mats over a vast rock ledge to host a grand banquet. This is a great spot to catch the sunset.

THE DRIVE
Carry on for 23km on Rte 101, then turn left onto the Melon Rd (signs for Shari). Continue for 18km through the countryside. This area has one of Japan's largest wind farms, and the turbines make a striking contrast with the bucolic surroundings. Turn left on Rte 228 to the entrance for the shrine; drive 1km to the car park.

06 TAKAYAMA INARI SHRINE (高山稲荷神社)

This photogenic shrine has gained attention on social media recently for the undulating rows of some 200 red **torii gates** that weave around the extensive grounds. That said, it still flies under the radar of most international visitors and generally maintains a peaceful atmosphere. There are also scores of fox statues around the shrine buildings on the hill above the *torii*. The animals are considered messengers to Inari Ōkami, the deity of rice and agriculture, enshrined here.

THE DRIVE
Drive 1km back onto Melon Rd and continue 1.5km, and turn left. Continue 6km and turn left onto Rte 184. Continue 13km via Rtes 184 and 151 to Goshogawara; park in the lot in front of the museum.

07 TACHINEPUTA MUSEUM (立佞武多の館館)

Nebuta matsuri (or *neputa*, based on regional variations) are summer festivals held across Aomori Prefecture, featuring parades of giant colourful floats made from paper. Each area adds its own spin on the festivities. The city of Goshogawara hosts the **Tachineputa Festival**, showcasing the tallest floats, which reach an astounding 23m high. See the towering creations on display at the Tachineputa Museum and discover how they are made. (You'll get to see Aomori City's dynamic version of the festival at the end of this drive.)

THE DRIVE
Take Rte 101 for 2.5km, turn right onto Rte 339 (signs for Hirosaki) and continue 16km, and then right onto 131. Proceed 8km to the castle. There is no designated parking for the castle; two nearby options for paid parking are the Hirosaki Municipal Tourism Information Centre and the Hirosaki Cultural Centre.

08 HIROSAKI CASTLE (弘前城)

Originally constructed in 1611, Hirosaki Castle is one of only 12 in Japan to have survived with its main tower intact. The castle is now part of **Hirosaki Park**, surrounded by over 2500 cherry trees. It's attractive at any time, but turns into a photographer's dream each spring, when pink blossoms frame the small castle and flutter down to cover its moat. The best viewing time is generally late April, but it varies from year to year, so check the latest forecasts for the flowers when planning your spring visit.

KUROKAWA MOKU/SHUTTERSTOCK

Takayama Inari Shrine

Apples to Apples

Aomori Prefecture produces more than half of the country's apple harvest, and you'll find apple motifs and products everywhere, from luscious apple pies to excellent ciders. Apple cultivation was introduced in the 1870s as a source of income for former samurai, after Japan transitioned from the feudal system to imperial rule. The cool climate, low rainfall and extreme temperature differences proved ideal for producing sweet, juicy fruit. The family-friendly **Hirosaki Apple Park** offers apple-picking experiences (August to mid-November), along with a cider brewery and apple-themed crafts and sweets.

MUHAMMAD ANUAR BIN JAMAL/SHUTTERSTOCK

Hirosaki Apple Park

THE DRIVE
Take Rte 41 and get on Rte 7 (Hirosaki Bypass) then drive for 16km. Turn and merge onto the Tōhoku Expressway (signs for Aomori). Drive 11km, exiting at the Aomori IC and proceed 4km, following signs for the Sannai Maruyama site.

09 SANNAI MARUYAMA ARCHAEOLOGICAL SITE (三内丸山遺跡)

Discover the lives and culture of Japan's first people at the country's largest and best-preserved Jōmon period (13,000–300 BCE) settlement – a UNESCO World Cultural Heritage Site. Walk around a reconstructed **Jōmon village**, which was built over the original excavation site, and check out artifacts unearthed from the area and other exhibits in the engaging museum.

THE DRIVE
Head to Aomori Station, driving 5km via Rte 44.

10 AOMORI CITY (青森市)

Your journey ends in central Aomori. Get a taste of the city's most iconic annual event – the **Aomori Nebuta Matsuri**, which draws over three million people in early August. Learn more at the hands-on **Nebuta Museum Wa Rasse** (paid parking available), then pick up some local crafts or souvenirs at the **A-Factory** complex next door. Both are located by the East Exit of the JR Aomori Station. Bullet trains depart from Shin-Aomori, one stop away on the JR Ou Line.

TOP TIP:

Modern Art

Combine ancient artifacts with modern art: from the Sannai Maruyama Archaeological Site, you can walk over to the nearby Aomori Museum of Art. The museum features contemporary works by artists associated with the prefecture. Don't miss the huge *Aomori Dog* sculpture by Nara Yoshimoto, one of the signature pieces.

Take a Break

A short walk from Hirosaki Castle brings you to the FUJITA MEMORIAL GARDEN, an expansive Japanese-style garden built in 1919 for Fujita Ken'ichi, a businessman and politician from Hirosaki. The facilities include the elegant ROMAN TAISHŌ TEA ROOM, located in Fujita's former home. The menu features a selection of apple pies – the tearoom's signature dish – as well as various other sweets and light meals. Afterward, work it off with a stroll in the garden.

22

Around the Shimokita Peninsula

BEST FOR SPIRITUALITY

Osorezan is revered as one of Japan's most sacred sites.

DURATION	DISTANCE	GREAT FOR
2 days	250km	Spiritualism, nature, hot springs & seafood

BEST TIME TO GO	
	May to early November; many of the routes between attractions are closed during the snowy season

SMCKE_M/SHUTTERSTOCK

Osorezan

Take the road less travelled, and explore the remote Shimokita Peninsula in Aomori, Honshū's northernmost prefecture. This rugged region is home to the Shimokita Geopark, with sacred sites, hot springs nestled in a valley, dynamic coastal scenery and natural beauty in abundance. Seafood lovers rejoice – the peninsula is brimming with bounty from the sea, straight from the nearest fishing village. While it takes some time and effort to reach this area, you'll be glad you did once you've experienced what it has to offer.

Link Your Trip

24 Hakodate to Sapporo

From Shimokita, drive about 50km north to Cape Ōma, then take the ferry to Hakodate in Hokkaidō.

21 Akita & Aomori Coast

It's about 2 hours along Route 279 to Aomori City.

01 SHIMOKITA STATION (下北駅)

From the major stations of Hachinohe (best route from Tokyo) or Aomori, depending on the time of the day, it's around 90 to 120 minutes on the Aoimori and Ominato Lines to reach Shimokita Station in Mustu, the gateway to the peninsula.

THE DRIVE

Drive 10km from the station, following Minorifureai Rd toward Shiriyazaki. Turn left onto Rte 6 and continue for 22km to the lighthouse at the cape.

CAPE SHIRIYAZAKI (尻屋崎岬)

Sitting at Aomori Prefecture's northeastern tip, Cape Shiriyazaki is where you can meet the **Kandachime horses**, a hardy local breed with thick coats suited to the region's harsh winters. Descended from horses formerly used for agricultural work, they graze freely on the cape from spring to autumn, and are moved to winter quarters when the colder weather sets in. Overlooking the cape is the historic **Shiriyazaki Lighthouse**, which was completed in 1867. Climb up inside for commanding Pacific Ocean views.

THE DRIVE

Return the way you came, following Rte 6 and then Minorifureai Rd toward central Mutsu for 27km, then turn right onto Rte 279. Continue for 16km and turn left onto Rte 4, and drive for 20km to Osorezan.

OSOREZAN (恐山)

Established in the 9th century, Osorezan (Fear Mountain) is considered one of Japan's top three sacred peaks. With bubbling **mud pits and sulphur vents**, this otherworldly landscape was thought to resemble the Buddhist vision of the afterlife. The major spots are atmospheric **Bodaiji Temple**, which was founded by legendary

Between Heaven & Hell

The Bodaiji Temple origin legend tells how the monk Ennin saw a vision while studying in China. Returning to Japan to search for a sacred mountain, his pilgrimage eventually led him to Osorezan, which fulfilled the conditions in his dream. Along with the harsh physical features, he found heavenly Lake Usori, surrounded by eight other mountains to correspond with the eight petals of a lotus, representing Buddha's land. Following the vision's instructions, Ennin carved a statue of the compassionate Jizō Bodhisattva, who helps lost souls find salvation and is the main deity of the temple.

Take a Break

A 17km drive from Ōma, the TSUGARU STRAIT CULTURE CENTRE ARUSASU is a community centre with tourist information, a small history museum and several restaurants. MANJUYA is popular for dishes using fresh local seafood, and there's an excellent bakery in the small block of shops adjacent to Arusasu. Interest and time permitting, you can also catch a sightseeing cruise for a closer look at the Hotokegaura Rocks (allow 90 minutes for the round trip).

monk Ennin and honours the Jizō Bodhisattva, protector of children and lost souls, and **Lake Usori**, whose turquoise blue water and white sands symbolise paradise. Day-trippers can bathe for free in the temple's onsen (hot springs); those wanting a more immersive experience should consider booking an overnight temple stay.

THE DRIVE
Continue along Rte 6, driving 16km to Yagen Onsen. Take your time and enjoy the drive on the winding country roads.

04 YAGEN ONSEN (薬研温泉)

Lying along the Ōhata River in a wooded valley, onsen fans will particularly enjoy this nature-rich area. Two storied baths await at Oku Yagen Onsen, up the mountain: the outdoor bath **Kappa-no-Yu** is free of charge, with set times for women and men, while **Fufu Kappa-no-Yu** charges a small entry fee for the two baths segregated by gender. Local legend says the baths were named in honour of a *kappa* (water sprite) that carried the injured monk Ennin to the healing hot waters. The entire Yagen Valley is particularly lovely in autumn.

THE DRIVE
Continue on Rte 6 for 10km, then turn left onto Rte 279 and follow the coast around for 30km to Cape Ōma. (Almost halfway between Yagen Onsen and Cape Ōma, the small hot-spring town of Shimofuro Onsen is a good place to stay overnight, where inns and guesthouses serve up local seafood.)

05 CAPE ŌMA (大間岬)

This is the northernmost point of the island of

Hotokegaura

IKEDA_A/SHUTTERSTOCK

Honshū, looking over to southern Hokkaidō. The region is famed for its blue fin tuna, which sells for high prices around Japan. A popular photo stop is the stone statue commemorating a **440kg tuna** caught in 1994, the largest in living memory. You can also take a small detour to climb up the observation deck near the 879m summit of **Mt Kamafuse**, the highest peak on the Shimokita Peninsula, or catch a ferry over to Hakodate in Hokkaidō.

THE DRIVE
Hug the coast on Rte 338 as you drive 40km toward the Hotokegaura Rocks. Drive with extra care on the final 6km of the narrow and winding road. Park at the designated spot for the lookout over the rocks.

Hop over to Hokkaidō

Cape Ōma faces Hokkaidō, Japan's northernmost island. Consider extending your journey and adding on a side trip over the Tsugaru Strait to the attractive city of Hakodate (p156) in southern Hokkaidō. Opened to American vessels in 1854, Hakodate was among the earliest ports to engage in international trade and once had a sizable foreign community. Attractions include the distinctive star-shaped Goryōkaku Fort, Japan's first Western-style fortress. The Tsugarukaikyō Ferry runs two daily departures year-round to Hakodate from the Ōma Ferry Terminal, for both people and vehicles (6.50am and 1.40pm from April to October).

06 HOTOKEGAURA (仏ヶ浦)

Hotokegaura (Buddha's Cove) is a majestic stretch of **rocks** shaped by weather and waves over millions of years. Enjoy the views from the cliffside parking area and follow a 1.4km **trail** down to the beach for another perspective.

THE DRIVE
Get back on Rte 338 heading inland toward Mutsu. Follow the winding road for 10km, at which point it turns into Rte 253. Continue straight for a further 10km, then turn left onto Rte 46 and drive 29km. You'll pass through the Kawauchigawa Valley on the way back to Shimokita Station, where your journey around the peninsula ends.

23

BEST FOR SCENERY

Jōdogahama Beach is considered one of Japan's most beautiful scenic spots.

Iwate Coast & Tōno

DURATION	DISTANCE	GREAT FOR
2 days	278km	Scenery, folklore & regional recovery tourism
BEST TIME TO GO	April to October	

MUSAS-II2001/SHUTTERSTOCK

Jōdogahama Beach

Iwate Prefecture combines stunning coastal views with charming countryside landscapes. Your starting point, prefectural capital Morioka, is known for its *wanko soba* dining experience: servers continuously refill your bowl with bite-sized portions of soba until you signal you're full. The Sanriku Coast, with its rugged cliffs and beautiful bays, has been working hard to recover from the 2011 earthquake and tsunami. The town of Tōno, steeped in folklore and legends, captivates the imagination. While highways connect most of the points on the route, taking the roads less travelled offers a more interesting drive without adding much time to the journey.

Link Your Trip

20 Zaō & Ginzan Onsen

From Morioka take the JR Tōhoku Shinkansen to Yamagata (two hours) to embark on Drive 20.

21 Akita & Aomori Coast

Drive 110km west on Rte 46 to Akita City to start Drive 21.

01 MORIOKA (盛岡)

Pick up your rental car at the station in Morioka, Iwate's capital city and a major stop on the Tōhoku bullet train.

THE DRIVE

Follow the signs for Tōno/Hamamaki from Morioka city centre and travel 6km, then turn left onto Rte 106 (signs for Miyako). Travel 71km and join Rte 45 then continue for 13km, exiting at the Tarō-minami IC. Follow signs for Central Tarō.

02 MIYAKO (宮古)

See the effect of the 2011 tsunami firsthand at the **Earthquake Heritage Tarō Kankō Hotel** in the fishing hamlet of **Tarō**, part of Miyako City. The tsunami destroyed the first three floors of the former hotel, which has been preserved as a visual reminder.

THE DRIVE

Turn left onto Rte 45 and drive for 12km, then left onto Rte 248 for 3km, following signs for Jōdogahama Beach. Parking lots 1 and 2 offer the easiest beach access.

03 JŌDOGAHAMA BEACH (浄土ヶ浜)

With white rocks topped with pine trees and clear waters, Jōdogahama Beach is a major attraction on the Sanriku Coast. Stop at the visitors centre for a map and to look around the free **museum**, then head down the **walking path**. For a different perspective, try one of the two short boat trips that leave from Jōdogahama – **Blue Cave Cruises** takes you to a cave known for its cobalt-blue water (March to November), while the bigger **Miyako Umineko-maru Pleasure Boat** operates year-round cruises out into the bay.

A Region's Recovery

The Tōhoku earthquake and tsunami of 11 March 2011 caused massive damage along the Sanriku Coast. Waves reached almost 40m high in some locations, taking thousands of lives and destroying homes and livelihoods. Despite the challenges, local communities have worked hard to rebuild. Efforts range from support for well-established industries such as fishing and agriculture, to opportunities for entrepreneurs to create new businesses. Regional tourism plays a valuable role in this ongoing recovery of local economies, helping to preserve cultural heritage and survivor stories while showcasing the region's resilience.

THE DRIVE
While the Rte 45 highway is the quickest way to get to Kamaishi, taking the coastal road (also named 45) adds only around 20 minutes to the journey, along with more chances to see the stunning Sanriku scenery. Take Rte 248 for 6km, following signs for Kamaishi/Central Miyako, then continue on 45. Travel 51km along the coast to Kamaishi, admiring the views of the dynamic rock formations, beautiful beaches and scenic bays.

04 KAMAISHI (釜石)

Another small coastal community that felt the full effect of the tsunami, Kamaishi is guarded by the **Kannon Daibutsu**, a towering 48.5m-high statue of the Buddhist goddess of mercy. Take a trip up inside to get a bird's-eye view of the region. The nearby **Steel and Iron Museum** commemorates the city's importance as the birthplace of Japan's modern steelmaking industry. Kamaishi is proud of its local rugby team: the **Kamaishi Recovery Memorial Stadium** was built for the 2019 Rugby World Cup and includes a quirky rugby-themed shrine.

THE DRIVE
Take Rte 283 for 4km, following signs for Hanamaki/Tōno. Turn left onto the E44/Sanriku Expressway ramp, following signs for Kamaishi Expressway and merging onto Rte 45. In just under 1km, at the Kamaishi Junction take the left lane and follow signs for Tōno/Hanamaki. Travel 15km and exit at Rōkandō IC toward Rte 167. It's 2km to the caves from there.

05 RŌKANDŌ CAVE (滝観洞)

Still unknown to most tourists, this limestone cave is worth a stop. Pay the entrance fee at the visitors centre and pick up your hard hat – you'll need it to traverse the challenging 880m journey into the heart of the cave, crouching down or squeezing past rocky outcrops. Your efforts are rewarded with **Iwato-no-taki**, one of Japan's highest underground waterfalls at 29m.

THE DRIVE
Skip the highway and get to Tōno almost as quickly by taking the local roads through bucolic scenery. Take Rte 167 for 12km, then turn right onto Rte 340, following signs for Tōno. Go through the city centre to reach the main points of interest in this itinerary on the other side.

06 TŌNO FURUSATO VILLAGE (遠野ふるさと村)

Brimming with rural charm, Tōno Furusato Village boasts a well-preserved collection of buildings from the Edo period (1603–1868) set out like a small farming village, including thatched *magiriya* (bent houses with a stable attached). Then drive to **Kappabuchi** pool and purchase a 'licence' to fish for river-dwelling sprites called

ZIGGY_MARS/SHUTTERSTOCK

***Magiriya*, Tōno Furusato Village**

Take a Break

Located along Rte 283, ROADSIDE STATION KAZE NO OKA is an ideal spot to try some Tōno specialities and select gift items for friends and family. There are several restaurants in the food court area. One local favourite is *hittsumi*, a kind of hotpot made from dumplings simmered with seasonal vegetables in a flavourful broth. Tōno is also a major producer of hops, so pick up some local craft beer to enjoy at your accommodation after a day of driving.

kappa with cucumber as bait – silly but surprisingly fun. You may run into Kappa Ojisan (Uncle Kappa), who serves as a *kappa* ambassador. Kappabuchi and the adjacent **Jokenji Temple** are best accessed from the car park at the **Denshōnen history museum**.

THE DRIVE It's a pleasant 66km along Rte 396 from Central Tōno back to Morioka Station.

Kappa Encounters

Folklorist Yanagita Kunio published *Tales of Tono* in 1910, and one of the best-known stories is about a *kappa*, a mischievous creature with a shell and a beak-like mouth. The *kappa* tries to drown a horse but gets dragged back to the village instead. *Kappa* motifs feature prominently around Tōno, ranging from creepy traditional versions to cute modern interpretations. Their strength comes from the fluid in a dish-like indentation on their heads, so bow to the creature if you happen to encounter one. Even the most malevolent *kappa* will bow back, spilling the fluid and allowing you to escape!

Also Try...

OMJAI C/SHUTTERSTOCK

Aomori City to Lake Towada

DURATION	DISTANCE
1 day	80km

Spend a day out in nature in the **Towada-Hachimantai National Park**. Hike part of the **Oirase Gorge**, a 14km stream laced with numerous waterfalls amid a lush forest, particularly lovely in the autumn. It takes four hours to cover the entire route, but even just a small section is rewarding. Renting a bicycle is another option for getting around. Nearby is **Lake Towada** (pictured), where you can learn more about the region's ecology at the visitors centre, take a relaxing lake cruise on the excursion boat and visit ambient **Towada Shrine**. On the way to or from Aomori, enjoy a trip up the **Hakkoda Ropeway** for panoramic views of the national park and surrounding mountains.

Akita City to Morioka

DURATION	DISTANCE
1 day	150km

There is plenty to see along this drive between two prefectural capitals. **Kakunodate** in **Senboku City** is known for its well-preserved samurai district and cherry blossoms. Several of the samurai residences *(bukeyashiki)* are open to the public. Take a refreshing 30-minute walk along the river in the pretty **Dakiageri Valley**, admiring the views from the suspension bridge on the way to the **Migaeri Falls**. Another scenic stop is Lake Tazawa, Japan's deepest lake, with sightseeing cruises and kayaking on offer. Located at the base of Mt Iwate, **Koiwai Farm** in bucolic **Shizukuishi** is one of Japan's largest privately owned farms. Enjoy some delicious ice cream and take a stroll around the farm's historical centre before continuing on to Morioka.

MTAIRA/SHUTTERSTOCK

Morioka to Hiraizumi & Genbeikei

DURATION	DISTANCE
1 day	115km

Hiraizumi (平泉) was Tōhoku's regional centre of power in the 12th century and is now a World Heritage Site. Visit **Chusonji Temple**, an extensive complex that includes the exquisite **Konjikidō**, a hall entirely covered in gold. Nearby, **Mōtsuji Temple** features a tranquil lake amid a traditional **Pure Land Garden**, designed to evoke a Buddhist paradise. Then, embark on a 90-minute scenic boat ride through the **Geibikei Gorge** as your boatman serenades you with folk songs. If time permits, continue to the similarly named **Genbikei Gorge** and snack on 'flying *dangō*' – dumplings delivered from the other side via a rope. Hiraizumi can also be accessed from Tonō (75km) and is convenient for onward travel to Sendai (90km).

Sendai City & Miyagi Loop

DURATION	DISTANCE
2 days	125km

The suggested route starts and ends in Sendai (仙台), Miyagi. Drive to **Matsushima Bay**, long celebrated for views of the pine-covered islets scattered throughout, and choose from a 50-minute cruise from **Matsushima Pier** or a ferry from **Shiogama Port** for island-hopping at your own pace. Then head inland to the storied hot-spring town of **Akiu Onsen** for a relaxing overnight stay. Nearby attractions include the 55m **Akiu Great Falls**, a stroll along Rairaikyō Gorge and a cluster of artisan workshops at the **Akiu Traditional Craft Village**. On the way back to central Sendai, visit a pair of 17th-century sites linked to the city's founder, Date Masamune: the beautiful Zuihōden Mausoleum, the warlord's final resting place, and the ornate **Ōsaki Hachimangu Shrine** (pictured).

100 km
50 miles
Sōya-misaki
Wakkanai
Rebun-tō
Rishiri-tō
Rishiri-Rebun-Sarobetsu National Park
Toyotomi
Hamatombetsu
Esashi
Embetsu
Teshio-gawa
Sea of Okhotsk
Sea of Japan
Haboro
Nayoro
Monbetsu
Shibetsu
Saroma-ko
Notoro-ko
Engaru
Abashiri
Shiretoko-misaki
Shiretoko National Park
Rausu-dake
Nemuro Strait
Rausu
Shari
RUSSIA
Rumoi
Asahikawa
Kamikawa
Kitami
Bihiro
Numata
Asahi-dake
26
Kushiro Shitsugen National Park
Kussharo-ko
Shibetsu
Naka-Shibetsu
Takikawa
Ishikari-gawa
Daisetsuzan National Park
Tokachi-dake
27
Teshikaga
Nemuro
Shibecha
Ishikari-wan
Bibai
25
Furano
Ashoro
Akan-Mashū National Park
Akkeshi
Shakotan Peninsula
Yoichi
Otaru
Ishikari
Ebetsu
Sapporo
Shimizu
Shiranuka
Kushiro
Iwanai
Eniwa
Obihiro
Kutchan
Yōtei-zan
Shikotsu-ko
Chitose
Shikotsu-Tōya National Park
Tomakomai
Poroshiri-dake
24
Toya-ko
Mukawa
Shiraoi
Setana
Date
Noboribetsu
Uchiura-wan
Yakumo
Muroran
Shinhidaka
Hirō
Urakawa
Okushiri-tō
Mori
Komaga-take
PACIFIC OCEAN
Esashi
Hakodate
Shiriuchi
Tsugaru Strait
Ōma
Fukushima
Matsumae

MAKIENI/SHUTTERSTOCK

Shiretoko National Park (p168)

Hokkaidō

Explore

Hokkaidō

It's like a different world up here, or at least it feels like it, with 20% of Japan's land area but only 5% of its population. Japanese identify this northern land with wildlife and mountains, greenery and agriculture, snowy winters, temperate summers and arrow-straight roads disappearing into the horizon. But there's more to Hokkaidō (北海道) than just the stunning scenery. As the homeland of Japan's indigenous Ainu people, it has a culture unlike other parts of the country, and a 'wild west' feel as the new frontier that was only really colonised by the Japanese from the 1870s onwards – it's an island ripe for a road trip.

Sapporo

The prefectural capital and fifth-largest city in Japan, Sapporo (札幌; population 2 million) is a dynamic and cosmopolitan urban centre that pulses with energy. Designed by European and American architects in the late 19th century, Sapporo is shaped by its wide grid of tree-lined streets and ample parks, giving it a high level of livability. It boasts a thriving food scene, stylish cafes, neon-lit nightlife and shopping galore. The population literally doubles during the legendary Snow Festival in February, while Sapporo beer and Sapporo ramen are household names throughout Japan. Get your city fix here before heading out into the wilds of Japan's largest prefecture.

Hakodate

Hokkaidō's southern gateway, Hakodate (函館; population 275,000) is the island's third-largest city. Built on a narrow strip of land between Hakodate Harbour and the Tsugaru Strait, the city is renowned for its night views from atop Hakodate-yama (334m) at the tip of the peninsula. It's one of the Nihon Sandai Yakei, the three most celebrated night views of Japan. Hakodate was one of two ports opened up to American ships under the Kanagawa Treaty of 1854. It hosted a small, diverse foreign community and the hillside Motomachi district is sprinkled with interesting European buildings and churches. The morning market and the waterfront's red-brick warehouse district are fascinating.

WHEN TO GO

Winter brings some of the best skiing and snowboarding on the planet, but also dangerous driving conditions; avoid winter for road trips. Cherry blossoms bloom from late April. *Tsuyu,* the rainy season, famously doesn't affect Hokkaidō, though some swear that's changing, along with the climate. Few typhoons make it this far north; summers are relatively cool and dry. For hills alive with autumn foliage, think late September.

Asahikawa

Hokkaidō's second-largest city, Asahikawa (旭川; population 330,000) carries the dual honour of having the most days with snowfall in all of Japan, plus the record for the coldest temperature (-40°C). It is mainly used as a transit point for those heading south to Biei and Furano, or into Daisetsuzan National Park. Others head north to Wakkanai for Rishiri and Rebun Islands, or east towards Shiretoko and Akan Mashū National Parks. Asahikawa Airport, 10km southeast of the city, receives flights from Japan's main cities, making it a good gateway to Hokkaidō.

Abashiri

To the Japanese, Abashiri (網走) is as synonymous with the word 'prison' as Alcatraz is to Americans. Just mention the city's name and Japanese will shiver involuntarily, for winters are as harsh as it gets and so is the prison's reputation, thanks in part to the 1965 cult classic movie *Abashiri Bangaichi* (Abashiri Prison). This east-coast city is also famous for the *ryūhyō* (drift ice) in the frozen Sea of Okhotsk, which can be explored on ice-breakers in the colder months. Once things warm up though, Abashiri is a great jumping-off point for Shiretoko and Akan Mashū National Parks.

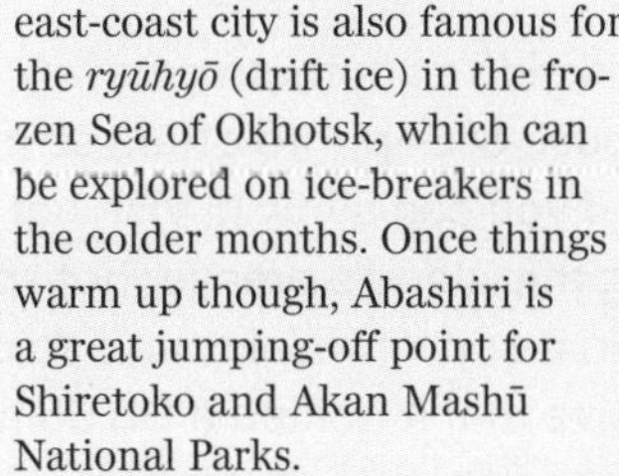

TRANSPORT

These days, a number of airports all over Hokkaidō receive flights from Japan's major cities, though the biggest, New Chitose Airport, 45km southeast of Sapporo, is considered the gateway airport, with domestic and a growing number of international flights. Ferry is a good option for getting to Hokkaidō, as well as train via the 54km Seikan Tunnel from the top of Honshū.

WHAT'S ON

Sapporo Yuki Matsuri
(Snow Festival) Taking place over a week in early February, this is one of Japan's top festivals. Lots and lots of winter fun.

Sapporo Summer Festival
For a month in summer, Ōdori-kōen in Sapporo becomes a massive playground of eating, drinking, singing and dancing.

Belly-Button Festival
Held in Furano (because it's in the middle!) in July; expect face-painting on people's torsos and a huge parade.

Resources

Hokkaidō Love *(visit-hokkaido.jp)* The prefecture's official tourism site.

Welcome to Sapporo *(sapporo.travel)* The capital's site for visitors.

Drive Plaza *(en.driveplaza.com)* Driving in Hokkaidō; download the Hokkaido Drive Guide.

Niseko Tourism *(nisekotourism.com)* One of the world's top mountain resorts.

Travel Hakodate *(hakodate.travel)* Info on Hokkaidō's third-largest city.

WHERE TO STAY

Hokkaidō has the full range of sleeping options, from campgrounds to business hotels, unusual lodgings run by eccentric characters, all the way up to luxury ryokan (traditional inns). Ski towns have lots of accommodation places with empty rooms out of the ski season; expect bargains in the warmer months. There are also deals to be had in onsen towns outside of weekends and holiday periods. Your best bet is to look at what's available online at travel.rakuten.com and trivago.com. Want a room in Sapporo during the Snow Festival? You'll need to book way in advance.

24

Hakodate to Sapporo

BEST FOR CULTURE

Upopoy is the National Ainu Museum and Park in Shiraoi.

DURATION	DISTANCE	GREAT FOR
4–7 days	480km	Ainu culture, nature & onsen

BEST TIME TO GO	May to October for warmer weather

TK*SZK/SHUTTERSTOCK

Upopoy: National Ainu Museum & Park

This enthralling drive linking Hokkaidō's southern gateway city of Hakodate to the prefectural capital and powerhouse of Sapporo offers so much of interest that you'll want to take your time – a week if you can allow it. Visit hot spots such as Upopoy: National Ainu Museum and Park; the island's premier hot springs resort of Noboribetsu Onsen; the world-class mountain resort of Niseko; and Yoichi, home of the Nikka Whisky Distillery. Lake Tōya is so attractive that it hosted a G8 Summit, and Otaru, an enticing city west of Sapporo, was once the financial centre of Hokkaidō.

Link Your Trip

22 Around the Shimokita Peninsula

Take a ferry between Ōma and Hakodate to link these drives.

25 Sapporo to Asahikawa

After some time in Sapporo, carry on north in Hokkaidō.

01 HAKODATE (函館)

Make sure to see the sights of Hakodate before you hit the road. One of the first ports opened to American ships in 1854, the city was home to a significant foreign community and interesting buildings remain in the hillside **Motomachi** district. Visit the **morning market**; red-brick **warehouse district** at the waterfront; and the intriguing **Goryōkaku Fort Park**, Japan's first Western-style

Irankarapte! Hello!

After almost dying out and being classified a 'critically endangered language' by UNESCO, the Ainu language is hopefully on an upswing, thanks to the Ainu finally being legally recognised as an indigenous people of Japan in 2019. Upopoy offers short Ainu language classes to visitors and the Foundation for Ainu Culture is training language instructors. The hope is for the Ainu language to be on Hokkaidō school curriculums some day, and eventually, for Ainu television programming. To learn some Ainu words, pick up a set of Ainu playing cards at Upopoy; each card has a different word to help with your Ainu study.

fort, completed in 1866 in the shape of a five-pointed star. Check out the legendary night views from atop **Hakodate-yama**.

THE DRIVE Head north out of Hakodate on Rte 5 for 30km to JR Ōnuma-kōen Station. Follow signage a few kilometres short of Ōnuma to get to the station and its surrounding resort village.

02 ŌNUMA QUASI-NATIONAL PARK (大沼国定公園)

Hakodate's version of a mountain-and-lake playground, Ōnuma sits beneath the impressive **Komaga-take** volcano (1131m). With sibling lakes – **Ōnuma** (big pond) and **Konuma** (small pond) – the park offers lake cruises, walking trails linking numerous small islands and good biking options. Ōnuma became famous in Japan when the Emperor Meiji turned up for a look in 1881, followed by members of the Italian and German royal families. Park near the station and enjoy a wander.

THE DRIVE Hop on the expressway for the 200km drive around Uchiura Bay, taking around 2½ hours to the Shiraoi IC. It's 4km from there to Upopoy. There are a number of service areas along the way with toilets and refreshments. This is the big driving leg on this road trip.

03 UPOPOY: NATIONAL AINU MUSEUM & PARK (ウポポイ国立アイヌ民族博物館)

Japan's northernmost national museum was opened in 2020, following the 2019 legal recognition of the Ainu as an indigenous people of Japan. After more than a century of forced assimilation and discrimination that saw the Ainu culture and language almost disappear, there is growing enthusiasm for an Ainu renaissance. Upopoy, charged with leading that renaissance, is a must-visit for anyone interested in indigenous peoples. The National Ainu Museum explores Ainu history, beliefs, language and daily life. Outside, the park sprawls

Take a Break

Like beer? There are a few interesting spots to try local brews along this drive, but whatever you do, don't drink and drive. Dine and taste the offerings at HAKODATE BEER before you leave. In Ōnuma, BRÄUHAUS ŌNUMA may look like a German-style brew house but makes beer from local apples, rice and spring onions. OTARU BEER is in a converted warehouse on Otaru Canal, while NISEKO TAPROOM in Niseko's Hirafu offers the opportunity to try craft beer from around the region.

around the southern end of Lake Poroto, with a *kotan* (village) of traditional Ainu buildings – try on Ainu clothing, watch performances, learn to play the *mukkuri* (mouth harp) and watch a dugout canoe demonstration.

THE DRIVE
Hop back on the expressway at Shiraoi IC and drive west, in the direction you came from. It's 23km to the Noboribetsu-Higashi IC; get off here and then drive 5km north up the valley to the hot springs resort.

04 NOBORIBETSU ONSEN (登別温泉)

Hokkaidō's premier hot springs resort became famous for its rejuvenating waters as a health resort for injured soldiers following the Russo-Japanese War (1904–05). These days it's a busy spot with numerous hotels and eating places along **Gokuraku-dōri** (Paradise St), below steaming **Jigoku-dani** (Hell Valley). A boardwalk leads out into the hissing valley to a boiling hot pool. Stay at the legendary **Takimoto-kan**, the biggest hotel in town, with its 35 onsen baths open 24 hours a day. Before you leave, make the winding drive up past Jigoku-dani to **Kuttara-ko**, a perfectly circular caldera lake, known as one of the clearest lakes in Japan. The road is a loop and will bring you back down to the valley not far from Noboribetsu-Higashi IC.

THE DRIVE
Head back down and out the valley to the expressway at Noboribetsu-Higashi IC; drive west for 52km to Abuta-Toyako IC, then 5km inland and through the tunnel to Tōya-ko Onsen.

05 TŌYA-KO ONSEN (洞爺湖温泉)

Tōya-ko is an almost classically round caldera lake with Tōya-ko Onsen on its southern shores. Views north of the near-perfect volcanic cone of **Yōtei-zan** (1898m) are stunning; it's such a lovely natural environment that the G8 Summit was held here in 2008. Consider cycling the 36km circumference of the lake on a rental bike, passing the giant volcano **Usu-zan** and its smoking neighbour, **Shōwa Shin-zan** (398m), which popped up out of a wheat field and surprised everyone in 1943. A highlight of the ride is **Tōya Gurutto Sculpture Park** with a total of 58 statues of stone, bronze, stainless steel and other materials carefully placed around the lake.

THE DRIVE
It's a gorgeous 44km drive, initially north from Tōya-ko, directly towards Yōtei-zan, then from the small township of Makkari, west along the base of the giant volcanic cone to Niseko town and train station. The ski resort known as Niseko is actually four interconnected resorts covering a huge area on the eastern slopes of the mountain, Niseko-Annupuri (1308m).

NISEKO (ニセコ)

Niseko may be synonymous with snow – a whopping 15m of the fluffy white stuff per year – but once the snow has melted away, the world-renowned resort area becomes a green playground. It's a great place to chill out and enjoy activities such as hiking, rafting, kayaking, canyoning, fishing, horseback riding and ziplining. Lots of accommodation, restaurants, cafes and hot springs too. The **Hirafu** area is the heart of the action, but there's also a lot going on around the base of **Niseko-Annupuri** mountain. Expect accommodation bargains in the green season.

THE DRIVE
Head north on Rte 5 for 52km to Yoichi; the last 10km or so is through a valley of orchards, with lots of roadside stalls selling apples, berries, cherries and more. Wineries too!

YOICHI (余市)

This small Hokkaidō town is where the father of Japanese whisky, Masataka Taketsuru, decided to build his distillery in 1934, after learning whisky-making techniques in Scotland and returning to Japan with his Scottish bride, Rita. He chose Yoichi for its earthy peat, crisp air and pure water, conditions ideal for him to re-create Scotch whisky. While tours of Nikka Whisky Yoichi Distillery are often booked out, it's free to turn up, check out the amazing museum and pay for whisky-tasting. Rita was a big hit in Yoichi and Rte 229, in front of JR Yoichi Station, was renamed

Yōtei-zan – a Fuji Lookalike

For hundreds, if not thousands of years, Mt Fuji, with its perfect shape and dominating height, has been the undisputed and unifying symbol of Japan, even for many Japanese who had never seen it. Throughout Japan, townsfolk began creating their own local version of Mt Fuji to worship, admire and be proud of. Today, there are at least 30 mountains called 'something-or-other Fuji', often attached to the old name of the province, before new prefectural names were adopted from 1868. Hokkaidō's Yōtei-zan is known as Ezo-Fuji, Kaimon-dake in Kagoshima Prefecture is Satsuma-Fuji, Iino-yama in Kagawa Prefecture is Sanuki-Fuji and so on.

KATAYAMA1492/SHUTTERSTOCK

Yōtei-zan

PAT LAW PHOTOGRAPHY/GETTY IMAGES

Otaru Canal

Rita Rd in her honour after she passed on in 1961.

THE DRIVE
Stay on Rte 5, along the coast, for the 21km drive to Otaru.

08 OTARU (小樽)

The financial centre of Hokkaidō in the early 20th century, Otaru was essentially Sapporo's port and a bustling base for trade with Russia and China. Stone and brick Western-style buildings were erected and **Nichigin-dōri** (Bank of Japan St) was known as the Wall St of the north. A host of elegant buildings remain in the city centre, while historic **Otaru Canal**, connected to the sea, is lined with late 19th- and early 20th-century warehouses, many of which have become museums and cafes. **Otaru Music Box Museum** has seven locations about town, with a staggering 80,000 music boxes in the main building alone. **Kitaichi Glass** virtually fills a street with shops, galleries, museums and cafes with everything imaginable made of glass.

THE DRIVE
Either take the expressway or stay on Rte 5 for the 38km drive southeast to Sapporo.

09 SAPPORO (札幌)

You've made it to the prefectural capital and it's easy to explore here for three or four days. In the 'don't miss' list should be the **Sapporo Beer Museum**; some Sapporo ramen at **Ganso Ramen Yokochō**, an atmospheric alleyway of 17 ramen shops that has been around since the early 1950s; and a stroll around the central park, **Ōdori-kōen**. **Susukino** is the largest entertainment district north of Tokyo and you'll recognise the neon Nikka Whisky Scotsman sign at **Susukino Crossing** if you dropped into the distillery at Yoichi on your way to Sapporo. The city is very visitor-friendly and its **Porocle rent-a-cycle** has 60 ports around Sapporo so you can rent and return a cycle wherever you like.

TOP TIP:

Try Local Whisky

Dropping into the Nikka Whisky Distillery in Yoichi? The Tasting Bar in the museum is open 9.15am to 4.15pm daily; enjoy a variety of Nikka whiskys (for a fee). Make sure you have a designated driver.

Take a Break

Hokkaidō is milk country and you'll find plenty of places selling tasty ice cream, gelato and more. Near Ōnuma-kōen Station, YAMAKAWA BOKUJŌ MILK PLANT has ice cream and all sorts of milk products in a large farm operation. High above Tōya-ko, on the road to Niseko, stop at LAKE HILL FARM and try their popular gelato. NISEKO GELATO is hard to pass by. Just up the road NISEKO TAKAHASHI DAIRY FARM MILK KŌBŌ serves up delicious soft-serve ice cream, yoghurt drinks, cream tarts and cheesecake.

25

Sapporo to Asahikawa

BEST FOR COLOUR

Furano's flower fields are a stunning rainbow of colour through summer.

DURATION	DISTANCE	GREAT FOR
4–5 days	250km	Scenery, nature & flowers

BEST TIME TO GO	May to October, once the snow has gone from mountain roads

GRACE'S PHOTO/GETTY IMAGES

Flower field, Furano

You could drive straight up the E5 expressway to Asahikawa in less than two hours, but that would be a great shame, as the wide valley to the south of Asahikawa is home to some of the most interesting places in Hokkaidō. Furano and Biei are enticing towns, and this area is the gateway to the western side of Daisetsuzan National Park – nicknamed 'the rooftop of Hokkaidō' – a vast wilderness of soaring mountains, with active volcanoes, remote onsen, clear lakes and dense forests. The mountains make an incredible backdrop that will have you constantly reaching for your camera.

Link Your Trip

24 Hakodate to Sapporo

Drive to Sapporo, the start of this tour, from southern Hokkaidō.

26 Asahikawa to Shiretoko National Park

Carry on to Hokkaidō's east coast from the end of the drive.

01 SAPPORO (札幌)

Make sure you've seen all the highlights of Hokkaidō's version of 'bright lights, big city' (p161) before heading out into the wilds of Japan's largest prefecture.

THE DRIVE

The first leg is a two-hour trip northeast that sets you up for days of fun in the central valley. Take the E5 expressway out of Sapporo northeast for 73km to the Mikasa IC; get off the expressway and head east into the

mountains, initially on Rte 116, then on Rtes 452 and 135, for an 89km drive through to Furano.

FURANO (富良)

A delight in all seasons, Furano is one of Japan's most inland towns and considered the centre of Hokkaidō, a distinction that has earned it the cute nickname of Heso-no-machi (Belly-Button Town). At 43.3°N, Furano is, somewhat surprisingly, the same latitude as Marseille in the south of France, and the resemblance doesn't end there. Furano produces wine, cheese and farm-fresh produce, boasts fields of flowers in summer, and offers excellent walking, hiking and biking opportunities. In winter, piles of powdery snow make Furano one of Japan's top skiing and snowboarding destinations. Book a place to stay for a few nights; out of ski season, rooms up near Furano Ski Resort are cheap as chips.

Spend a day driving around the Furano area. Places not to miss are Furano Cheese Factory, producing butter, ice cream and cheese from Furano milk; Ningle Terrace, with 15 log cabins in a forest below the Furano Prince Hotel, each with a different art or craft; Furano Winery, a municipal winery producing a large variety from Furano grapes; and to complete your Furano French odyssey,

Sprawling Flower Fields

Furano's lavender fields have changed focus from the 1950s, when lavender was simply a profitable agricultural product. With the arrival of cheaper, imported lavender in the 1970s, Furano's growers put their thinking caps on, went a bit lateral, and came up with a scheme for the blossoming domestic tourism market. They planted carefully organised, sprawling flower fields to attract visitors to Furano in summer. While the lavender is at its best mid-July to early August, you'll see poppies, lupins and canola blossoms in June, lilies from July and cosmos, salvias and sunflowers in August and September. It's a raging summer spectacle of colour.

visit Furano Marché, with its cafes and home-made bread shop (the Japanese word for bread is pan!).

THE DRIVE
Drive north up the valley 34km to Biei.

Detour
Fukiage Roten-no-yu
Start: 02 Furano

Drive 10km up the valley to **Farm Tomita**, with its astounding array of fields of flowers. This place is known Japan-wide and is so popular it even has its own seasonal JR train station; while lavender was the original here, expect to be dazzled by a rainbow of colour between June and September, with fields of flowers with staggered blooming seasons. It's a 25km drive on Rte 353 to **Shirogane Blue Pond**, seen on computer screens worldwide due to being used as a Mac wallpaper. Carry on driving into the mountains on Rte 966 for 12km to reach **Fukiage Roten-no-yu**, a wonderful, free outdoor onsen in the forest a short walk down from the car park. It's *kon-yoku* (men and women together), you'll need to get naked, and there are no facilities whatsoever. It's not for the bashful. From here, it's a 32km drive down and out to Furano.

03 BIEI (美瑛)

This gorgeous little town is known for its stunning scenery, rolling hills and the mountains of **Daisetsuzan National Park** as a backdrop to the east. Pick up maps at the Biei Tourist Centre at the station for the **Patchwork Road** (18km) and **Panorama Road** (24km) courses, which highlight local scenery and link art studios, galleries and all sorts of fun spots. While many cycle these courses on rental bicycles, it's perfectly legit to do it in your car.

THE DRIVE
It's a 38km foray east up into the mountains on Rte 213, then Rte 1160, to Asahidake Onsen.

04 ASAHIDAKE ONSEN (旭岳温泉)

Sitting at 1100m, this place is magical. Drop into the National Park Visitor Centre, then take Asahidake Ropeway up to 1600m. Just coming for the views is worth it, but hikers should contemplate a four- to five-hour return hike to the highest peak in Hokkaidō, Asahi-dake (2290m). Alternatively, there's a lovely 1.7km loop trail at the top of the ropeway.

THE DRIVE
It's a 45km drive west out of the mountains to Hokkaidō's second-largest city.

05 ASAHIKAWA (旭川)

While many view Asahikawa as a transit point to head elsewhere, the city has charm and some excellent **sake breweries**.

Take a Break

There are some great spots to eat in Furano. YUIGA DOXON is a rustic log cabin-type place, only a few minutes' walk from JR Furano Station, serving popular 'omelette curry rice' *(omu-kare)*, homemade venison sausages and beer. A very relaxed, top spot. Almost next door, MASAYA, run by the effervescent English-speaking Masa, has a wide menu, from *okonomiyaki* (savoury pancake) to *omu-kare* to grilled steak. Sit at the counter, sup on cold beer and chat with Masa or whoever is cooking, right in front of you.

THONGCHAI.S/SHUTTERSTOCK

Daisetsuzan National Park

Bohemian Biei

The small town of Biei has a bit of a different feel, with lots of arty types and alternative lifestylers around here. Biei's surrounds boast rolling hills and meandering country lanes passing through fields of flowers and white birch. This is primarily a summer destination and visitors come to explore the countryside, maybe pick up local produce from farm stands, and visit a cute little cottage cafe or two. Local scenery, in particular, attractive trees and fields with mountains in the background, have been used in popular television commercials over the years, and many Japanese come to see where they were filmed.

26

Asahikawa to Shiretoko National Park

DURATION	DISTANCE	GREAT FOR
3–5 days	330km	Nature, wildlife & adventure

BEST TIME TO GO	May to October, once the snow has gone

CHEN MIN CHUN/SHUTTERSTOCK

Kurodake Ropeway

This enjoyable drive links Daisetsuzan National Park – 'the rooftop of Hokkaidō' and Japan's largest national park – in the centre of the island, with World Heritage–listed Shiretoko National Park on the east coast. There's magical mountain country to explore, remote onsen, some stunning natural attractions, intriguing Hokkaidō history and the chance to meet wildlife on a personal basis. The roads between Asahikawa and Abashiri were originally constructed by prisoners in the early 1890s – men sent to Abashiri Prison to develop Hokkaidō during their sentences and then to populate it later. Two hundred are said to have died in harsh conditions building these 'prisoners' roads'.

Link Your Trip

25 Sapporo to Asahikawa
Drive between Hokkaidō's main city and Asahikawa.

27 Shiretoko National Park to Kushiro
Carry on through Akan Mashū NP to Kushiro City.

ASAHIKAWA (旭川)

Make sure to check out Hokkaidō's second-largest city (p164) before heading out east.

THE DRIVE
Take Rte 39 northeast out of town as it makes a wide curve around the top of the mountains to Kamikawa, then continues southeast to Sōunkyō Onsen; 65km in total.

02 SŌUNKYŌ ONSEN (層雲峡温泉)

This lovely little onsen village tucked away in the mountains (at 670m) is the main access point to Daisetsuzan National Park from the northeast and a great spot to overnight. The popular **Kurodake Ropeway** and a chairlift whisk hikers and sightseers up to 1520m for a relatively easy hike up **Kurodake** (1984m). The ropeway is especially popular for viewing autumn foliage. The village has good sleeping and eating options.

THE DRIVE
Only 3km south of the village, Ryūsei-no-taki (Shooting Star Falls) and Ginga-no-taki (Milky Way Falls) are worth a stop to view from their observation points. 7km further on, stay right at Taisetsu Dam on Rte 273; 5km on, follow signage to turn right for Daisetsu Kōgen Onsen, the most remote spot you will visit in Japan. It's 10km west on the unsealed road.

03 DAISETSU KŌGEN ONSEN (大雪高原温泉)

While the rambling mountain hut Daisetsu Kōgen Sansō is only open 123 days per year, from 20 June, this is a place to stay if you like remote adventures. Even if you're not staying, you can use the onsen for ¥900. Wildlife lovers come to hike the **Kōgen-numa Meguri**, a four- to five-hour walk that will give you an excellent chance to see a *higuma*

Higuma (Brown Bears)

Hokkaidō is bear country, and let's face it, these aren't those small black bears that inhabit Honshū. These are *higuma*, much bigger, much more aggressive, thought to be the ancestor of the North American grizzly, and every hiker's nightmare. If you're going to do any hiking, make sure you have a *kuma-yoke* (bear repeller), in the form of a small bell tied to your backpack. The theory goes that if a bear hears you coming, it will head the other way. Much better than rounding a corner for a surprise meeting! Bear activity is at its peak in spring and early summer.

(brown bear) in the wild. In order to avoid overly close encounters, hikers must attend a lecture at the **Brown Bear Information Centre**; they are only allowed to head out on the track between 7am and 1pm, and must be back by 3pm. Staff with radios are out on the trail, keeping track of the whereabouts of both bears and hikers.

THE DRIVE
Head back to Taisetsu Dam, then turn east on Rte 39; it's 29km in total to the mountain pass.

04 SEKIHOKU MOUNTAIN PASS (石北峠)

At 1050m, this is the highest point on Rte 39 between Asahikawa and Abashiri, and it's worth making a stop to take in glorious views of the mountains.

THE DRIVE
It's a long 115km drive out of the mountains on Rte 39, through Kitami, then on to Abashiri on the east coast.

05 ABASHIRI (網走)

This east coast port city of 35,000 is known for two things to Japanese – its prison, originally built in the Meiji-era 1880s, and *ryūhyō* (drift ice) out in the frozen Sea of Okhotsk. You can visit the fascinating **Abashiri Prison Museum** year-round. The 1965 movie *Abashiri Bangaichi* (Abashiri Prison) really put Abashiri on the map; it was so popular that it spawned 17 sequels and turned star Ken Takakura into the Clint Eastwood of Japan. If you show up between January and March, head out into the sea of white on an **ice-breaker tour**.

THE DRIVE
Sixteen kilometres east of Abashiri, Koshimizu Gensei Kaen is a good place to stop to see wildflowers and take a short walk out to the sandy beach. Drive east for another 59km around the coast to Utoro, the best spot to base yourself in Shiretoko NP.

06 SHIRETOKO NATIONAL PARK (知床国立公園)

Known to the Ainu as 'the end of the world', World Heritage–listed Shiretoko National Park is a magnificent finger of wilderness poking out northeast into the sea. It's mostly inaccessible, but excellent nature cruises of varying lengths head out from Utoro. **Shiretoko NP Nature Center**, 5km northeast of Utoro, has excellent displays and information, while another 9km up the road, **Shiretoko-go-ko Nature Trail** is a lovely 800m-long boardwalk, 2m to 5m high off the ground (to make it safe from bears!). Cross the peninsula in your car; the views from **Shiretoko Pass**, at 740m, are superb. There are plenty of open-air onsen in the area, such as **Kuma-no-yu**, and if you want to summit one of Japan's 100 Famous Mountains, climb **Rausu-dake** (1660m).

Take a Break

Beer lovers, except perhaps the purists, should head to ABASHIRI BIRU-KAN to try colourful brews produced by Abashiri Beer. These are the innovative guys who brought us 'Bilk', made of 70% beer and 30% Hokkaidō milk. It didn't survive, but these guys keep trying. They now produce some of the most mind-bogglingly colourful beer on the planet. Ryūhyō Draft, made with water from drift ice, is startlingly blue; Shiretoko Draft, in the colours of the national park, is an emphatic green; Oto-no-Shizuku, made from local cherries, is bright red.

LEE WARANYU/SHUTTERSTOCK

Shiretoko National Park

Northern Territories Dispute

That big island you can see looking east from Shiretoko Pass is Russia! Known to the Japanese as Kunashiri-tō, it's the southernmost major island of the Kuril Islands, a volcanic archipelago that stretches 1300km to the Kamchatka Peninsula. With tit-for-tat squabbles between Japan and Russia over who owned what since the 1800s, the southern Kurils belonged to Japan until the end of WWII. Not party to the Potsdam Declaration under which Japan surrendered, Russia took the Kurils after Japan believed the war was over – a bone of contention ever since and the two countries have yet to sign a post-WWII peace treaty.

27

Shiretoko National Park to Kushiro

BEST FOR WILDLIFE

Kushiro Wetlands NP is home to the red-crowned crane.

DURATION	DISTANCE	GREAT FOR
4–5 days	250km	Ainu culture, nature & wildlife

BEST TIME TO GO	May to October, when there's unlikely to be snow

DIGI-LAB/SHUTTERSTOCK

Kushiro Wetlands NP (p172)

While Shiretoko NP may hold UNESCO World Heritage status, eastern Hokkaidō is also blessed with two other stunning national parks that are best visited with your own wheels: Akan Mashū NP, with its lovely lakes, hiking trails, open-air onsen and Ainu communities; and Kushiro Wetlands NP, where visitors can view the legendary red-crowned crane. If you love nature and a bit of wilderness, it would be easy to potter around out here for a week or more. Our wildcard: turn up at Sakura-no-taki between June and late August to watch salmon try to swim up the 3.7m-high falls.

Link Your Trip

26 Asahikawa to Shiretoko National Park

This drive continues on from the end of Drive 26.

24 Hakodate to Sapporo

Drive the expressway to Sapporo and do Drive 24 in reverse.

01 SHIRETOKO NATIONAL PARK (知床国立公園)

With so much of interest in the World Heritage-listed national park (p168), don't head off until you've seen what you want to see.

THE DRIVE

It's a 62km drive in total – southwest to Shari, then on Rte 115 through Kiyosato to Aoba Shrine; turn left, cross the river, then turn south on the unsealed road to the falls.

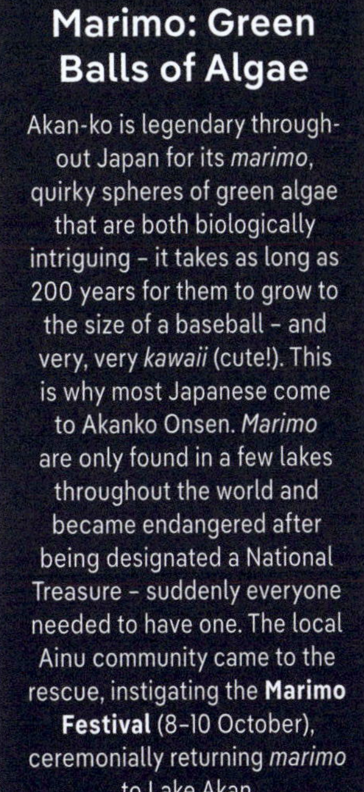

Marimo: Green Balls of Algae

Akan-ko is legendary throughout Japan for its *marimo*, quirky spheres of green algae that are both biologically intriguing – it takes as long as 200 years for them to grow to the size of a baseball – and very, very *kawaii* (cute!). This is why most Japanese come to Akanko Onsen. *Marimo* are only found in a few lakes throughout the world and became endangered after being designated a National Treasure – suddenly everyone needed to have one. The local Ainu community came to the rescue, instigating the **Marimo Festival** (8–10 October), ceremonially returning *marimo* to Lake Akan.

02 SAKURA FALLS (さくらの滝)

Each year, from June until late August, *sakura-masu* (cherry salmon) jump up 3.7m-high Sakura-no-taki as they head upriver to spawn. It's an amazing sight, watching the salmon trying to defy gravity by hurtling themselves at these remote falls. Keep your wits about you, as bears are also interested in salmon.

THE DRIVE
Head back to Rte 115, then 3km over to Rte 391, before heading south into Akan Mashū NP; it's 24km in total to Iō-zan.

03 IŌ-ZAN (硫黄山)

Considering Japan's standard 'safety at all costs' attitude, this hissing mountain (512m), known as Atosa-nuppuri (Naked Mountain) in Ainu, is remarkably accessible. Park and wander as far as the ropes will let you, right up to steaming sulphuric-yellow **vents** and bubbling water. Vendors sell *onsen tamago* (eggs boiled in hot springs) at the car park.

THE DRIVE
It's a winding 12km drive up to Viewpoint 3 overlooking Lake Mashū; a further 3km along to Viewpoint 1.

04 MASHŪ-KO (摩周湖)

Long considered one of Japan's most beautiful lakes, Mashū-ko is not accessible at lake level, but you can drive up onto the caldera rim for stunning views on clear days. Hikers wanting to climb Mashū-dake (857m) should allow five to seven hours for the 14km (return) hike from Viewpoint 1.

THE DRIVE
Continue down from the southern end of the caldera rim towards Teshikaga, then head northwest to the southern end of Lake Kussharo (22km).

05 KUSSHARO-KO (屈斜路湖)

This beautiful caldera lake is well worth a visit. There's a small Ainu *kotan* (village) at its southern end; take a soak in lakeside **Kotan-no-yu**, a free-to-use, open-air onsen with superb views. Virtually next door, **Marukibune** offers local Ainu cuisine; the small restaurant doubles as a venue in the evenings with impromptu Ainu music sessions, and upstairs it has Ainu-styled accommodation (pre-book). Take a 7km drive up the lake's eastern side, to **Suna-yu**, where you can bury your feet in hot water coming up through the sand or dig a hole and wallow.

THE DRIVE
It's a 52km drive over to Akanko Onsen, the small township in western Akan Mashū NP.

06 AKANKO ONSEN (阿寒湖温泉)

The Ainu *kotan* here is your best chance to see Ainu culture in a modern community setting. Some 120 residents make a living by promoting their culture, singing and dancing daily on stage at the theatre **Ikor**, cooking Ainu cuisine in restaurants such as **Poronno** and selling Ainu handcrafts in a number of shops. Akanko Onsen is also a popular destination for its *marimo*, green balls of algae that are remarkably spherical and famous Japan-wide. Take a cruise to the far side of the lake to the **Marimo Observation Centre**. There is also excellent hiking around Akanko Onsen.

THE DRIVE
It's a 53km drive south on Rte 240 to the Kushiro Japanese Crane Reserve. Keep your eyes peeled for flying cranes.

07 KUSHIRO WETLANDS NP (釧路湿原国立公園)

Japan's largest undeveloped wetland, the area containing **Kushiro Shitsugen NP** sits south of Akan Mashū NP and north of Kushiro City. There are a number of viewing spots and observatories around the wetland, as well as roads that you can drive. Near Kushiro Airport, the **Kushiro Japanese Crane Reserve** has a small resident population that can be viewed year-round.

THE DRIVE
Head the 20km or so into Kushiro City.

08 KUSHIRO (釧路)

The most populous city in eastern Hokkaidō, Kushiro (population 170,000) is a big industrial port, relatively free of ice in winter. It's easy to drive by expressway to Sapporo in four hours or fly direct to Japan's major cities from here.

Take a Break

Trains are few these days on the JR Senmō train line that runs between Kushiro and Abashiri; many of the stations are now *mujin-eki* (no-staff stations). The 1936-built JR Kawayu Onsen Station, in Akan Mashū NP, only 2km east of Iō-zan, features ORCHARD GRASS CAFE, an eclectic little place with an iron stove serving top *omu-raisu* (omelette and rice) and beef curry options. Top off your visit by warming your feet in the *ashi-yu* (foot bath), also in the old station building.

AUTTAPON NUNTI/SHUTTERSTOCK

Red-crowned cranes

Red-Crowned Crane

The elegant *tanchō-zuru*, said to live for 1000 years, is a symbol of longevity, Japan Airlines and of Japan itself. In the early 20th century, the cranes were thought extinct due to overhunting and habitat destruction. In 1926, however, some 20 birds were discovered in the marshlands north of Kushiro City. With concentrated conservation efforts, they now number over 1000. Cranes can be seen year-round, but the best time is during winter when they gather at feeding spots. You can visit various viewpoints around Kushiro Shitsugen National Park, Japan's largest wetland. There's a small resident population at Kushiro Japanese Crane Reserve.

Also Try...

RUJIN/SHUTTERSTOCK

Kushiro to Sapporo

DURATION	DISTANCE
2 days	300km

This drive, from eastern Hokkaidō back to the prefectural capital, follows on from the four main drives in this chapter, which end in Kushiro (釧路). While it's possible to complete this drive in four hours on the expressway, it passes through the Tokachi region, a name as synonymous with wine in Japan as Beaujolais is in France. In particular, the small town of **Ikeda**, 100km west of Kushiro, is worth a stop. It started experimenting with winemaking in the 1960s and boasts a giant corkscrew sculpture and wine-glass fountain at its train station. Drop in to **Ikeda Wine Castle**, plus galleries, cafes and farm stores. The city of **Obihro** (population 170,000) is 23km further west.

Asahikawa to Wakkanai

DURATION	DISTANCE
1 day	250km

The four-hour drive from Asahikawa (旭川) through to Wakkanai (稚内), Japan's northernmost city, is for those heading out to Rishiri (pictured) and Rebun islands in **Rishiri-Rebun-Sarobetsu National Park**. These remote islands, 40km west of Wakkanai, are the reason to make the trip; virtually abandoned in winter months, from May to August they burst to life with wildflowers, drawing hikers and visitors by the boatload. One spot definitely worth a stop during the long drive north is the **Sarobetsu Wetland Centre**, in the mainland part of the national park, 45km south of Wakkanai. Wildflowers bloom in the wetlands between May and September and can be viewed from a series of boardwalks built out onto the marsh.

MUSASHI2001/SHUTTERSTOCK

Wakkanai to Abashiri

DURATION	DISTANCE
1 day	325km

This full-day drive from Wakkanai (稚内) along Hokkaidō's northeastern coast down to Abashiri (網走) connects into Drive 26 (p166). It will defy any preconceptions you may have about Japan being a densely populated, crowded country. A highlight is **Sōya-misaki** (pictured), the northernmost point on mainland Japan, 31km northeast of Wakkanai. On a good day, you can see **Sakhalin**, Russia, 43km north across **La Pérouse Strait**. Continue south-east, down the Sea of Okhotsk coastline all the way to Abashiri. The Japanese never had a name for the sea on the eastern coast of Hokkaidō, so they adopted the Russian name, and this part of Japan is known as the Okhotsk region.

Hakodate to Esashi

DURATION	DISTANCE
1 day	161km

Head southwest from Hakodate (函館) on Rte 228, initially to the tiny town of **Fukushima**. The **Seikan Tunnel Museum** is here, where the 54km underwater tunnel that links Hokkaidō and Honshū emerges. Sumō fans can visit **Yokozuna Museum** – Fukushima has produced two grand champions, Chiyonoyama in the 1950s and his protégé, Chiyonofuji (the Wolf), a legend from 1981 to 1991. **Matsumae** is home to the only Japanese-style castle on Hokkaidō; the Matsumae clan maintained Japan's only outpost on Hokkaidō through the mid-1800s. Its grounds boast 10,000 cherry trees. Up the western coastline, **Esashi** was a prosperous fishing town, with a fascinating street of old houses. Join up with Drive 24 (p156) at **Yakumo**, just north of Ōnuma Quasi-National Park.

Hiroshima
Mihara
Onomichi
Fukuyama
Miyajima
Kure
Eta-jima
Iwakuni
Ikuchi-jima
Inno-shima
Ōmi-shima
Hakata-jima
Ō-shima
Seto-nai-kai National Park
Inland Sea
Sea of Aki
Yanai
Yashiro-shima
Imabari
Sea of Hiuchi
Takamatsu
Marugame
31
Shido
Kotohira
Kanonji
Inland Sea
Sea of Harima-nada
Naruto Strait
Awaji-shima
Naruto
Kii Channel
Tokushima
Komatsushima
Mima
Iyomishima
Niihama
Saijō
Matsuyama
Iyo
Sea of Iyo
Ishizuchi-san
30
Mt Tsurugi
Anan
Ōtoyo
Yuki
Minami
29
Ōzu
Yawatahama
28
Kōchi
Nankoku
Kainan
Shishiku
Tōyō
Sakawa
Tosa
Aki
Yusuhara
Susaki
Tosa-wan
Muroto
Muroto-misaki
Uwajima
Kubokawa (Shimanto-chō)
Kuroshio-machi
Shimanto City (Nakamura)
Sukumo
Tosa-Shimizu
Ashizuri-misaki
PACIFIC OCEAN
0 50 km
0 25 miles

SEAN PAVONE/SHUTTERSTOCK

Kōchi (p180)

Shikoku

Explore

Shikoku

Nestled between its larger neighbours of Honshū and Kyūshū in the country's southwest, Shikoku (四国) is the smallest and least populated of Japan's four main islands. Shikoku means 'four provinces', and today's modern-day prefectures of Kagawa, Tokushima, Kōchi and Ehime, linked by an ancient pilgrimage route of 88 temples, maintain a deeply reflective culture served well by the flexibility of having your own wheels. With the incredible island-dotted expanse of the Inland Sea (Seto-nai-kai) to the north and the wild waves of the Pacific Ocean to the south, and an undulating mountainous interior in between, Shikoku is a place that insists you stay a while.

Takamatsu

The only rail link from outside Shikoku makes Kagawa and its capital of Takamatsu (高松) a popular starting point. Find a good concentration of the prefecture's 540 dedicated *sanuki-udon* restaurants here; this delightfully chewy wheat-based noodle is Kagawa's speciality. In Takamatsu, expect a happening downtown with an array of dining options, lively bars and shops, as well as bountiful nature on the city's doorstep. The magnificent Ritsurin-kōen, awarded the maximum three stars in the *Michelin Green Guide* for attractions 'worth a special journey', is undoubtedly a highlight. It's a quick boat ride to some of Shikoku's most renowned art islands.

Tokushima

Capital city of the prefecture of the same name, Tokushima's (徳島) downtown is concentrated on a gourd-shaped sandbar encircled by the Suketō and Shinmachi Rivers. Its extensive river promenades entice residents for relaxed strolls, weekend markets, buskers and river cruises. Many rich art forms have developed out of Tokushima, including the country's indigo dyeing trade; *ningyō jōruri* puppet theatre; and the traditional summer dance, Awa-odori. A special place for pilgrims embarking on the Shikoku 88 Temple Pilgrimage, Tokushima is the location of Ryōzen-ji, Temple 1 on the 1140km circuit, which can be completed by car in around 10 days.

WHEN TO GO

As a general guide, April to November provides good conditions for road trippers. Try to avoid rainy season around June, be prepared to crank the air-con in August, and keep an eye on typhoon updates around September. From December to March, winter snowfall brings road closures to some of the island's more remote and mountainous locations.

Kōchi

Another city that shares its prefectural name, Kōchi (高知) has palm-tree-lined streets that couldn't be a better visual representation of its relaxed persona. Food and drink underpin its welcoming *okyaku* culture – a gathering in which spontaneously inviting strangers to eat and have a tipple together is second nature. Visitors can infiltrate this local custom at the lively Hirome Market, open every day and night of the week. Beyond its food markets and drinking culture, find one of Japan's most unique original castles, Kōchi-jō, and stroll Makino Botanical Garden, an 8-hectare green space with a three-level greenhouse featuring towering palms and streaming waterfalls.

Matsuyama

Matsuyama (松山), the capital of Ehime Prefecture, brings modern convenience and romanticism for the past in equal measure. Among the numerous shopping streets and arcades, trundling streetcars run between the city's lofty Edo-era castle, Matsuyama-jō, and its historic bathhouse, continuing a 3000-year legacy of bathing at ancient Dōgo Onsen. A soak in the restorative and extremely hot waters of the main bathhouse, Dōgo Onsen Honkan, feels like a rite of passage, while various free footbaths around town offer quick pick-me-ups. With a warm coastal climate ideal for growing citrus, mikan (mandarin orange) juice can be found on tap here.

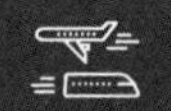

TRANSPORT

Each of the prefectural capitals has an airport for easy domestic transfers from major Japanese cities. Numerous ferries link Shikoku with ports in Honshū and Kyūshū, while three major bridge connections allow you to drive to the island on your own schedule. The only rail link from outside Shikoku is from Okayama to Kagawa via the Great Seto Bridge.

WHAT'S ON

Oyama Biraki Matsuri
A 10-day festival in July marking the beginning of the official climbing season on Mt Ishizuchi.

Awa-odori Matsuri
Plan far ahead for this sizzling summer dance festival attracting more than one million visitors to Tokushima over four days in August.

Setouchi Triennale
One of Japan's largest contemporary art festivals; held every three years over approximately 100 days on 12 islands in the Inland Sea.

WHERE TO STAY

In Shikoku's major hubs, you'll have options at just about any price point, from high-end hotels and ryokan (traditional inns) to hostels and holiday rentals. As a pilgrim island, there are numerous small, family-run guesthouses *(minshuku)* offering basic amenities along the pilgrimage route. Wild camping is highly contentious and discouraged; use official campgrounds or other paid accommodations that support the local economy instead. With a gorgeous coastline and a largely mountainous interior, opportunities for lodgings with a view abound, including no-frills mountain huts near the summits of Shikoku's two major peaks, Mt Ishizuchi and Mt Tsurugi, from where you can catch a memorable sunrise.

Resources

Tourism Shikoku *(shikoku-tourism.com/en)* Shikoku's official tourism site provides sample drive itineraries with a 'create your own course' function for completely customised trip planning.

Tokushima Welcome Center (トクシマウェルカムセンター) Information centre near Tokushima Station with excellent English-language assistance for Tokushima and beyond; a must for anyone attempting the 88 Temple Pilgrimage.

28

Kōchi & the Shikoku Karst

BEST FOR ARCHITECTURE

Yusuhara is an otherworldly mountain town of Kengo Kuma–designed buildings.

DURATION	DISTANCE	GREAT FOR
2 days	135km	Landscapes & architecture

BEST TIME TO GO	May to October, with cooler mountain temperatures in summer

TANYA JONES/SHUTTERSTOCK

Kōchi City

Of Shikoku's four prefectures, Kōchi (高知県) is the largest but least populated, giving bountiful terrain for its natural land and waterscapes to flourish, and relative solitude for visitors to enjoy it all. This 135km drive will take you from Kōchi City into the prefecture's mountainous interior via pristine rivers, gorges and highlands, and the Shikoku Karst's 'road in the sky', one of the most scenic routes in the country. Along the way, learn the art of *washi* paper-making, a local speciality thanks to abundant water sources, and tour a remote mountain village of Kengo Kuma–designed buildings.

Link Your Trip

29 Tokushima to Kōchi Coast

Make your way to Kōchi City on a freeing ocean drive from Tokushima down the region's renowned surf coast.

01 Shimanami Kaidō

Continue onto Ehime's Imabari to cross the Inland Sea by bridge-connected islands to Onomichi, or by ferry and bridges to reach Hiroshima on Drive 2.

01 KŌCHI CITY (高知市)

Washi (Japanese paper) has been handcrafted in Kōchi for more than 1400 years. Around 15km from Kōchi City, visit the town of **Ino** (いの町) and its **Ino-chō Paper Museum** to learn about the history and evolution of Kōchi's 'Tosa *washi*', and the raw materials and tools used to make it. Watch an artisan demonstrate *nagashi-suki*, a method in which a screen is repeatedly submersed in water with plant fibre until layers of paper are formed. For an

Ishizuchi Quasi National Park
Tsuchi-goya
Yoshino River
SHIKOKU
Motoyama
Kuishi-yama
KŌCHI PREFECTURE
Kuma
Ikekawa
START
Kōchi 01
Nankoku
Nakatsu Gorge 02
Ino
Ochi
Shikoku Karst 03
Sakawa
Tosa
Ōnogahara
FINISH
Yusuhara 04
Susaki
Tosa-wan
0 20 km
0 10 miles

additional fee (¥500), try a simplified method to make your own set of postcards or coloured paper (five to 20 minutes).

THE DRIVE
Head west on Rte 33 via Sakawa to Nakatsu Gorge (40km).

02 NAKATSU GORGE (中津渓谷)

One of the most renowned spots along the 124km-long Niyodo River, Nakatsu Gorge has a gorgeous riverside hike to **Uryu-no-taki**, a 20m waterfall that's exhilaratingly powerful after rain. The river itself, consistently ranked as Japan's purest water source, is so pristine that the colour of its exquisite waters has been bestowed its own name: Niyodo blue. A variety of illusive shades, the colour changes depending on the time of day, the weather and – some even say – depending on who is viewing it. Try to decipher the hue for yourself on the one-hour return hike. A car park across the road from the trailhead makes it easily accessible for road trippers.

Niyodo River Detours

In addition to Nakatsu Gorge, there are several other stunning locations along the Niyodo River. Detour to **Yasui Gorge** with its popular hiking trail known for **Suishōbuchi**, a basin with the most transparent waters in the entire Niyodo River system, as well as a number of waterfalls. Further west is plunge pool **Nikobuchi**, considered one of the best places to view the river's trademark Niyodo blue. Access is via a long staircase from the road. For locals this is a sacred place where it is believed a water serpent deity resides, and therefore no swimming, eating or drinking is allowed here.

THE DRIVE
Drive 40km southwest on Rte 439, before heading north on the increasingly winding Rtes 304 and 48.

03 SHIKOKU KARST (四国カルスト)

The Shikoku Karst is one of Japan's three largest karsts. A distinctive topography, a karst is formed by the dissolution of carbonate bedrock, creating an interesting surface of mounds and depressions, and a complex sub-surface network of underground caves, streams and springs. The 25km-long Shikoku Karst straddles the border between Kōchi and Ehime, with a 15km stretch of road (Rte 383) down its middle, known as the **Shikoku Karst Longitudinal Line** (四国カルスト縦断線), to admire it from. At an elevation of over 1400m, it's often referred to as the 'road in the sky' (天空の道) and is considered one of the top 100 scenic roads in Japan.

Starting from the east, the road starts at the **Tengu Highlands**, where you'll find the **Hoshifuru Village Tengu** hotel and the trailhead to the **Tengu Highlands Therapy Road**, a roughly 4.5km-long, out-and-back woodchipped course (around one hour). For stereotypical imagery of the karst, continue west to the **Godan Highlands** to see the limestone mound-dotted grasslands and grazing dairy cows. Weather pending, coffee van **Karst Coffee** is stationed by the **Mezurudaira** parking area from around March to November. Check Instagram for updates (@karstcoffee). The scenic road ends at **Ōnogahara**.

THE DRIVE
Backtrack along Rte 383 to the Jiyoshi Pass, before turning right on Rte 440 toward Yusuhara (17km).

04 YUSUHARA (檮原町)

Dubbed the 'town above the clouds', Yusuhara is a misty mountain town deep in Kōchi's interior. Interestingly, it's where acclaimed Japanese architect Kengo Kuma designed his first full-scale wooden building and the place he credits for his foray into wood as a central medium used in so many of his now iconic designs.

That first building was **Machi-no-Eki** – a roadside station and lodging facility. There are now a further five Kengo Kuma–designed buildings in the town, from the **Town Hall** to the popular **Yusuhara Community Library** with its striking wooden beams and bouldering wall for kids (note Kuma-no-Ue-no Hotel is undergoing indefinite restoration works). All within 2km of one another, it's a lovely architecture walk that Kuma himself believes showcases his evolution as an architect –it's a rarity to see so many examples of one person's work over an extended period in one location.

A 15-minute drive away is **Kamikoya**, a guesthouse and *washi* studio, where you can learn the art of Japanese paper-making in a unique, sustainable setting (reservations required: info@kamikoya-washi.com). From Yusuhara, connect with Kōchi's Shimanto or Ehime's Uwajima, Uchiko, Ōzu or Matsuyama (p199).

Take a Break

Nearby Nakatsu Gorge, craft beer brewery MUKAI CRAFT BREWING *(mukaicraftbrewing.com)* is on a mission to revitalise the small village of Niyodogawa, threatened by depopulation. Its on-site taproom, BLUE BREW, offers numerous thoughtfully curated bottled and on-tap beers using local ingredients, such as green tea, sweet potato, ginger and wild herb *kuromoji*. Buy some nibbles or reserve the BBQ, and dangle your feet riverside with a drink in hand. If you don't have a designated driver or just want to linger, there's a hotel and campground next door.

HASETETSU/SHUTTERSTOCK

Shikoku Karst

Cycling the Karst

Once at the Shikoku Karst, some visitors like to further connect with the landscape by switching four wheels for two. There are two options for rental e-bikes along Rte 383. One is **Karst Terrace** *(karstterrace.com)*, near Hoshifuru Village Tengu in the Tengu Highlands. The other is **Karst Rental Cycle** *(event.kuma-kanko.com)* in Mezurudaira, which also offers cross bikes. While Karst Terrace at the top of Rte 383 can still be reached in snow, the remainder of the road is closed during winter and therefore bike rental is also suspended.

29

BEST FOR SURF

Kaiyō is the laid-back centre of Japan's pumping surf coast.

Tokushima to Kōchi Coast

DURATION	DISTANCE	GREAT FOR
3–4 days	245km	Sea & surf

BEST TIME TO GO	July to August for beach weather. Torrential rain and typhoons can cause town-wide closures.

NORIMORI303/SHUTTERSTOCK

Kaiyō (p186)

Facing the Pacific Ocean, the long stretch of coast from Tokushima to Kōchi feels worlds apart from Shikoku's calm and sheltered Inland Sea side. Dubbed the 'surfing capital of Japan', expect dynamic waves, craggy cliffs and ocean spray as you cruise this invigorating coastal route, from the swirling whirlpools of Naruto in Tokushima to the palm-tree-lined capital of the adjoining prefecture, Kōchi. Among the surf action, find carefree beach towns and protected bays for a more casual splash, along with some innovative attractions that can only be found here (and don't require getting your feet wet).

Link Your Trip

28 Kōchi & the Shikoku Karst

Swap coast for mountains and venture into some of the region's most remote and unique elevated landscapes.

14 Kyoto to Kōya-san

From Shikoku connect, via Naruto and Awaji Island, to some of Kansai's greatest cultural and religious centres.

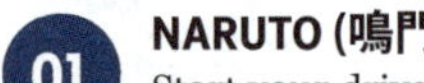

01 NARUTO (鳴門市)

Start your drive northeast of Tokushima in the city of Naruto. First stop is the **Uzu-no-Michi Walkway** on Ōnaruto Bridge for an overhead view of the **Naruto Whirlpools** in the Naruto Strait – a natural phenomenon that occurs due to a unique interaction of tidal currents and underwater topography. Align your visit with the day's tide timings.

Nearby, dedicate the better part of a day to the outstanding **Ōtsuka Museum of Art**, which showcases

more than 1000 Western masterpieces meticulously recreated on ceramic boards, including life-sized historical reconstructions of famous art-filled buildings, such as the Sistine Chapel. In what would usually require a visit to 190 museums in 25 countries, at Ōtsuka you can see a compilation of some of the greatest contributions to the art world all in one place. Free buses shuttle visitors between the car parks and the museum entrance.

THE DRIVE
Head 25km (40 minutes) on Rte 11 to Tokushima City.

02 TOKUSHIMA (徳島市)

The prefectural capital is a convenient overnight base with plentiful cultural attractions. Visit **Tokushima Castle Museum** on the site of the old castle grounds, along with the attached former palace garden, and see a live performance of the city's famed summer dance Awa-odori any time of year at **Awa Odori Kaikan**.

Delve further into traditional arts at **Awa Jūrōbē Yashiki Puppet Theatre and Museum** for captivating puppetry, and **Aizumi-chō Historical Museum** for excellent multilingual exhibits related to the prefecture's indigo dyeing trade, and to experience dyeing your own cloth at a walk-in workshop.

THE DRIVE
Start the 50km coastal drive south on National Rte 55.

Seeing the Whirlpools

The **Naruto Whirlpools** are an attraction where timing is everything, and the difference between seeing huge whirlpools up to 20m in diameter or nothing at all. Check the tide timetable online (uzusio.com/en/siomi) to view when they'll be most active on the day of your visit. It's even better if your schedule can align with the 'spring tides' (approximately every two weeks) when the whirlpools put on their biggest show. Note the different timings for the 'south' current (occurs directly below the Uzu-no-Michi Walkway) and the 'north', 300–400m from Ōnaruto Bridge and best viewed by boat (see Uzushio Kisen, Aqua Eddy and Wonder Naruto services).

MINAMI (美波町)

Formerly known as Hiwasa, the town of Minami is home to the **Hiwasa Sea Turtle Museum**, a dedicated marine turtle museum by local egg-laying spot **Ōhama Beach**. After a comprehensive two-year renovation, the complex is set to reopen with brand-new facilities in mid-2025. Less than 2km away is **Yakuō-ji**, Temple 23 on the 88 Temple Pilgrimage, famous for warding off bad luck during the supposed unlucky years – age 42 for men and 33 for women.

THE DRIVE
Switch Rte 55 for Prefectural Rd 147, also known as the Minami Awa Sunline, for a 30km (45-minute) coast-hugging drive with a number of observation points.

KAIYŌ (海陽町)

From Kaiyō's cultural village, **Awa-Kainan Bunkamura** (阿波海南文化村), have someone else do the driving for a while by taking a ride on the **DMV** *(asatetu.com)*. The world's first commercially operated dual mode vehicle, the DMV can drive on both road and rail tracks. The full route (35 minutes) utilises a 10km stretch of defunct rail line and goes through two 'mode changes' as it switches from 'bus' to 'train' (and back again), ending at **Shishikui Onsen**. Take the DMV in the opposite direction to return to your vehicle. Whether you're looking for challenging swells or just a splash around, the cluster of towns around Kaiyō make an ideal base for a relaxed couple of days.

THE DRIVE
Head 8km south on Rte 55 to the beginning of the region's most popular surf beaches.

SHISHIKUI (宍喰町)

Tokushima's Shishikui is popular with surfers, divers and sea kayakers, while over the border in Kōchi, **Shirahama** is great for a beginner-level paddle (it's a swim-only beach July–August). Two kilometres south, **Ikumi** attracts beginner to mid-level surfers with good waves all year round. Observe local parking etiquette by using dedicated car parks. For the uninitiated, rent equipment and take a surfing lesson (by reservation) from one of the beachside accommodation options, such as **Beach House Shishikui**, **Pavilion Surf & Lodge** and **Haryugetu Guesthouse**.

THE DRIVE
Continue following coastal Rte 55 down Cape Muroto. Otherwise use Rte 439 to bypass the cape, stopping at Monet's Garden (closed winter), before rejoining Rte 55 to Kōchi City.

KŌCHI CITY (高知市)

Enjoy the **castle**, market and gardens of Kōchi's relaxed palm-filled capital (p180).

Take a Break

The huddle of waterfront eateries overlooking Shishikui Beach have several top options to fuel your surf coast wanderings, including TAKE SAND (テイクサンド), an organic-focused restaurant with excellent burgers, mixed plates and a vegetarian menu, and BAHATI, a local favourite serving curry, pasta and rice dishes. By appointment, visit INBETWEENBLUES *(inbetweenblues.jp)* for a surf-inspired indigo-dyeing workshop and indigo tea at the on-site cafe.

Kōchi Castle

Ride the DMV

DMV (dual mode vehicle) operations began in December 2021 in the hope of reviving local tourism and a railway struggling for survival. The innovative fleet of 'bus-trains' uses regular roads in bus mode and the rail line between Awa-Kainan Station (Tokushima) and Kannoura Station (Kōchi) in rail mode. So, how does it make the switch? While passengers remain aboard, steel guide wheels descend, lifting the front road tyres off the track while the rear tyres remain down, allowing the vehicle to propel forward as a train. It all happens to the sound of a melody and within 10 to 15 seconds, and in reverse at the other end.

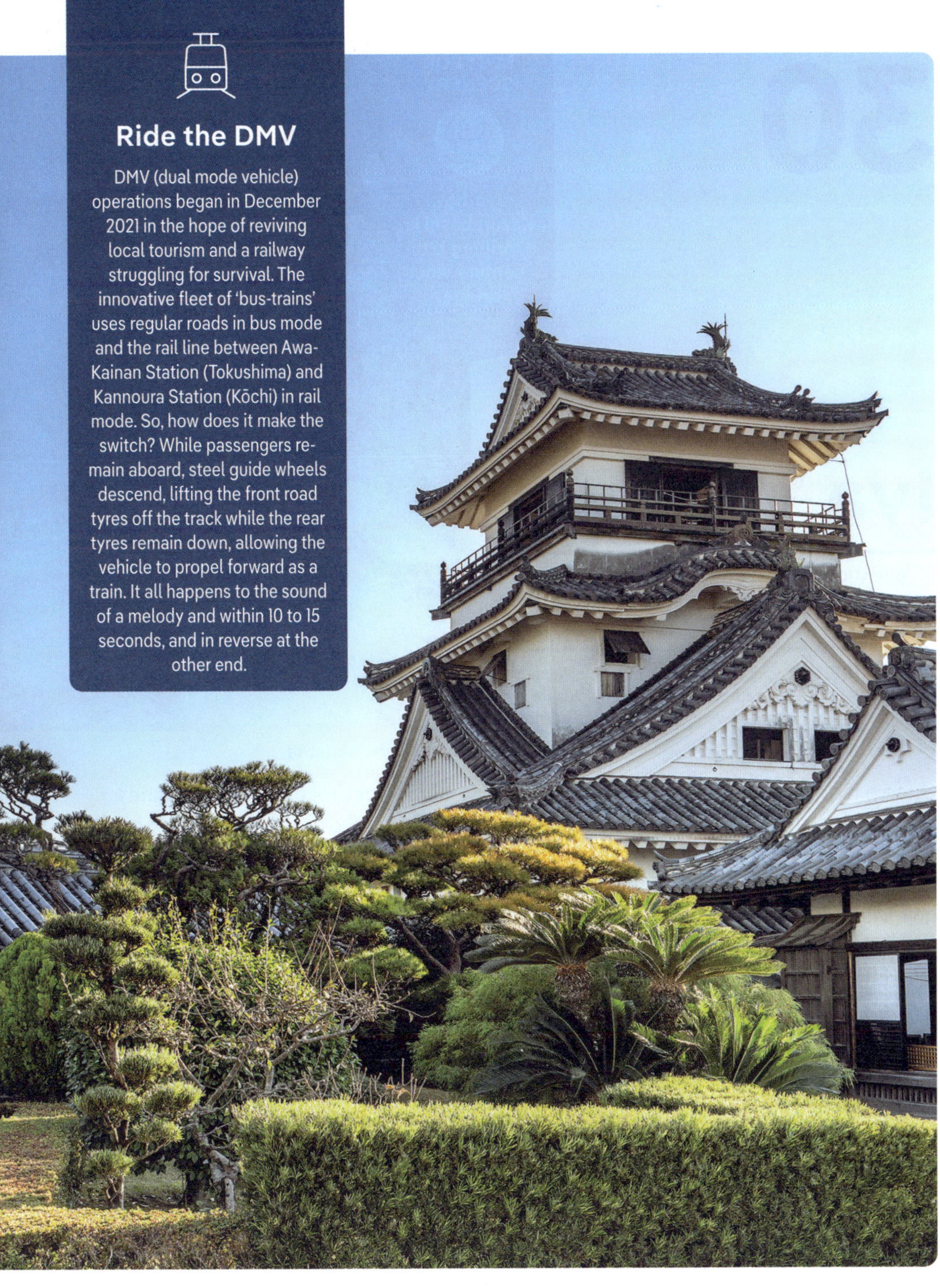

30

BEST FOR SCENERY

Iya-no-Kazurabashi is a thrilling 12th-century vine bridge.

N_FUJITA/SHUTTERSTOCK

Iya-no-Kazurabashi (p190)

Iya Valley

DURATION	DISTANCE	GREAT FOR
3 days	70km	Nature & history

BEST TIME TO GO	April to November; expect inclement weather around June and closures from November to March due to snow

Once a hideout for defeated warriors, the allure of far west Tokushima's Iya Valley (祖谷渓) has always been its remoteness. Dramatic gorges, expeditious rivers and mountain peaks have both graced and challenged the valley's inhabitants to work within its striking and notoriously formidable landscape. Today, sealed roads and cable cars give visitors a leg up over the vine bridges of 800 years ago, allowing access to what were once impenetrable parts of the valley. Whether you choose the thrill of rapids or lean into history and culture, Iya's superb natural scenery is worth the winding drive.

Link Your Trip

31 Western Kagawa

Explore Takamatsu's famed feudal garden and do a loop of the prefecture's more remote cultural highlights.

29 Tokushima to Kōchi Coast

Continue from the valley's deep east onto Tokushima City, where an epic drive down the region's surf coast awaits.

01 KOBOKE & ŌBOKE GORGES (小歩危・大歩危)

The neighbouring gorges of Koboke and Ōboke at the gateway to the Iya Valley were carved out by the Yoshino River, the fastest torrent in Japan, over the course of 200 million years. Meaning 'small dangerous steps' and 'big dangerous steps', the once perilous scramble across their rocky topography is now appreciated at leisure from spectacular roadside viewpoints and river rafts.

Koboke Observation Deck, off National Rte 32, is worth the short detour, as is a stop at **Ōboke Gorge Sightseeing Boat**. The echoing mic commentary aside, this walk-up 30-minute tour is an easy way to view the gorge's geologically significant crystalline schists from river level.

Extend your exploration of Yoshino-gawa, one of Japan's premier rafting destinations, with a half- or full-day **white-water rafting tour**. Numerous adventure outfits operate out of the gorges ranging from family-friendly water fun to faster-paced expeditions (advance booking required).

Sea of Clouds

The Iya Valley is a destination that rewards early risers. From sunrise to approximately 7am, witness low-lying clouds called *unkai* forming in the valleys in and around Ōboke. From above, the fog appears like a sea of clouds and the mountaintops like islands peeking through. Recommended viewing points include Ahashi Unkai Viewpoint and Mt Kunimi Trailhead – both less than 20 minutes by car from Ōboke town centre. The phenomenon occurs during periods of climactic change, with highest likelihood from March to April and October to December, or, with a bit of luck, anytime there is a stark temperature difference from one day to the next.

THE DRIVE
Cross Ōboke Bridge to Ōboke town centre and start the winding drive east on Rte 45. Albeit small, at Ōboke you'll find the valley's train station terminus (JR, unstaffed), a taxi rank and grocery store.

02 NISHI-IYA (西祖谷)

An 8km or 15-minute drive from Ōboke, at the junction of the more touristed, western side of the valley, is Nishi-Iya, with aerial playground **Forest Adventure** *(iya.gogo-adventure.com)*. Popular with families and active travellers, the two-hour adventure course here spans 31 obstacles among the treetops. Included in

Take a Break

Aside from the colossal Ōboke cruise complex, the roadside precinct RIVERSTATION WEST WEST between Koboke and Ōboke is the last of the more developed highway stops before heading into the valley proper. Find noodle restaurants, souvenirs, an outdoor adventure store, and the valley's only chain convenience store. Stretch your legs at the riverside facilities, which include an observation deck, elevated 'tree trekking' course and dog run. A five-minute drive south, HANAN COFFEE is a top spot for a caffeine fix, smoothies and small bites overlooking the river.

the ticket is a thrilling return trip on a 50m-high, 360m-long zipline across the open valley. If time doesn't permit, a zipline-only option (30 minutes) is available. Reservations are recommended.

THE DRIVE
Gain some elevation and increasingly breathtaking valley views as you head 6km north on Rte 32, following the bends of the Iya River.

03 IYAKEI GORGE (祖谷渓)

Make your mountain ascent toward Iyakei Gorge, stopping at the **Iya River Bend Observation Point** for stunning views of the sharp **Hi-no-ji bend**, named after its resemblance to the Japanese hiragana character 'hi' **(ひ)**. Funnily enough, the main tourist draw to this stretch of the valley is the unexpected landmark, the **Statue of a Peeing Boy**. This playful monument symbolises an old local tradition: young boys would stand on the edge of this 200m precipice and urinate into the gorge to test their bravado. With no dedicated car parks and narrow passes, limit your time at each stop to five or 10 minutes in consideration of others.

TOP TIP:

Rent a Car in Advance

For this Shikoku drive, you'll need to secure your car rental outside the valley. Be sure to make an advance reservation as it's common for rental companies, especially in urban locations where space is a premium, to keep their vehicles off-site until reserved.

THE DRIVE
Turn around and head back in the direction you came, stopping at Hotel Iya Onsen (a one-minute drive) or Hotel Kazurabashi (15 minutes) for a hot spring break, or continue a few minutes' further south to famed vine bridge, Iya-no-Kazurabashi. Small, paid parking areas for visitors operate on either side of the adjacent Iyakei Bridge.

04 IYA-NO-KAZURABASHI (祖谷のかずら橋)

The largest of Iya's three surviving vine bridges, **Iya-no-Kazurabashi** in Nishi-Iya is the centre of the valley's tourist trail. Stand on the **Iyakei Bridge** for photos, then proceed down to the entrance via the short forest path near popular **Mori-no-Kumasan** cafe. For a fee, traverse the 45m vine bridge one carefully placed foot at a time while looking through the rungs at the heart-pumping 14m drop to the Iya River below. Once you reach the other side, turn left and walk 50m to **Biwa-no-taki**. According to local folklore, fleeing Heike warriors played the *biwa* (a Japanese lute) at this waterfall in longing for their homeland.

THE DRIVE
Start your exploration of the quieter side of the valley, Higashi-Iya (東祖谷), by heading 17km east on local road 32 merging onto National Rte 439. Note the roads from here are typically closed from January through March due to snow.

05 OCHIAI VILLAGE (落合集落)

Designated as a Nationally Important Preservation District for Groups of Traditional Buildings, Ochiai Village is an ode to an Iya fast disappearing. This small hamlet clinging to a 390m vertical section of remote mountain slope is an example of the historically resilient architecture and farming practices that have made an otherwise difficult landscape habitable.

While its precise origins are hazy, the village's legacy continues thanks to the foresight of writer and anthropologist Alex Kerr who spearheaded restoration efforts of the hamlet's thatched-roof houses. A group of eight thoughtfully restored thatched homes, collectively referred to as **Tōgenkyo-Iya** *(tougenkyo-iya.jp)*, on the upper reaches are now available for private overnight stays and offer optional village tours and

The Valley's Vine Bridges

There were once 13 *kazura-bashi* crossing the valley's Iya River. First suspended by the Heike clan who retreated here after their 12th-century defeat in the great Genpei War, the vine bridges facilitated movement through the challenging landscape, and importantly could be cut down momentarily to fend off enemy pursuit. Today, only three survive with locals spending six weeks every three years to replace the hardy kiwi vines, gathered from the nearby mountains. Nowadays the bridges are also reinforced with planks and wire for the safety of the hundreds of tourists who arrive daily to make an exhilarating river crossing.

SEAN PAVONE/SHUTTERSTOCK

Ochiai Village

RETIREMENTBONUS/SHUTTERSTOCK

Nagoro Scarecrow Village

soba making experiences (enquire at booking). On the lower reaches, **Nagaoka-ke Historic House** is free and open to the public.

Expect a largely quiet visit; it's mainly worthy of a stop for its cultural significance, along with steep gravel paths that markedly up the driving (and walking) game. For those less confident of the terrain, try the more accessible **National Heritage Area Ochiai Village Observatory** on the opposing side of the valley, which fortunately also provides the best vantage point for photos of the entire villagescape.

THE DRIVE
Back in the driver's seat, continue following the Iya River along Rte 439 for another 13km.

06 NAGORO SCARECROW VILLAGE (名頃かかしの里)

You'll know you've reached Nagoro Scarecrow Village once you start seeing scarecrow-like dolls by the roadside, set up as if doing various everyday activities about town. They are the work of local resident Tsukimi Ayano, who pursued doll-making as a way of re-energising the dwindling village, now home to only two dozen human inhabitants. In fact, some of the 350 life-sized characters are made in the likeness of former residents and each one has a name and either real or imaginary backstory that's kept in the artist's 'Scarecrow Register'.

Most of the dolls are centred along a 150m-stretch from Nagoro Lower bus stop to the bridge by the **former elementary school**. If unlocked, visitors are free to enter the school, which features more dolls in the gym and upstairs classrooms, along with the **old kindergarten** (look for the blue peaked roof) that also functions as Tsukimi-san's workshop. Enquire directly for her three-hour **scarecrow making workshops** *(090-8659-4691, Japanese language only)*.

THE DRIVE
After Nagoro, Rte 439 draws you further into the deepest part of the valley, Oku-Iya (奥祖谷). Take it slow for another 3.5km of mountain driving.

07 OKU-IYA DOUBLE VINE BRIDGE (奥祖谷二重かずら橋)

Beyond the route of most tour buses, the Oku-Iya Double Vine Bridge allows visitors to experience *kazura-bashi* in a more secluded setting. Here you'll find a pair of 'husband and wife' bridges, spanning 44m and 22m respectively, as well as the **Wild Monkey** – a self-propelled cart used to transport goods and people (including you!) over the river by pulling a rope.

THE DRIVE
The turns on Rte 439 become decidedly more twisty from here. It's a further 15 minutes from the Oku-Iya vine bridges to the trailhead of Mt Tsurugi.

08 MT TSURUGI (剣山)

At an elevation of 1955m, only 30m separates Mt Tsurugi and Shikoku's highest mountain, Mt Ishizuchi, yet it is significantly easier to summit. The most direct route takes just 40 minutes, after an easy-breezy 15-minute ride on the **Mt Tsurugi Chairlift**, in operation from mid-April to late November. Keen hikers can skip the lift altogether, which adds only 50 minutes to the climb.

Mt Tsurugi means 'sword mountain', and legend has it that when the Heike clan finally succumbed to defeat in the decade-long Genpei War, they buried their emperor's sword atop this peak. The trail to the summit includes rocky steps and gravel paths before becoming a boardwalk in the last few hundred metres. Mountain lodging **Tsurugi-san Chōjō Hyutte** (five minutes from the summit) is open for a hot meal and drink from 6am to 4pm, late April to late November.

Take a Break

Try an OPEN-AIR ONSEN accessible only by cable car at two of the valley's hotels, where you can enter as a daytime guest during set hours. The use of self-operated cable cars to take you there – they auto-depart on arrival and can be called back with the push of a button when done – adds to the seclusion. At HOTEL KAZURABASHI, travel two minutes to its hot springs with valley views, while at HOTEL IYA ONSEN, make a spectacular 170m, 42-degree-angle descent to its riverside baths over five minutes.

31

BEST FOR CULTURE

Zentsū-ji is the largest temple on the 88 Temple Pilgrimage.

SANGA PARK/SHUTTERSTOCK

Zentsū-ji

Western Kagawa

DURATION	DISTANCE	GREAT FOR
3 days	130km	Culture & views

BEST TIME TO GO	All year round. Kagawa gets little snowfall, but monitor weather updates and prepare for mountain driving accordingly.

With public transportation getting thinner, the western side of Kagawa Prefecture (香川県) is ideal for a road trip. This 130km route will take you through some of the region's oldest and most sacred places of worship, from the largest to the highest temples on the 88 Temple Pilgrimage, and lofty Konpira-san shrine and its long forest staircase of 1000-plus steps. Find spectacular views of the Inland Sea and mountain ranges from castles, observation parks and ropeways, as well as plenty of interest for culture aficionados, from Edo-era architecture and landscaped gardens to hands-on traditional craft and culinary workshops.

Link Your Trip

30 Iya Valley

Continue an hour south to explore the dramatic scenery and 12th-century vine bridges of the Iya Valley.

18 San'in–Shimane & Tottori

From Takamatsu, connect with Sea-of-Japan-facing prefectures Shimane and Tottori via Okayama.

01 TAKAMATSU (高松市)

With all the amenities of a prefectural capital, Takamatsu is an excellent starting point. Before you depart, visit **Takamatsu-jō**, considered one of Japan's three best castles on the sea, and stunning Edo-era garden, **Ritsurin-kōen**.

THE DRIVE
From Takamatsu, take an easy 50-minute (30km) drive west on either of the two major arterials to Marugame.

MARUGAME (丸亀市)

The small seaside city of Marugame has cemented its inclusion on just about any Kagawa itinerary thanks to 17th-century **Marugame-jō**, one of Japan's 12 remaining original castle keeps and, among them, Shikoku's oldest. Enthusiasts of traditional arts can learn about Marugame's round hand-held paper fan *(uchiwa)* industry – the city accounting for an incredible 90% of *uchiwa* made in Japan. By prior reservation, fan-making workshops are available at the castle's information centre and dedicated **Marugame Uchiwa Museum**.

THE DRIVE
Take a detour into Kagawa's interior on Rte 319 for two important cultural and religious centres.

ZENTSŪ-JI (善通寺)

The largest of the 88 temples, **Zentsū-ji** (Temple 75), in the city of the same name, is worshipped as the birthplace of Kōbō Daishi, the founder of the pilgrimage and Shingon Sect of Buddhism in Japan. In the eastern precinct, admire the two gargantuan **camphor trees**, said to date to Kōbō Daishi's childhood. In the western precinct, visit Kaidan Meguri in the basement of **Mieidō**, built on the site

Plan Ahead

To stem congestion on narrow mountain roads, some destinations have special traffic rules in place during their busiest periods. Note the road to the upper car park at Takaya Shrine (a five-minute walk to the main shrine and *torii*) is closed to private vehicles on weekends and public holidays (plan to take the shuttle bus or use the lower car park and make the 50-minute hike instead). If visiting Mt Shiude Observation Park during cherry blossom season, an advance reservation and fee for use of the car park applies (mitoyo-kanko.com/shiude-access). The car park is free and without restriction during the rest of the year.

Take a Break

Before or after your hike up to Konpira-san, recharge on Omotesandō, the main street before the steps leading to the shrine. Find food outlets serving Kagawa's speciality *sanuki-udon* and NAKANO UDON SCHOOL *(nakanoya.net)*, where by prior reservation you can participate in a high-energy workshop to make your own. Afterwards sample *oiri* (round colourful sweets) on soft serve at KOTOHIRA TERRACE, before a relaxing soak in the free footbath (opposite). For a longer sojourn, stay in the accommodation at KOTOHIRA ONSEN.

of his birth, to follow a 100m mandala-lined passageway in pitch darkness.

THE DRIVE
Continue a further 15 minutes (8km) south to Kotohira.

04 KOTOHIRA (琴平町)

Dedicate at least a half-day to explore the cultural attractions on Kotohira's **Mt Zōzu**, spread out along a lengthy ascent of 1368 steps. A revered place of worship for centuries, the main destination is **Kotohira-gū** (also known as Konpira-san), a Shintō shrine dedicated to the deity of seafarers.

THE DRIVE
Retrace your drive back to Zentsū-ji, then head 40 minutes (25km) west to the Sanuki Cape.

05 SANUKI CAPE (讃岐岬)

In Kagawa's extreme west, the Sanuki Cape brings blooms and sea views. On the northern rim, **Flower Park Urashima** is a pretty seaside photo spot when the marguerite daisies and poppies bloom in May. Outside the season, head directly to the southern side and up the winding mountain road to **Mt Shiude Observation Park**. Explore the different walking paths, each one giving their own superb lens out to the Inland Sea, and pack a picnic to enjoy under the abundant cherry trees.

THE DRIVE
Descend back down the mountain and follow the coastal highway south toward Kanonji.

Flower Park Urashima

06 KANONJI (観音寺市)

A number of attractions entice road trippers down the Kanonji coastline. If you can time your visit for dusk (particularly during low tide), **Chichibu-ga-hama Beach** provides a playful setting for reflection photography. Further south, **Takaya Shrine** and its breathtaking '*torii* in the sky' on the precipice of **Mt Inazumi** is worth the tight mountain drive to get there. Round out your coastal jaunt at the unusual **Zenigata Sunae**, a 345m-circumference sand sculpture in the shape of a coin, maintained since the Edo period. The best views are had from the observation points on the eastern boundary of **Kotohiki Park**.

Explore Konpira-san

The stairs up to Kotohira-gū's main shrine take around 45 minutes (785 steps), however, there are various other points of interest to explore. At the 22-step mark, take a short detour to **Kanamaru-za**, Japan's oldest kabuki theatre, where you can self-tour or have a volunteer guide show you how all the fascinating mechanisms work. Just over halfway up, in the mountain's art precinct, Edo-era **Omote Shoin** and its impressive screen paintings is an Important Cultural Property. While at the main shrine, from 9am keen hikers can continue through the forest for another 583 steps (30 minutes) to **Oku-sha**, the inner shrine.

THE DRIVE
From the city of Kanonji, it's 11km (20 minutes) to Unpen-ji Ropeway.

07 UNPEN-JI (雲辺寺)

At an elevation of 900m, Unpen-ji (Temple 66) is the highest of the 88 temples. Also known as 'the temple in the clouds', the ethereal atmosphere here makes it a highlight of the pilgrimage route. While you can drive all the way up to the temple (on another winding mountain road), most visitors head to the large car park by **Unpen-ji Ropeway's Sanroku Station** and allow the cable car to whisk them to the foggy mountain summit over the border in Tokushima in just seven minutes. En route to the main temple, walk among the 500 life-sized stone **Arhat statues** of Buddha's disciples in the cedar forest.

SAND555UG/SHUTTERSTOCK

Also Try...

YOSHINORI OKADA/SHUTTERSTOCK

Mt Goken & Mt Yashima

DURATION	DISTANCE
1 day	27km

An easy day trip from Takamatsu, this short route features two road-accessible peaks just east of the capital. Tabletop mountain and famous 12th-century battleground **Yashima** (屋島) has a large summit car park to welcome visitors taking the walking loop around the 8th-century temple **Yashima-ji** and incredible sunset spot, **Shishi-no-Reigan Observatory**. On the lower reaches, **Shikoku-mura** is a popular open-air museum exhibiting relocated and restored buildings from all over Shikoku. At adjacent **Mt Goken** (五剣山), visit the money-lucky, matchmaking temple of **Yakuri-ji** perched among the cliff faces (avoid narrow roads by switching to cable car at Yakuri Tozanguchi), and nearby, by reservation, tour **Isamu Noguchi Garden Museum** to view 150 of the internationally renowned sculptor's works in natural surrounds.

Imabari to Mt Ishizuchi

DURATION	DISTANCE
1–2 days	55km

Easily combined with Drive 1 (p22), this northern Ehime course brings together a number of cultural and natural attractions, culminating at western Japan's highest peak, **Mt Ishizuchi** (石鎚山; pictured). Use **Imabari** (今治) as a starting point, visiting the city's castle **Imabari-jō** and car-accessible-only **Towel Museum**. An easy-going highway connects with 'spring water capital' **Saijō** (西条), the gateway city to Mt Ishizuchi, where an incredible 90,000 tons of natural spring water, originating from the mountain, spouts daily from the city's approximately 3000 self-priming wells. From Saijō, make a winding mountain drive to the parking areas by **Ishizuchi Mountain Ropeway** for a seven-minute cable car ride to 1300m elevation. For summit climbers, it's a further six-hour return hike via **Jōju Shrine**.

AMEHIME/SHUTTERSTOCK

Ehime Historic Course

DURATION	DISTANCE
1–2 days	120km

From Ehime's capital **Matsuyama**, follow a southerly route of the region's architectural highlights. Explore **Uchiko** (内子), a preserved Meiji-era townscape with an impressive kabuki theatre (pictured) that built its wealth on sumac wax production, and the historic city of **Ōzu** (大洲) for the restored 14th-century castle **Ōzu-jō** and **Garyu Sanso**, a mountain villa and garden where feudal lords came to unwind. Further south in **Uwajima** (宇和島), visit Edo-era **Uwajima-jō**, one of Japan's 12 remaining original castle keeps, before taking Rte 37 along the pearl-farming Uwajima coast with some of the prettiest sea views in the country. End on the **Yusu Peninsula** (遊子水荷浦) at the stone-terraced potato fields of **Yusumizu-gaura-no-Danbata**, overlooking the Uwa Sea.

Shimanto River & Cape Ashizuri

DURATION	DISTANCE
1 day	From 125km

Japan's only undammed river and the longest in Shikoku, the serpentine **Shimanto River** (四万十川) is an easy introduction to Kōchi's splendid natural environment. One of the most exciting aspects for visitors is the numerous *chinkabashi*: submersible bridges without railings that allow water and debris to flow unimpeded when the river swells. Start your drive in the wider downstream area, where the bridges tend to be larger and can accommodate one-way car traffic; use **Sada Chinkabashi** as a starting point. In the middle-upper-stream sections, the bridges become pedestrian-only and gentle *yakatabune* boat rides turn to faster-paced water activities. Combine your river wanderings with a coastal loop of **Cape Ashizuri** (足摺岬) and its breathtaking clifftop temple and shrine.

0 50 km
0 25 miles
Korea Strait
Iki
Sea of Genkai
Shimonoseki
Yamaguchi
Iwakuni
Ashiya
Kitakyūshū
Ube
Hōfu
Kudamatsu
Yanai
Nogata
Yukuhashi
Sea of Suo
Hime-jima
Fukuoka
Iizuka
Bungo-Takada
Sea of Iyo
Kunisaki Peninsula
Hirado
Karatsu
Hirado-shima
Taku
Imari
33
Kitsuki
Sasebo
Saga
Kurume
Hita
Kusu
Beppu
Beppu-wan
Kashima
Yufu
Ōita
Gotō-rettō Islands
Oshima Island
Ōmura-wan
Sea of Ariake
Oguni
Ōmuta
Kujū-san
Usuki
Ōmura
Unzen-Amakusa National Park
Isahaya
Aso-Kujū National Park
Taketa
Saiki
Fukue
Sea of Sumō
Nagasaki
Shimabara
Tachibana-wan
Kumamoto
Nagasaki Peninsula
32
Shimabara Peninsula
Takachiho
Shimabara-wan
Hondo
Kunimi-dake
Yatsushiro
Nobeoka
Kami-jima
Amakusa Islands
Shimo-jima
Sea of Yatsushiro
Hitoyoshi
Minamata
Nagashima
Izumi
Ebino
Saito
Takanabe
Kirishima-Kinkōwan National Park
Kobayashi
Satsumasendai
Miyazaki
35
Kirishima
Koshiki Islands
Miyakonojō
Kagoshima
Sakura-jima
Nichinan
Shibushi
Satsuma Peninsula
Kinkō-wan
Kanoya
Kushima
Shibushi-wan
Makurazaki
Ibusuki
Ōsumi Peninsula
Ikeda-ko
Minamiosumi
Ōsumi Straits
Mishima
Nishinoomote
Ōsumi Islands
Tanegashima
East China Sea
34
Yakushima
Yakushima National Park
Okinawa (400km)
Okinawa
Iheya-jima
Izena-jima
Ie-jima
Nago
36
Ishikawa
Kerama Islands
Okinawa City
Naha
Itoman
0 50 km
0 25 miles

SEAN PAVONE/SHUTTERSTOCK

Naha (p220)

Kyūshū & Okinawa

Explore

Kyūshū & Okinawa

The prefectures of Japan's south, including the seven of mainland Kyūshū (九州) and the string of islands that make up the remote prefecture of Okinawa (沖縄), merge mountains and sea in a mild, largely subtropical climate that feels unlike the rest of Japan. In Kyūshū, bubbling craters and steaming onsen go hand-in-hand as you tour the country's most active volcanoes and celebrated hot springs. The seaside paradise of Okinawa has a distinctive history as an independent kingdom, along with periods of domestic and international administration, which have shaped a rather remarkable assemblage of language, culture and cuisine.

Fukuoka

The largest city in Kyūshū, Fukuoka (福岡) makes for a convenient starting point for drives in any direction. Known for its food culture, the city is home to around 100 independently run *yatai* – small street-food stalls of eight to 10 seats that start up their grills at sundown. One dish you're sure to find with ease is Hakata ramen, Fukuoka's fine ramen noodles with a *tonkotsu* pork-bone broth. During the daytime, explore the grounds of Ōhori Park; ascend exterior staircases to the 14th floor of the 50,000-plant-strong outdoor 'Step Garden' ACROS; and admire the gigantic Reclining Nehanzō Buddha at Nanzōin Temple.

Kumamoto

The capital of Kumamoto Prefecture, Kumamoto (熊本) is a modern city epitomised by its feudal past. The city's centrepiece, the 17th-century Kumamoto Castle, along with its feudal gardens and samurai residences, are among its most popular attractions. A history of East Asian trade, migration and cultural exchange, contribute to a cuisine with distinct Chinese and Korean influences. From the city, it's an easy trip to Aso-Kujū National Park and fiery Mt Aso, where you can stare directly into the smouldering active crater and traverse a network of hiking trails across barren volcanic peaks and vast grasslands.

Kagoshima

The city of Kagoshima (鹿児島), on the shores of Kagoshima Bay, has one of the most visually interesting skylines you'll find.

WHEN TO GO

From cherry blossoms to the onset of rains, seasonal changes occur earlier this far south. Expect rain from mid-May to early July, and typhoons from June to November. Kyūshū has two or three typhoons per year, while Okinawa averages seven or eight. Plan island visits for the beginning or midpoint of your trip to account for potential travel disruption.

Commanding the city from the centre of the bay, active volcano Sakura-jima is a daily spectacle, with perpetual volcanic plumes rising from its dynamic crater. Here in the former Satsuma province, find the legacy of one of the most powerful domains in feudal Japan. A multitude of history, art and culture museums make for more learned wanderings. Kagoshima City is a gateway to the islands of Kagoshima and Okinawa – a plane or ferry extends your journey south.

Naha

The capital of Okinawa Prefecture, Naha (那覇) on the main island, Okinawa-Hontō, differs from the archipelago's stereotypical imagery of seclusion. A contemporary city of modern hotels, lively restaurants and shopping streets, it's emblematic of a divergent history, from the former palace of the Ryūkyū Kingdom, Shuri Castle, through to its continued US military presence harking from the Battle of Okinawa in the final days of WWII. Take a walk down Kokusai-dōri ('International Street'), feast on fresh fish at Makishi Public Market, and head to Nami-no-Ue, Naha's only swimming beach, for a taster of the coastline beyond.

TRANSPORT

All seven of Kyūshū's prefectures are serviced by an airport, with easy connections from Tokyo and Osaka. If you've rented a car outside the region, cross the Kanmon Strait from Honshū via the Kanmon Bridge. For Okinawa, Naha is the largest and most connected of the archipelago's airports. Ferries can get you to some of the more remote islands.

WHAT'S ON

Aso Fire Festival
On separate dates in March, see the kanji for 'fire' set ablaze on Mt Aso and dynamic fire-swinging at Aso Shrine.

Beppu Hatto Onsen Matsuri
A five-day celebration of hot springs in early April, featuring street parades, free onsen entry and a fire festival on Mt Ōgi.

Zentō Eisā Matsuri
Over three days in August, experience Okinawa's largest festival dedicated to the islands' traditional folk dance, *eisā*.

WHERE TO STAY

With so much volcanic activity, Kyūshū is the ideal opportunity to enjoy *onsen ryokan* (traditional hot-spring inns) and to experience walking the streets in *yukata* (light kimono) from one public bathhouse to the next. Ōita's Beppu and Yufuin, and Kumamoto's Kurokawa are some of the region's more famous onsen towns. In Okinawa, island life lends itself well to resort-style accommodation. On main Okinawa Island, large hotel chains with pools, international buffets and a full swathe of amenities dominate. On more remote islands, smaller, family-run guesthouses are a good choice for those looking to disconnect for a few days.

Resources

Ministry of Environment
(env.go.jp) Plan your exploration of Kyūshū and Okinawa's national parks, with suggested driving, hiking and water-based routes.

Visit Okinawa
(visitokinawajapan.com) The dedicated driving and typhoon safety resources on Okinawa's official tourism website are of particular use to road trippers.

32

Kumamoto, Aso, Takachiho

DURATION	DISTANCE	GREAT FOR
2–3 days	200km	Culture, scenery & hiking

BEST TIME TO GO	April to November; from December to March, foliage can be sparse and icy conditions can close roads to Mt Aso.

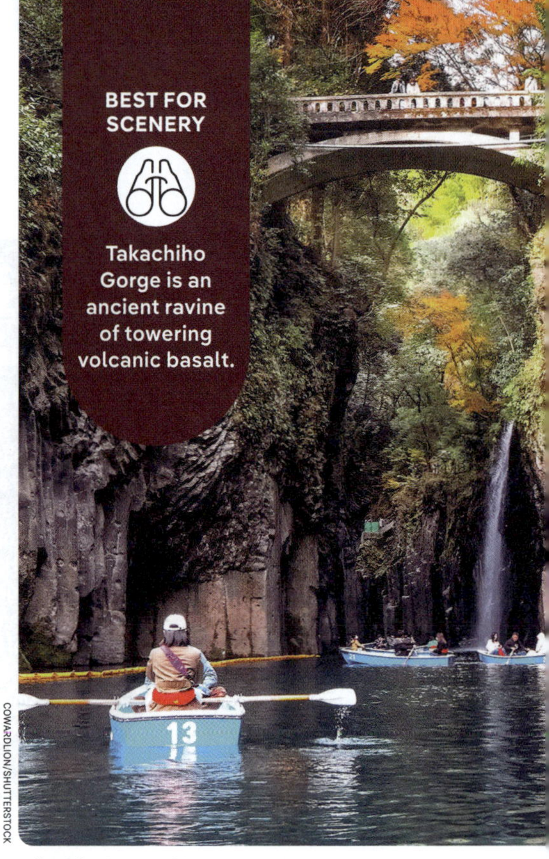

COWARDLION/SHUTTERSTOCK

Takachiho Gorge (p206)

From the castle city of Kumamoto to Miyazaki's most famous gorge, this exceptional loop drive includes some of the region's most esteemed highlights. Admire the stone-by-stone handiwork of artisans past, dig into ancient stories from Shintō mythology, and get up close to the gas-spewing crater of one of the most active volcanoes in the world. A car is all that's needed to reach prime viewing positions, while a hike, boat trip or elevated train ride allows you to experience the landscape from different perspectives.

Link Your Trip

33 Kunisaki, Beppu, Usuki

Continue east to Ōita's hillsides of Buddhist statues and the voluminous hot spring waters of Beppu.

35 Kirishima Kinkōwan National Park & Kagoshima City

Head south for Kagoshima's most famous volcano and get acquainted with Satsuma's feudal history.

01 KUMAMOTO CITY (熊本市)

Start at Kyūshū's western city of Kumamoto and its most visited attraction, **Kumamoto Castle**. The main keep, a historical reconstruction of the 17th-century castle tower, reopened to visitors in 2021 following extensive damage in the Kumamoto earthquakes of 2016. Further restoration of the castle complex, including its 13 Important Cultural Properties, will be reopened in stages, with completion set for 2052. Visitors have the rare opportunity to view reconstruction efforts via elevated walkways.

A 4.5km drive away is **Suizenji Jōjuen**, a landscaped Edo-era garden representing the 53 post stations of the Tōkai-dō, the route that linked Tokyo and Kyoto during feudal Japan. It includes a miniature Mt Fuji.

THE DRIVE
Head 35km east on the E77 or Rte 445 to Yamato.

YAMATO (山都町)

In the town of Yamato in eastern Kumamoto, find **Tsūjun-kyō** *(tsujunbridge.jp)*, a stone-arched aqueduct bridge built in 1854 to supply water to the Shiraito Plateau. The bridge, designated a National Treasure in 2023, continues to irrigate about 100 hectares of rice paddies 170 years after its construction. On set days from April to early May and mid-July to November, water is released from the 78m-long, 21.3m-high bridge, resulting in a remarkable cascade of water spouting dramatically into the river below. The spectacle takes place at 1pm for 15 minutes; check the website for dates. On water release days, visitors can enter the top of the bridge for a fee, while observing from river-level is free.

Also visit **Gorō-ga-taki**, a 50m-high waterfall best viewed from the nearby suspension bridge.

THE DRIVE
Continue 40km east on Rte 218, crossing into Miyazaki.

Legend of Amaterasu

Takachiho is the site of one of the most renowned stories in Japanese Shintō mythology. According to legend, the sun goddess Amaterasu, angered by her brother the storm god, hid in a cave northeast of the gorge, thus plunging the universe into darkness. Other deities were unsuccessful in convincing Amaterasu to re-emerge until revelry goddess Uzume provocatively danced, prompting cheers and laughter. Puzzled by the commotion, Amaterasu came forth and, bedazzled by her own reflection in a mirror, was pulled from the cave. The entrance was quickly sealed with a sacred straw rope and the world regained light. Visit the cave at Amano-Iwato Shrine.

03 TAKACHIHO GORGE (高千穂峡)

The striking, 80–100m volcanic basalt columns of **Takachiho Gorge** *(eipro.jp/takachiho1/)* were formed by multiple eruptions of nearby Mt Aso over hundreds of thousands of years. Between the narrow chasm, blue-green **Gokase River** and picturesque **Manai Waterfall** come together with seasonal foliage to create a scene that borders on magical.

There are two options for enjoying the gorge scenery: by an **upper walking route** of around 1km, or at river-level on a 30-minute **self-operated row boat**. It's best to book boats online as same-day tickets may not be available. Reservations can be made from two weeks up to two days before the booking date, pending availability.

Nearby, **Amaterasu Railway** *(amaterasu-railway.jp)* operates an open-air trolley train ('super cart') between Takachiho Station and the 105m-high **Takachiho Iron Bridge**, the highest railway bridge in Japan, including a breathtaking five-minute stop on the bridge. Same-day tickets only.

THE DRIVE
Head 55km northwest to Aso-Kujū National Park via Takamori.

04 MT ASO (阿蘇山)

Mt Aso is the collective term for five individually named peaks (and an outer mountain range) that form one of the largest calderas in the world. Spanning 350 sq km, it includes active volcano **Naka-dake** (Mt Naka) and its seven craters. Naka-dake's active crater (the '**1st crater**') is the main destination for visitors to Mt Aso. Conveniently, road trippers can drive directly to the crater car park via the Aso-san Kōen Toll Road (¥1000). View the craters, including crater one's constant volcanic plumes and dramatic crater wall, from Zone B. You can explore further on foot with hiking trails leading to the summit of Naka-dake (1506m) for elevated crater views, and to **Taka-dake** (1592m), the tallest of the five peaks.

Note that entry to the crater is condition dependent; accessible areas vary based on the warning level issued. Check the mountain's status online before arrival (aso-volcano.jp/). Visitors can typically reach **Aso Volcano Museum** and the **Kusasenri Grasslands** even when toxic gas concentration is high at the crater. See the visitor centre website (aso-visitorcenter.com) for facilities and hiking routes, both within and outside the restriction zones.

Take a Break

Sample local produce at TAKACHIHO GAMADASE MARKET (高千穂がまだせ市場). Open from 9am to 5pm daily, this roadside station has a comprehensive range of agricultural products from fresh fruit and vegetables to honey and yoghurt. Try the homemade Takachiho beef croquettes and hamburger patties made from the region's branded *wagyū* beef and enjoy the outdoor seating. The adjacent restaurant, NAGOMI, serves Takachiho beef steak (reservations not accepted) and *yakiniku* (reservations required at least one working day prior; phone 0982-73-1109).

GRANDSPY_PHOTOS/SHUTTERSTOCK

Yo-kagura

Evening Kagura

Takachiho's **Yo-kagura** (夜神楽) or 'Evening Kagura' is a Shintō ritual of song and dance revering local deity Ujigami-sama for a successful harvest. Established 850 years ago, the 33-part all-nighter is performed in and around 20 local villages from mid-November to early February, each depicting a scene from ancient folklore. At **Takachiho Shrine**, view four representative scenes, including the cave legend of Amaterasu, from 8pm to 9pm every night (¥1000). Tickets are available online (120 spots; takachiho-kanko.info/kagura) or from the on-site ticket office from 7pm (80 spots). Seating is tatami flooring; most accommodation provides cushions for attending guests.

33

BEST FOR HOT SPRINGS

Beppu is Japan's largest source of thermal spring water.

Kunisaki, Beppu, Usuki

DURATION	DISTANCE	GREAT FOR
3 days	150km	Culture & hot springs

BEST TIME TO GO	March to May and September to November have moderate temperatures

SEAN PAVONE/SHUTTERSTOCK

Beppu

Situated in Kyūshū's northeast, Ōita Prefecture's mountainous places of worship stand in contrast to the manicured rock gardens and botanical displays that often accompany temples and shrines elsewhere. Here the forested hillsides of moss-enveloped statues and hike-accessible cliff carvings remain untouched except by the passage of time. Explore the prefecture's incredible concentration of Buddhist statuary across the Kunisaki Peninsula and Usuki, while the abundant hot spring waters of onsen towns Beppu and Yufuin allow for a near-limitless tour of the region's bathhouses.

Link Your Trip

32 Kumamoto, Aso, Takachiho

Venture west for Miyazaki's picturesque gorge and Kumamoto's outstanding, fiery Mt Aso.

17 Yamaguchi Prefecture

A ferry runs between Takedatsu in Kunisaki and Tokuyama in Yamaguchi, covering the 50 km distance in about 2 hours.

01 FUTAGO-JI (両子寺)

The mountainous Kunisaki Peninsula (国東半島), with its deep connection to the spiritual practices of Rokugō Manzan, contains more than half of Japan's stone Buddhist statuary (and some of its oldest). Start your exploration of Kunisaki's distinct landscape of sacred relics near the peak of the 721m **Mt Futago**. Here you'll find Futago-ji, a 1300-year-old temple and the principal temple of Rokugō Manzan, well known for its large

Rokugō Manzan

The Kunisaki Peninsula in Ōita's northeast is home to Rokugō Manzan ('Six Districts, Full of Mountains'), a reference to both the region's traditional division into six areas and the unique spiritual culture that evolved from it. Containing elements of Buddhist, Shintō and mountain worship, the culture is practised across dozens of mountain temples and shrines. Thousands upon thousands of rock statues and carvings seamlessly merge with the surrounding vegetation. According to local folklore, the peninsula means 'land's end' and was created by demons in the service of powerful gods.

pair of stone **Nio guardian statues** marking the beginning of the 10-minute stone-step ascent to the inner temple grounds.

About 15km away, the main temple hall of **Fuki-ji** is a designated National Treasure and the oldest wooden structure in Kyūshū (c 794–1185). Visitors can stay overnight at the on-site inn **Ryoan Fukinotō** and have meals prepared by a monk. Optionally, guests can participate in an early morning *zazen* (seated meditation) experience.

A further 10km south is **Kumano Magaibutsu**, the largest Buddhist reliefs carved directly into natural rock in Japan. One is an 8m-tall depiction of deity Fudō Myō-ō and the other a 6.7m-tall Dainichi Nyorai Buddha. The cliff carvings are reachable by a 20- to 30-minute forest walk, including a 10-minute climb up uneven cobblestone steps, which, according to legend, were built by a devil in one night.

THE DRIVE
Head 30km south on Rte 10 via Hiji to Beppu, one of Japan's most renowned hot spring centres.

02 BEPPU (別府市)

Beppu has more than 2300 hot spring sources, making it the world's second-largest source of thermal spring water after Yellowstone National Park in the United States. There are eight onsen towns in the area collectively known as '**Beppu Hatto**'. Take your pick of more than 100 public bathhouses and even try sand bathing at Meiji-era **Takegawara Onsen**.

Perhaps the most well-known of the region's hot springs, however, are the ones you can't enter at all. The '**Hells of Beppu**' are a circuit of seven scalding to-be-looked-at-only onsen, so-called since their beginnings, as their searing waters and violent natural displays led locals to believe the springs were cursed. Find bubbling mud and geyser-spitting pools, and waters ranging from vermilion red to azure blue. Each pool is individually ticketed; to see them all, grab the more cost-effective joint admission ticket (Jigoku Meguri).

THE DRIVE
Detour 10km inland to Yufuin via Prefectural Rd 11 with an optional stop at Beppu Ropeway for views from Mt Tsurumi.

03 YUFUIN (湯布院町)

A district of the city of Yufu, Yufuin has more hot springs and a popular 1.5km pedestrian shopping street, **Yunotsubo Kaidō**, leading you on a town walk from the station to picturesque Lake Kinrin. Car parks near the pedestrian street are often full; be prepared to search for a free spot during peak times.

Commanding the town is the twin-peaked 1584m-tall **Mt Yufu**. From the **Yufu-tozan-guchi** main trailhead, the east peak takes two to three hours return and is suitable for beginner or leisure hikers, while the west peak requires more climbing, including scrambling over rocks and use of chains, and will take around four or five hours (return) to summit.

THE DRIVE
Loop back toward Beppu on the Ōita Expressway and take a 60km highway drive southeast to the city of Usuki.

04 USUKI (臼杵市)

In the former castle town of Usuki, find an impressive collection of Buddha statues carved directly into consolidated volcanic ash from an ancient eruption of Kumamoto's Mt Aso.

The **Usuki Stone Buddhas**, designated National Treasures, are dispersed across four hillside sites, numbering 61 in total. Much remains unknown about the origins and purpose of the carvings, although they are estimated to date to the late Heian period (c 1185). The clusters are connected by an 800m route of path-covered slopes and stone steps, and take around 30 minutes to self-tour.

In Usuki city centre, visit the **Usuki Castle Ruins** and **Niōza Historical Road**, while in the extreme east of Sagonoseki, stargazers will enjoy **Sekizaki Ocean and Astronomical Observatory** *(kaiseikan.jp)*.

Take a Break

Reimen (cold noodles) were introduced to Beppu from cooks returning from Manchuria after WWII, and a tweaked recipe for local tastes has made it a signature dish of the region. A chewier version of a buckwheat noodle similar in thickness to spaghetti, the toppings typically include a few slices of well-seasoned beef, kimchi and boiled egg, served in a clear, cold soup. Find it at numerous local restaurants; the signature *reimen* at IKKYŪ-NO-NAMIDA (closed Thursday) features an elevated beef bone and *kabosu* citrus broth.

SUCHART BOONYAVECH/SHUTTERSTOCK

Jigoku-mushi Kōbō Kannawa

Jigoku-mushi

Meaning 'hell steaming', *jigoku-mushi* is a traditional method of cooking using the steam of a hot spring. A custom of Beppu since the Edo period, around town you'll find soft-boiled eggs and custard pudding naturally flavoured by mineral-laden 'hell' waters (the restaurant Okamoto-ya is a favourite). To try cooking hell-steamed cuisine for yourself, visit the popular and slightly chaotic **Jigoku-mushi Kōbō Kannawa**, where you can rent an onsen steam vat and purchase food sets (expect long waits at peak times). Hybrid ryokan-hotel **Sally Garden Yanagiya** *(beppu-yanagiya.jp)* also offers shared steam vats for guests in a relaxed garden setting.

34

BEST FOR NATURE

Seibu Rindō is a World Heritage–listed forest path of monkeys and deer.

IWANAMI PHOTOS/SHUTTERSTOCK

Macaque ***(yaku-saru)*****, Seibu Rindō**

Yakushima

DURATION	DISTANCE	GREAT FOR
3 days	150km	Hiking & nature

BEST TIME TO GO	March to November; May to September for turtles. Typhoons, typically August to October, significantly impact travel

The subtropical island of Yakushima (屋久島), south of mainland Kagoshima, has such extraordinary environmental diversity that one-fifth of the island is a natural World Heritage Site. Coral reefs and turtle egg-laying beaches quickly give way to primeval cedar forests and alpine conditions culminating at Kyūshū's highest peak, the 1936m Miyanoura-dake, earning it the nickname 'the Alps of the ocean'. This 150km driving route will take you on a full circumnavigation of the island, coupled with interior hiking detours to Yakushima's jaw-dropping ancient cedars.

Link Your Trip

35 Kirishima Kinkōwan National Park & Kagoshima City

Connect with this epic trail of volcanoes from Kagoshima Bay to the Kirishima mountain range.

36 Okinawa Main Island

From Kagoshima, fly south to the modern, resort city of Naha for a Japanese prefecture that's unlike the others.

01 SHIRATANI UNSUI RAVINE (白谷雲水峡)

From **Miya-no-ura Port**, venture 10km south on Rte 594 to Shiratani Unsui Ravine to hike the forest that inspired Studio Ghibli's *Princess Mononoke*. There are three hiking routes: **Yayoi-sugi** (one hour), **Bugyō-sugi** (three hours) and **Taiko-iwa** (four hours), featuring Yakushima's famed cedars. Note that Typhoon No 10 (Shanshan) in August 2024 caused extensive damage in Yakushima, including the ravine. While

Sea Turtles

Yakushima is a critically important location for the conservation of green sea and loggerhead turtles. Japan is the only area in the North Pacific where loggerheads lay their eggs and, of those, around half do so on Yakushima, with approximately 90% choosing Nagata-hama (永田浜) – a collective term for three adjacent beaches on the northwest of the island. At night from May to August, the period of highest turtle activity, access to **Nagata-hama** is by guided observational tour only, preceded by a safe viewing lecture. Tours are limited to 50 people per night; advance reservations essential (nagata-umigame.com).

the Yayoi-sugi course reopened in February 2025, the course's namesake and main draw, the 3000-year-old Yayoi cedar, was blown over in the storm. At the time of research, the Bugyō-sugi route remains closed, however, the superb Taiko-iwa course, including the moss forest, is fully accessible. Follow on-site signage for open trails during your visit.

Japanese cedar *(Cryptomeria japonica)* or *sugi* is a coniferous evergreen endemic to Japan, and Yakushima's are so ancient they are differentiated by age – the term *yaku-sugi* is reserved for Yakushima cedars over 1000 years old and *ko-sugi* for those younger. A substantial number of both can be found at the ravine, which also features **Kokemusu Mori**, a vivid moss forest of 600 species that required Studio Ghibli to use an extreme number of green shades to emulate it on screen.

THE DRIVE
Return to Miya-no-ura Port, before travelling 8.5km west on Rte 78 to Issō Beach.

02 ISSŌ BEACH (一湊海水浴場)

Cradled in an inlet flanked by Cape Yahazu, calm and protected Issō Beach is one of the best snorkelling and diving spots on the island. White sand meets exquisitely clear waters, and below the surface, you can view coral reefs and bountiful sea life, including sea turtles in summer.

Swim and snorkel comfortably from June to October (rent snorkels and floatation devices from beachside vendors), while scuba diving is year-round, with numerous guided tour outfits to choose from.

THE DRIVE
Follow Rte 78 west for approximately 25km to Seibu Rindō.

03 SEIBU RINDŌ (西部林道)

Meaning 'Western Forest Path', Seibu Rindō is a 20km

stretch of road on the island's west. More than a through-road, the vast majority falls within the World Heritage Area, and it's the domain of Yakushima's endemic species of macaque *(yaku-saru)* and deer *(yaku-shika)*.

Find monkey troops sprawled across the path and deer emerging from the primeval forest. Drive with caution; be prepared to stop frequently for crossing animals, and oncoming vehicles along the narrowest sections. Feeding or interfering with wildlife is strictly prohibited.

THE DRIVE
Continue a further 10km south on Rte 78.

04 ŌKO-NO-TAKI (大川の滝)

Dropping 88m from the slope of Mt Nagata, Ōko-no-taki is a striking waterfall that's equal parts menacing and gorgeous. The falls are well fed by Yakushima's large volume of annual rainfall, ranging from 3000mm on the coast and up to 10,000mm in the mountains, making the island the wettest place in Japan.

Ōko-no-taki can be reached in a couple of minutes by foot from the car park.

THE DRIVE
Round out the southern part of the island, stopping at ocean hot springs, before venturing north on Rte 77 to the town of Anbō.

05 YAKUSUGI MUSEUM (屋久杉自然館)

Once you reach Anbō (安房), take Rte 592 for several opportunities to explore Yakushima's ancient cedars. First, stop by **Yakusugi Museum**, worthwhile for English speakers with the accompanying audio guide. Learn about the area's rich cedar history and see a branch that fell from the island's oldest tree, Jōmon-sugi.

It's approximately 20km from here back to Miya-no-ura Port.

Detour
Yakusugi Land (ヤクスギランド)
Start: 05 Yakusugi Museum

Thirteen kilometres inland from Yakusugi Museum is Yakusugi Land (¥500), a popular hiking area with five hiking trails ranging from 30 minutes (with a boardwalk) to 3½ hours and suitable for beginner hikers. Another 5.5km find **Kigen-sugi** (紀元杉), the only ancient cedar that's accessible by car. It's viewable from the road, but a short walk (which includes some stairs) will get you closer.

Take a Break

On the southern coast of Yakushima, you'll find two natural seaside hot springs right on the beach; entry for either is a ¥200 donation. YUDOMARI ONSEN (湯泊温泉) is generally accessible 24/7 unless the waves are particularly choppy. A five-minute drive away, HIRAUCHI KAICHŪ ONSEN (平内海中温泉), our pick of the two, is only accessible for a three-hour window between high and low tide. Prepare to release your inhibitions, as despite being mixed gender and outdoors, both onsen are no-swimsuit zones (although a modesty towel is permitted).

IMPREZASTI/SHUTTERSTOCK

Jōmon-sugi

Hike to Jōmon-sugi

The oldest cedar on Yakushima, with upper estimates of its age as high as 7200 years old, is Jōmon-sugi, a 10-hour round trip from Arakawa Trailhead via an old logging rail route. From March to November, the 4km stretch of road before the trailhead is closed to private vehicles; take the bus from Yakusugi Museum instead. Tickets can be bought from either the Yakushima Mountain Environmental Council Office by the bus stop (open 5am to 6am and 3pm to 6pm), or from the Tourist Information at Anbō or Yakushima Airport (best option for 5am departures). Overnighters must use mountain huts or designated camping areas. Bus timetable and ticket info: yakushima-tozan.com.

35

Kirishima Kinkōwan NP & Kagoshima City

DURATION	DISTANCE	GREAT FOR
3–4 days	200km	Scenery, hiking & history

BEST TIME TO GO	Year-round, with most moderate temperatures in April–May and OctoberNovember.

SEAN PAVONE/SHUTTERSTOCK

Once known as Satsuma province, the western half of modern-day Kagoshima Prefecture has both an important feudal history and some of the most iconic volcanic scenery in the country. This route will focus on the three distinct areas that form Kirishima Kinkōwan National Park (霧島錦江湾国立公園), from the dense cluster of more than 20 volcanoes in the Kirishima mountain range bordering Miyazaki, to billowing Sakura-jima in Kagoshima Bay and sand-bathing capital Ibusuki on the Satsuma Peninsula. Outside the park's boundaries, Kagoshima City provides an interesting look into Japan's transition to the Meiji Restoration.

Link Your Trip

34 Yakushima

Take a plane or ferry from mainland Kagoshima to the prefecture's subtropical island of ancient cedars.

32 Kumamoto, Aso, Takachiho

About 120 km north of Ebino is Kumamoto City, where you can connect with Drive 32.

01 EBINO PLATEAU (えびの高原)

Begin your national park exploration at Ebino Plateau, the trailhead for various hikes, by way of scenic road the **Ebino Skyline**. Drop into the highly informative **Ebino Eco-Museum Center** for exhibits on the area's natural history and the latest on hiking trails.

One of the most popular hikes is to **Mt Karakuni** (1700m), the tallest peak in the Kirishima volcano range. The steep 2.5km ascent from the trailhead,

Sakura-jima (p218)

BEST FOR SCENERY

Sakura-jima is a stunning active volcano on the doorstep of a city.

Sakura-jima Ferry

The Sakura-jima Ferry (for passengers, bikes and cars) conveniently operates 24 hours a day, departing every 20 minutes from its Kagoshima Terminal (one service per hour overnight). Ferry tolls are handled exclusively on the Sakura-jima side, so you can simply drive on (no reservation or ticket required) and pay at the highway toll booth after disembarking. The fare depends on vehicle size and number of passengers; expect a minimum of ¥1700 for a car of 3m to 4m and one occupant (¥250 for each additional passenger). On the return journey, pay again at Sakura-jima before boarding and freely drive off on arrival at Kagoshima.

located just 500m from the museum, takes around two hours. From the summit, view the striking lava dome of **Mt Shinmoe**, which, owing to several eruptions since 2011, has replaced the previous crater lake, and to the west, Karakuni's own gargantuan **Ōnami Crater Lake**.

Opposite **Takachiho-gawara Visitor Center** (closed Monday) in the park's east is the trailhead to **Mt Takachiho** (1574m), a site of great reverence in Japanese Shintō mythology. Nearby, visit shrine and National Treasure **Kirishima Jingū**.

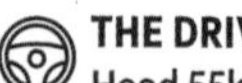

THE DRIVE

Head 55km southwest to Kagoshima Port for the Sakura-jima Ferry. Located in Kagoshima Bay (also known as Kinkō-wan), Sakura-jima was an island until lava flows from a major eruption in 1914 connected it with Kagoshima's Ōsumi Peninsula. While there is road access from the east, it's a 90-minute detour. Easier is the 15-minute Sakura-jima Ferry from Kagoshima Port.

02 SAKURA-JIMA VISITOR CENTER (桜島ビジターセンター)

Looming over Kagoshima City, the 1117m-tall volcano of Sakura-jima is so active it has a minor eruption almost every day. Start a circumnavigation of the volcano by the ferry terminal, where you'll find **Sakura-jima Visitor Center** and its on-site volcano museum, a small beach, public hot springs and the excellent open-air **Nagisa Park Footbaths**. On a separate internal road nearby, **Yunohira Observation Point** is the closest you can get to the craters.

For insight into past eruptions, take the **Nagisa Lava Trail**, 3km of walking tracks through lava fields south of the port, and visit **Kurokami Buried Torii**, a buried shrine gate on the volcano's east, both from the 1914 eruption. Near the gate is a **lava field** from an eruption in 1946. If visiting from late August to February, see the volcano's renowned gigantic radishes at various stages of development at **Sakura-jima Daikon Field** by northern Shirahama Port.

THE DRIVE

Return to Kagoshima mainland by ferry to explore Kagoshima's downtown highlights.

03 KAGOSHIMA CITY (鹿児島市)

History enthusiasts have much to look forward to on this side of the bay. Don't miss **Sengan-en**, a 5-hectare landscaped bayside garden with Sakura-jima as its backdrop, and the former residence of the powerful Shimazu clan, who ruled this region from the 12th to the 19th centuries. Early adopters of industrial technologies, their legacy lives on in remnants like furnaces, sluice gates and adjacent **Shōko Shūsei-kan**, Japan's first modern factory, which form the UNESCO 'Meiji Industrial Revolution Heritage Sites of Japan'.

A 5km drive away, an observation deck atop 107m-tall **Shiro-yama** ('castle mountain') affords stunning volcano views. Shiro-yama is where 'last samurai' Saigō Takamori and his supporters barricaded themselves in the final throes of the Satsuma Rebellion (1877). In the vicinity, find statues of Takamori, the cave where he took refuge, and the site of his death. At the mountain's base, history and culture museum **Reimei-kan** (closed Monday) operates on the site of the **Kagoshima Castle Ruins**.

THE DRIVE

Head 50km southeast on Rte 226 to the southern tip of the Satsuma Peninsula.

04 IBUSUKI (指宿市)

Right at the mouth of Kagoshima Bay, the coastal city of Ibusuki has several sand-bathing *(suna-mushi)* locations, where you can be buried up to your neck in geothermally heated black sand. A fortuitous result of the region's high volcanic activity, the naturally occurring hot sand is said to provide benefits three or four times greater than a hot-spring bath.

Popular locations include **Sand Bath Hall 'Saraku'** *(ibusuki-saraku.jp)*, 1.5km from Ibusuki Station, and **Yamakawa Hot Sand Bath 'Sayuri'** *(ibusuki.or.jp/spa/sunamushi/sayuri)* with views of Mt Kaimon.

Take a Break

On GOURMET STREET (グルメ通り) in Kagoshima City, you'll find eateries serving up local Satsuma cuisine. Known as *Satsuma-ryōri*, this regional fare reflects Kagoshima's relative isolation in Kyūshū's extreme south, along with the province's centuries-long control of Okinawa, which led to a distinct melding of southern flavours. Dishes include *Satsuma-age* (deep-fried fish cakes), *kibinago* (raw herring fish), *tonkotsu* (a pork-and-miso-based stew), *kuro-buta* (black pork), *kuro-ushi* (black beef) and *tori-sashi* (raw chicken). Wash it down with Satsuma *shōchū*, a distilled liquor made from sweet potato.

The Last Samurai

Kagoshima-born Saigō Takamori (1828–77) is considered one of Japan's most notable samurai. He was a key leader in the Meiji Restoration that brought an end to feudal Japan, effectively ending the samurai class, and ultimately rebelled against the regime he helped create. He is memorialised at numerous points around Kagoshima City's Shiro-yama Park, where he and his failed Satsuma Rebellion met their final moments. Takamori is remembered fondly in Japan, viewed as a tragic hero who honourably fought for his ideals until the end. Hollywood period action drama *The Last Samurai* (2003) was based on his story.

KPG-PAYLESS/SHUTTERSTOCK

Saigō Takamori statue, Kagoshima

36

BEST FOR BEACHES

Enjoy snorkelling the Blue Cave.

PETESPHOTOGRAPHY/GETTY IMAGES

Blue Cave, Cape Maeda

Okinawa Main Island

DURATION	DISTANCE	GREAT FOR
2–3 days	285km	Families, snorkelling & beaches

BEST TIME TO GO	Year-round; winter is too chilly for swimming

The main and largest island of Okinawa Prefecture, Okinawa Hontō (沖縄本島) is long and skinny, about 100km from top to bottom and at its narrowest, only 3km wide. The south part of the island is congested with traffic, so head north as soon as you get your fill of the city. Rte 58 follows the coast almost the whole length of the west coast, winding past postcard-perfect beaches and coral reefs to your left and jungle-encased castle ruins in the interior. You could easily spend two or three days exploring this route, but feel free to make it a week if you're feeling lazy.

Link Your Trip

32 Kumamoto, Aso, Takachiho

Fly 90 minutes from Naha to Kumamoto to embark on Drive 32.

35 Kirishima Kinkōwan National Park & Kagoshima City

Ferries travel between Naha and Kagoshima three times per week for Drive 35.

01 NAHA AIRPORT (那覇空港)

Most travellers will fly into Naha Airport and rent a car there. The capital of Okinawa Prefecture, Naha is full of shopping, nightlife, and the island's only train service, the Yui Rail serving Naha and Urasoe. While you're here, you may want to shop at **Makishi Public Market**, drink on **Kokusai-dōri**, or see digital art at **teamLab FuturePark**.

Shīsā Spotting

Keep your eyes peeled as you drive around Okinawa and you'll soon notice pairs of *shīsā* popping up everywhere: gates, shop entrances and on roofs. These mythological creatures are sometimes called lion dogs and exist in various forms throughout much of Asia, though the associated folklore varies from place to place. In Okinawa you'll see them deployed liberally, from private homes to castle gates, meant to ward off bad luck and protect inhabitants from evil spirits. The first *shīsā* in Okinawa were found near Shuri Castle and date from the 1400s.

THE DRIVE
Pick up Rte 58 just north of the airport. Traffic can get hairy down here, but the road will open up soon enough; it's 20km to Chatan.

02 HAMAGAWA FISHING PORT (浜川漁港)

If you're visiting in winter, you're in luck: humpback whales migrate here from Russian and Alaskan waters each winter to breed and raise their calves; whale-watching tours leave from the port (cerulean-blue.co.jp/); book ahead. If you're peckish, the adjacent open-air mall **American Village** has dozens of shops and restaurants with both Okinawan and US-style cuisine.

THE DRIVE
Head north on Rte 58 for 11km, then fork left when you see signs for Ryūkyū Mura, 2km further on the left.

03 RYŪKYŪ MURA (琉球村)

This theme park recreates the Ryūkyūan way of life via a village featuring traditional structures and musical and dance performances. The Eisā dance held in a **cave theatre** is particularly stirring. On nearby Cape Maeda is **Blue Cave**, a limestone cave famous for snorkelling and diving. Go in the early morning to avoid the crowds.

THE DRIVE
Here the scenery really starts to sing. Leaving behind the more developed part of the island, head north on Rte 58 following the coast. You're now in the Yambaru region, a densely forested area home to Yambaru National Park. You'll enter Onna Village and stretches of unbroken ocean views. It's 24km to Busena Marine Park, on the left.

04 BUSENA MARINE PARK (ブセナ海中公園)

This underwater observatory showcases one of Okinawa's most important treasures: the **coral reef**. Villagers are collaborating with the nearby Okinawa Institute of Science and

Technology (OIST) to preserve and reseed the reefs, which are suffering from coral bleaching.

THE DRIVE Continue north on Rte 58, then west on Rte 84 for 15km in total.

05 NAGO PINEAPPLE PARK (ナゴパイナップルパーク)

If you have kids, or even if you don't, consider a stop at this fun and kitschy **amusement park** dedicated to the locally grown pineapple. Taste pineapple treats, learn all about the crop, and take a spin through the wacky dinosaur park populated with animatronic reptiles.

THE DRIVE Travel north on Rte 58 for 50km to the tippy top of the island.

06 CAPE HEDO (辺戸岬)

This lonely, windswept cape is where the top of Okinawa Hontō meets the Pacific Ocean and East China Sea. Views stretch north to the islands of Kagoshima Prefecture, and a **monument** here marks the end of US occupation. There's an observatory, walking paths, and basic tourist facilities.

THE DRIVE Rte 58 crooks southward for a few kilometres before becoming Rte 70 at Oku, then Rte 331 at Higashi-son for this 63km leg.

07 HIGASHI VILLAGE FUREAI HIRUGI PARK (東村ふれあいヒルギ公園)

Salt and freshwater mix here and create the growing ecosystem for the island's mangroves, a designated national Natural Monument. You can take a **canoe tour** *(yanbaru-experience.com)* while learning about the precious local environment.

THE DRIVE Continue south on Rte 331 for 23km, where it merges with Rte 329. If you prefer, take the tolled expressway (E58) running parallel; it's easiest to pick it up near Ginoza. Otherwise, continue for 60km until the turnoff onto Rtes 38, 155 and 29.

08 SHURI CASTLE (首里城)

This was the palace of the Ryūkyū Kingdom for more than 400 years. It has been destroyed by fire several times, most recently in 2019, and was still being rebuilt at the time of writing, slated to reopen in late 2025. The castle serves as a **museum** to Ryūkyūan history and offers beautiful – and strategic – views of the surrounding area.

THE DRIVE It's about 10km back to Naha Airport.

Take a Break

At Michi-no-eki Ogimi is the YAMBARU FOREST VISITORS CENTER, with a gift shop, food stalls and a tourist information centre (TIC). Snack on *sata-an-dagi* (Okinawan doughnuts), *shikuwasa* (Okinawan lime) juice, and curly Okinawan soba with simmered pork. You'll find plenty of souvenirs, from food gifts to T-shirts to local crafts, local Okinawan produce and a large parking area with a beach across the street. The TIC has information on wildlife and a few bicycles for rent if you feel like a side quest.

MXTRAVEL/SHUTTERSTOCK

Sanshin

The Sound of Sanshin

If you're lucky, you'll catch some Okinawan folk music during your trip. The cornerstone of the island's sound is the *sanshin*, the three-stringed instrument similar to the Japanese *shamisen*. In fact, the *sanshin* is the precursor, having come here first from China before continuing up the island chain. Distinctively covered in snakeskin (usually python), its plaintive notes instantly evoke images of sun, wind and sea. The instrument is widely played at festivals and local concerts, or seek out a performance at **Ryūkyū Mura**, the **National Theatre Okinawa**, or at an *izakaya* with live music nightly, such as **Chinuman** (locations in Naha and Onna).

Also Try...

VICHIE81/SHUTTERSTOCK

Nichinan Coast

DURATION	DISTANCE
1 day	90km

From **Mizayaki City**, take your pick of beaches, waterfront parks and surf spots as you cruise the prefecture's southern Nichinan Coast (日南海岸). Explore subtropical coastal forests and botanical gardens filled with cycads, hibiscuses and jacarandas. Along the way, stop at **Aoshima Shrine** via the scenic **Devil's Washboard** rock formations, shoreside park **Sun Messe Nichinan** to view the giant 5.5m Moai statues, and fascinating Shintō shrine **Udo Jingū**, set in a cave on a rocky ocean outcrop. End at **Cape Toi**, a scenic promontory with a lighthouse and wild horses roaming the hillsides, said to be descendants of samurai steeds left to graze here some 300 years ago. There's a small entry fee per vehicle to enter the cape.

Northern Kyūshū Culture Trail

DURATION	DISTANCE
2 days	140km

This multi-prefecture cultural route connects the hub of Fukuoka with eastern Ōita and western Kumamoto. Start on the outskirts of **Fukuoka City** (pictured) at the scholarly shrine **Dazaifu Tenman-gū**, with its thousands of plum trees, and marvel at national treasures in the adjacent **Kyūshū National Museum**. Head east to explore the traditional pottery villages of **Tōhō** and **Onta**, along with historic **Hita**, considered the 'Kyoto' of Kyūshū. For manga culture, visit the 'Attack on Titan' exhibits at **Hita Museum** and go on a real-world quest using its augmented-reality sightseeing app. In nearby **Kusu**, find a recreated door from anime *Suzume-no-Tojimari* at **Bungomori Rail Park**. Continue south to **Kurokawa Onsen** for impressive outdoor hot-spring baths.

REI IMAGINE/SHUTTERSTOCK

Fukuoka, Saga, Nagasaki

DURATION	DISTANCE
3 days	190km

From Fukuoka, head southwest to the castle and hot-air ballooning city of **Saga** (佐賀). In late October to early November, don't miss the captivating **Saga International Balloon Fiesta** (pictured), with up to 100 hot-air balloons decorating the skies by the Kase River; a dedicated **Balloon Museum** serves visitors the rest of the year. Continuing west, see the legacy of **Nagasaki's** merchant history as one of few ports open to foreign trade during Japan's self-imposed period of isolation. Find multiple European-style theme parks, including Sasebo's **Huis Ten Bosch**, a replicated 17th-century Dutch town. In **Nagasaki City**, experience Japan's oldest **Chinatown**, top night views from **Mt Inasa**, and solemn WWII memorials at **Atomic Bomb Hypocenter** and **Peace Park**.

Miyako-jima

DURATION	DISTANCE
3–4 days	100km

Fly from Naha to the remote Okinawan island of Miyako-jima (宮古島) in under an hour. A full island circumnavigation by car is easily achieved in a day, but plan for multiple days to enjoy the breathtaking coastline, which even by Okinawan standards is regarded as some of the archipelago's best. For swimming, the white sand **Yonaha-Maehama Beach** on the island's southwest stretches 7km, and for snorkelling, explore the coral reefs off **Yoshino Kaigan** in the east. In between, tour gardens and farms featuring fruits and foliage of the tropics. Bridges connect Miyako-jima with three smaller, neighbouring islands. Be sure to cross the spectacular, undulating 3540m **Irabu Bridge**, the longest non-toll bridge in Japan, to **Irabu-jima**.

TOOLKIT

The chapters in this section cover the most important topics you'll need to know about in Japan. They're full of nuts-and-bolts information and valuable insights to help you understand and navigate Japan and get the most out of your trip.

Ryokan, near Kanazawa (p73)

ALLA TSYGANOVA/SHUTTERSTOCK

Arriving

Most international visitors will arrive in Japan by air, to Haneda (HND) or Narita (NRT) in Tokyo, or Kansai (KIX) in Osaka. The next largest international airports are Nagoya (NGO), Fukuoka (FUK), Sapporo (CTS) and Naha (OKA). All these airports are accessible by rail.

Airport Car Rentals

Most airports in Japan have a car rental counter or counters representing the major companies. Expect to find Toyota Rent a Car, Nippon Rent a Car, Orix Rent a Car, Times Car Rental, etc. Most counters will be on the arrivals floor, just after leaving the baggage claim area.

It's best to reserve in advance, as counters might not be staffed if there are no bookings, especially after hours or at smaller airports. Many agencies will close overnight, so make sure your rental company will be open if you've got a late flight.

Though sometimes cars are kept on-site, the rental offices are often a few kilometres from the airport. The best companies will have a free shuttle; allow an extra 20 minutes for transit. Cheaper or smaller outfits may ask you to take a taxi; some may reimburse the cab cost.

Airport to City Centre

	Narita (Tokyo)	Haneda (Tokyo)	Kansai (Osaka)
TRAIN	60 min **¥2750**	30 min **¥510**	60 min **¥1680**
BUS	75 min **¥1500**	25 min **¥1000**	70 min **¥1800**
TAXI	60 min **¥30,000**	30 min **¥7000**	50 min **¥21,000**

IMMIGRATION

Japan is visa-free for 70+ countries, for periods between 15 and 90 days. Entry tends to be efficient, though all foreign nationals are photographed and fingerprinted.

WI-FI

Free wi-fi has become more ubiquitous in recent years, and is available at most hotels, airports and many stations and stores. E-sims have also become cheap and plentiful and can close the gap between free spots.

ATMS

ATMs will often offer a better exchange rate than money changers. Look for machines in convenience stores and post offices; bank ATMs often serve only their own customers.

TOUCH & GO

Credit cards and other cashless payments have proliferated. With a stored-value IC card like Suica or Pasmo you can pay for not only transit but also goods at convenience stores and many restaurants.

Getting Around

PARKING

Parking can be expensive, especially in cities and near large tourist attractions. City parking is often at 'coin parking' lots and charged in 20-minute increments with mechanical plates that keep your car in place until you've paid. Machines will take ¥1000 notes but may not take anything larger, so be prepared with coins and smaller bills. Some shops and attractions will give you an hour or two of free parking in exchange for your business; inquire at the information desk.

Drive on the left.

Stop signs in Japan may not have English.

.03

Blood alcohol limit is 0.3g/L

Speed

The speed limit on urban or residential roads is generally 30km/h to 50km/h, and 60km/h on larger roads. On expressways, the maximum speed is generally 100km/h; a few stretches allow 120km/h. Speed cameras are in regular use.

Rail

The train network is extensive, comfortable and fast, and will take you right to the city centre. Stored-value IC cards like Suica work across most transit networks. Trains can convey you to a hub city to rent a car for further exploration.

Rental Cars

Driving in Japan is possible and even pleasurable outside of big city centres thanks to multilingual navigation systems. International Driving Permits are almost certainly required; check your country's requirements.

Ferries

Ferries connect all main islands and many smaller inhabited ones. This isn't the speediest method (eg Tokyo to Kitakyūshū takes 34 hours, ¥20,020). Cars are allowed on larger ferries for an extra fee.

Car rental

From ¥7000 per day

Petrol

Approx ¥185 per litre

Tokyo-Kyoto by shinkansen

¥14,000

Tokyo-Okinawa by plane

From ¥12,000

FROM LEFT: G-FISHER/SHUTTERSTOCK, MR ILLUSTRATION/SHUTTERSTOCK, MARKUS MAINKA/SHUTTERSTOCK

Accommodation

HOW MUCH FOR A NIGHT IN...

Regional business hotel room

From ¥7000

Farm stay with two meals

From ¥12,000

Shukubō lodging with two meals

From ¥10,000

Shukubō

Pilgrims making a visit to a sacred temple to pay their respects would stay at *shukubō*, temple lodging (japan.travel/en/guide/temple-stays). Many temples still offer accommodation, even to the casual traveller. *Shōjin ryōri* (Buddhist vegetarian devotional cuisine) is usually included. Expect to sleep on tatami mats and wake up early for prayer. Try this at Mt Kōya after Drive 14 or before Drive 15.

Farm Stay

Stay on a working farm, often in a *kominka* (traditional Japanese house; see www.japan.travel/en/guide/homestay-farmstay). You'll sleep on a futon, and you may have the opportunity to cook with or do simple farm chores with your host. Two meals are generally included. Tōno (Drive 23) is a great place to look for a farm stay.

Onsen Ryokan

The traditional Japanese inn with on-site hot springs and elaborate *kaiseki ryōri* set meals is the ultimate relaxation experience in Japan, and can have a price tag to match. Resort towns such as in Drive 6 Izu Peninsula, Drive 20 Zaō & Ginzan Onsen and Drive 33 Kunisaki, Beppu, Usuki will have a number of options.

Business Hotels

Designed as a port of call on domestic work trips, business hotels are compact and economical but with everything you need. Clean, narrow rooms usually have a desk and wi-fi, a prefab ensuite shower and toilet, simple amenities like toothbrushes and combs, and a basic breakfast. City-centre hotels may not offer parking.

Capsule Hotels

If you're not claustrophobic, capsule hotels (pictured) are fun to experience at least once. Sleeping quarters are in stacked pods about the size of a single bed, with power outlets and a door or curtain. There are common areas for lounging and shared bathing facilities. Some are men only. Try one after turning in your rental car after Drive 24 as they won't offer parking.

CAMPING

Japan's dense forests and imposing mountains mean that there are loads of campers and climbers from casual to hardcore. Camping (japan.travel/en/guide/camping) is especially popular in the warmer months, and there are an increasing number of glamping sites as well. Bring your own gear or stock up with domestic brands like Mont Bell and Snow Peak. Don't try to camp on private property without permission; you'll find plenty of campsites near places on Drive 7 Fuji Five Lakes and Drives 25-7 in Hokkaidō. Expect to pay a few thousand yen for a tent site.

Cars

Car Rental

Car rental agencies are fairly common in Japan, especially since public transportation infrastructure is so good that many city dwellers choose not to own cars and instead rent a vehicle whenever they want to go for a country drive.

You'll find rental offices at almost every airport and near most major train stations. Additionally, car sharing services use parking garages, petrol stations and shopping centres as bases for their fleets.

The majority of available cars are the *kei* (light) and compact-style vehicles, holding four to five passengers. If you're hoping to rent something larger, expect to pay at least twice as much; minivans, ATVs and the like are not in regular rotation.

Automatic transmissions are the norm; manual transmissions require a special designation on your licence.

Electric Vehicles (EVs)

EVs (pictured) are available in Japan, though hybrids are still much more common. Most car-rental outfits will not keep EVs in stock; if you want to drive one, be sure to reserve ahead.

Charging stations can be few and far between but are generally available at highway rest areas, airports and some larger shopping centres.

GoGoEV *(ev.gogo.gs)* has a map of EV chargers, normal (100v) and rapid (200v). At the time of writing, there were about 25,000 nationwide.

OTHER GEAR

Car navigation systems are standard issue in most rentals, and nowadays they tend to be bilingual, with searching available by address, keyword and phone number. Depending on the age of the system and the newness of your destination, your phone's map application may be more accurate.

Electronic Toll Collection (ETC) machines are standard issue in most rentals, and you may be able to rent an ETC card to go with it, allowing you to fly through toll gates and pay what you owe when you return your rental.

Car seats and winter tyres are available add-ons at most agencies for a small additional fee.

FROM LEFT: PAJOR PAWEL/SHUTTERSTOCK, SONGSAK C/SHUTTERSTOCK

Health & Safe Travel

Natural Disasters

There's no getting around it: Japan has a lot of natural disasters. Placed on the Pacific Ring of Fire, Japan experiences regular earthquakes, and residents are used to intermittent small shakes. There are also yearly typhoons, and the ever-present risk of volcanic eruptions and tsunamis. Keep an eye on the news for any developing situations. JNTO has a 24-hour visitor hotline for emergencies (050-3816-2787).

INSURANCE

Travel insurance is always a safe bet. Clinics and hospitals will require payment at the time of service, which you'll need to claim back from your insurance provider. There is generally no extra charge for an ambulance ride. Car rental fees will include basic liability and collision insurance, with upgrades available to cover additional items, such as damage and theft.

Theft & Fraud

Theft is rather rare in Japan, though of course it happens. Regular security such as locking the car should be sufficient in most cases. If you are the victim of theft or scam, make a report to the nearest *koban* (police box) and leave your contact information; ask for an interpreter if you have any trouble communicating.

Rail Crossings

There are tens of thousands of level crossings (pictured) in Japan, and you must always stop before proceeding. If you hear the bell or see flashing lights, it's a signal that a train is coming, usually accompanied by barrier gates that descend until the coast is clear. Wait until gates are lifted and all lights and alarms have ceased before moving ahead.

CAR BREAKDOWN

In the event of a breakdown or flat tyre, first ensure you're in a safe place, then call the rental agency. They will be able to advise about flats etc. The American Automobile Association (AAA), Fédération Internationale de l'Automobile (FIA) and Alliance Internationale de Tourisme (AIT) have reciprocal agreements with the Japan Automobile Federation (JAF) for roadside service in Japan.

FROM LEFT: KIMBERRYWOOD/SHUTTERSTOCK, D3_PLUS/SHUTTERSTOCK

Responsible Travel

Climate Change & Travel

Lonely Planet urges all travellers to engage with their travel carbon footprint, which will mainly come from air travel. While there often isn't an alternative, travellers can look to minimise the number of flights they take, opt for newer aircrafts and use cleaner ground transport, such as trains.

One proposed solution - purchasing carbon offsets - unfortunately does not cancel out the impact of individual flights. While most destinations will depend on air travel for the foreseeable future, for now, pursuing ground-based travel where possible is the best course of action.

The UN Carbon Offset Calculator shows how flying impacts a household's emissions:

The ICAO's carbon emissions calculator allows visitors to analyse the CO_2 generated by point-to-point journeys:

Resources

Japan National Tourism Organization

www.japan.travel Japanese tourism authority.

Japan Times

japantimes.co.jp Japan's largest English-language newspaper.

NHK World

*www3.nhk.or.jp/nhkworld*Japan's public media orgnisation.

REDUCE PLASTIC

Plastic bags now come with an extra fee in Japan to encourage eco-bag use. Consider using a reusable water bottle; the app mymizu shows free water refill spots around Japan and the world.

SUPPORT LOCAL

There are many family-run businesses and heritage craftspeople in Japan, many of whom have been plying their trades for generations. By supporting local, you're sure to have a one-of-a-kind experience.

GIVE BACK

Get souvenirs and support local causes: **35 Coffee** *(35coffee.com)* in Okinawa donates a portion of proceeds to coral conservation, while **Watalis** *(watalis.co.jp)* in disaster-affected Miyagi Prefecture creates accessories from recycled kimono made by local women.

Nuts & Bolts

Currency

Yen ¥ (円, en in Japanese)

Best Ways to Pay

Cashless payments have gained a lot of ground in the last decade, with payment apps battling for supremacy with credit cards, but there are still places where cash is king, especially in small businesses. Keep some coins and notes on hand for vending machines.

Tipping

Tipping is not done in Japan and tips are almost never expected. *Izakayas* may add a small service charge (¥300 to ¥500 per person), and some high-end and luxury places may add a service charge of around 10%, but there is no place for discretionary tips. Tips are not necessary in other restaurants, taxis or hotels.

Payment Kiosks

Increasingly, businesses like supermarkets, chain restaurants and convenience stores are relying on payment kiosks to handle the cash part of a transaction, though your purchase might still be rung up by a human. You'll then be instructed to insert your money and use the touch screen to complete the sale.

Toilets

They're starting to disappear, but squat toilets still exist, especially in rural areas. Since you don't touch anything, they're quite hygienic - as long as you don't lose your balance.

Smoking

Smoking has become much less common in recent years, with a number of bans on smoking indoors, in restaurants and while walking. You'll find designated smoking areas outside of large train stations.

Tap Water

Tap water is generally safe all over Japan, though taste will vary depending on the source. If it's not potable, there will be a warning sign over the tap.

ELECTRICITY 100V/50-60HZ

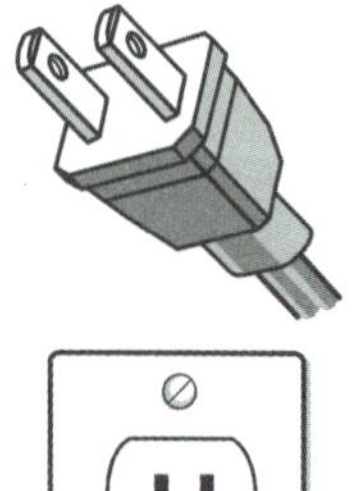

Type A
100V/50-60Hz

Type B
100V/50-60Hz

Index

Routes 000
Map Pages 000

F

G

H

I

K

Routes 000
Map Pages 000

L

M

N

O

U

V

W

Y

Z

THE WRITERS

Selena Takigawa Hoy
Selena loves coffee, animals, and old farm houses in the Japanese countryside, preferably all at the same time. She is a writer and editor in Tokyo. Instagram @selenahoy

Louise George Kittaka
Louise is a Tokyo-based writer who chases waterfalls and sweet treats with equal enthusiasm, always willing to take the scenic (and tastier) route. Instagram: @louisegeorgekittaka

Kimberly Hughes
Kimberly Hughes is a Tokyo-based freelance writer originally from the southwestern U.S. whose stories often land at the intersection of food/drink, travel, art/culture and social issues. Kimberlyhughes.online

Jessica Korteman
Jessica is a travel writer and Japanese culture expert, passionate about raising the profile of women in the travel industry. jessicakorteman.com

Craig McLachlan
Craig has hiked the 3200km length of Japan, climbed the Hyakumeizan (Japan's 100 Famous Mountains), summited all 21 of Japan's 3000m peaks, walked the 88 Sacred Temples of Shikoku Pilgrimage and driven all over Japan. He's been writing Lonely Planet guidebooks for 25 years. Instagram @yuricraig

BEHIND THE SCENES

This book was researched and written by Selena Takigawa Hoy, Louise George Kittaka, Kimberly Hughes, Jessica Korteman and Craig McLachlan. It was produced by the following:

Production Editor Will Allen

Destination Editor Selena Takigawa Hoy

Book Designer Dorota Michalec

Cartographers Mark Griffiths, Anthony Phelan

Cover Design & Researcher Kat Marsh

Assisting Editors Imogen Bannister, Monique Choy, Ailbhe McMahon, Darren O'Connell, Charlotte Orr, Gabrielle Stefanos

Thanks to Karen Henderson, Akanksha Singh, Norihiro Togasaki

ACKNOWLEDGMENTS

Digital Model Elevation Data
Contains public sector information licensed under the Open Government Licence v3.0 website http://www.nationalarchives.gov.uk/doc/open-government-licence/version/3/

Cover photograph Yasaka shrine, Kyoto (p82), Rintaro Kanemoto/Lonely Planet